People Making A Difference

Family Bookshelf offers the finest in good wholesome Christian literature, written by best-selling authors. All books are recommended by an Advisory Board of distinguished writers and editors.

We are also a vital part of a compassionate outreach called **Bowery Mission Ministries**. Our evangelical mission is devoted to helping the destitute of the inner city.

Our ministries date back more than a century and began by aiding homeless men lost in alcoholism. Now we also offer hope and Gospel strength to homeless, inner-city women and children. Our goal, in fact, is to end homelessness by teaching these deprived people how to be independent with the Lord by their side.

Downtrodden, homeless men are fed and clothed and may enter a discipleship program of one-on-one professional counseling, nutrition therapy and Bible study. This same Christian care is provided at our women and children's shelter.

We also welcome nearly 1,000 underprivileged children each summer at our Mont Lawn Camp located in Pennsylvania's beautiful Poconos. Here, impoverished youngsters enjoy the serenity of nature and an opportunity to receive the teachings of Jesus Christ. We also provide year-round assistance through teen activities, tutoring in reading and writing, Bible study, family counseling, college scholarships and vocational training.

During the spring, fall and winter months, our children's camp becomes a lovely retreat for religious gatherings of up to 200. Excellent accommodations include heated cabins, chapel, country-style meals and recreational facilities. Write to Paradise Lake Retreat Center, Box 252, Bushkill, PA 18324 or call: (717) 588-6067.

Still another vital part of our ministry is **Christian Herald magazine**. Our dynamic, bimonthly publication focuses on the true personal stories of men and women who, as "doers of the Word," are making a difference in their lives and the lives of others.

Bowery Mission Ministries are supported by voluntary contributions of individuals and bequests. Contributions are tax deductible. Checks should be made payable to Bowery Mission.

 Fully accredited Member
of the Evangelical Council
for Financial Accountability

Every Monday morning, our ministries staff joins together in prayer. If you have a prayer request for yourself or a loved one, simply write to us.

 Administrative Office:
40 Overlook Drive, Chappaqua,
New York 10514 Telephone: (914) 769-9000

SEASONS
OF THE
LORD

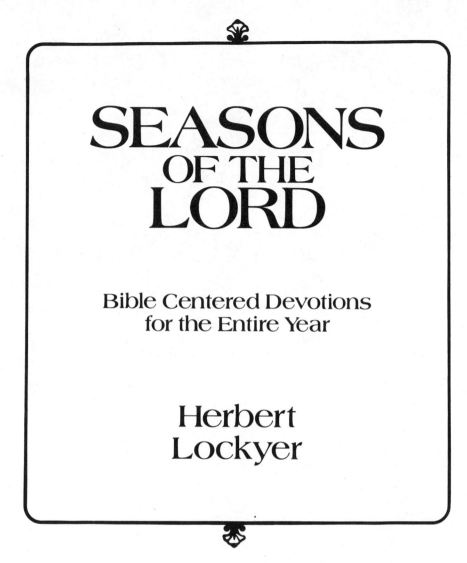

SEASONS
OF THE
LORD

Bible Centered Devotions
for the Entire Year

Herbert
Lockyer

1817

Harper & Row, Publishers, San Francisco

New York, Grand Rapids, Philadelphia, St. Louis
London, Singapore, Sydney, Tokyo, Toronto

FIRST EDITION

Library of Congress Cataloging-in-Publication Data

Lockyer, Herbert.
    Seasons of the Lord : Bible-centered devotions for the entire year / Herbert Lockyer. — 1st ed.
      p. cm.
    Contents: v. 1. Bible-centered devotions on purity and hope — v. 2. Bible-centered devotions on resurrection and glory — v. 3. Bible-centered devotions on fulfillment and splendor — v. 4. Bible-centered devotions on silence and remembrance.
    ISBN 0–06–065260–8
    1. Devotional calendars.   I. Title.
  [BV4811.L593   1990]
  242′.2—dc20   89–46445
                                                            CIP

90   91   92   93   94   FAIR   10   9   8   7   6   5   4   3   2   1

This edition is printed on acid-free paper that meets the American National Standards Institute Z39.48 Standard.

Contents

PART I

Purity and Hope

That life is made up of new beginnings is a truism we cannot escape as we enter the circle of another year. With two faces, one looking back and the other forward, we approach the opening month on our calendar. It signifies life and promise and seems to say to our hearts, "Grow old along with me, the best is yet to be." This season welcomes the dreary scene of the worm, but it is also a time of laughter and hope; so let us gladly receive this fresh beginning as it overtakes us with the gaiety of youth.

Forcing their way through the hard and frosty soil as the forerunners of the riotous flowerage of summer, the little white heads of the lovely snowdrops seem to proclaim the message of purity. These fair maids of February send, in advance, a commendable virtue every human should covet.

The next flowers to give us pleasure are the attractive yellow daffodils, helping to make the year more golden. As they stand erect like a company of soldiers, they remind us of energy in action in spite of adverse weather. They also bid us remember that often the slender things survive the strife and storm, smiting the strong as well as the weak. Difficulties can be steppingstones to a higher life. Martin Luther faced a great deal of the stormy side of life, but his words were like battlefields winning spiritual victories for his Master.

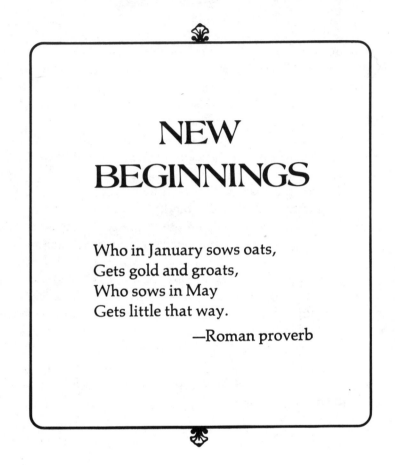

NEW
BEGINNINGS

Who in January sows oats,
Gets gold and groats,
Who sows in May
Gets little that way.

—Roman proverb

Where I Did Begin, There Shall I End

"In the beginning, God." *Genesis 1:1.*

In this marvelous opening of the Bible, simplicity and sublimity walk together in blissful harmony. Language cannot describe the majesty enshrined in the little monosyllable, or the first name of Scripture which represents the Hebrew *Elohim*, in which the Trinity—Father, Son, and the Spirit—are latent. This then is the revelation of his greatness and grace God has stamped upon the very forehead of his Book. *God first!* Is this not the message, not only of Genesis, but of the whole of Scripture? God first in everything—creation, redemption, providence, and personal experience?

As we face hidden cares, trials, and responsibilities, let us begin where the Bible does, namely, with God. All his august name suggests will be the rock on which the wildest storm will spend its strength for nought. May the young begin the first chapter of life with him, and let the aged begin its last chapter with him. As each day dawns, may it be *God first* in the books we read, in the letters we write, and in all our labors and enterprises. What trouble and sorrow have been ours because of wrong beginnings! Let this day register for you, not only the turning over a new leaf, but impartation of new life from above, even from him who has "neither beginning of days" (Heb. 7:3).

Not Let His Eyes See Sin, but through My Tears

"Thou God seest me." Genesis 16:13.

Is it not surprising that these four words constitute a further name for the Almighty? Sarai "called the name of the Lord that spake unto her, Thou God seest me: for she said, Have I also here looked after him that seeth me?" Then she called the well, where this revelation took place, *Beer-lahai-roi*, which means, "the well of him that liveth and seeth me."

Truly, there is no nobler way to live. We may be as grasshoppers in his sight and feel a sense of inferiority, but what a joy it is to know that he who sees a sparrow fall watches over us. We may count ourselves as worms of the dust; yet we are never out of God's sight, whose care of his children is personal and intimate. The days before us will be the most blessed we have experienced if we are daily conscious and confident that "the eyes of the Lord are on the righteous" (Ps. 34:15).

The seventeenth-century hymn by Phineas Fletcher is recalled:

> *In your deep floods*
> *Drown all faults and fears,*
> *Not let His eyes see sin,*
> *But through my tears.*

No Good Thing

"No soundness . . . but wounds and bruises." *Isaiah 1:6.*

Apart from divine grace, human beings are riddled with the disease of sin. Like Lazarus, they are "full of sores." Or as the prophet Isaiah stated, "From the sole of the foot even unto the head there is no soundness in it; but wounds and bruises and putrifying sores." Such a description is humiliating, but there it is, and the sooner it is recognized and confessed the better. "In me [that is, in my flesh], dwelleth no good thing" (Rom. 7:18). Isaiah urged the evildoers of his day to "wash and be clean" (1:16). Filthy hands, however, cannot cleanse a foul body. Apart from Christ and his healing blood, we are both helpless and hopeless. It is therefore fitting that the evangelical prophet of old should point all who are bruised and broken by sin to the one who can turn scarlet into snowy white, crimson into the lustrous purity of the unstained fleeces of sheep in green pastures. The healing balm of Gilead is more than able to deal effectively with all the filthiness of flesh and spirit. Charles Wesley wrote:

> *His blood can make the foulest clean,*
> *His blood avails for me.*

Soundness of soul or body can only be effected as the efficacious remedy is appropriated. *Confess, believe,* and *receive* are the key words of the Gospel. Calvary made deep cleansing from sin possible, but only personal faith can make it actual.

When God Is Deaf

"Many prayers, I will not hear." *Isaiah 1:15.*

This is one of those startling phrases in the Bible which compel us to stop and think. Jesus taught his disciples to pray to God, assuring them that he would hear and answer. But Isaiah declared that there are some prayers God cannot, and will not, answer. Jeremiah spoke of the Lord covering himself with a cloud so that our prayers should not pass through to him (Lam. 3:44). Isaiah agreed with this when he said that our sins cause God to hide his face from us and that he will not hear our prayers (Isa. 59:2). "Ye make many prayers" (Isa. 1:15).

But why waste our breath and time turning out prayers on a mass production basis if we only talk into air and not into ears? God is very positive about those prayers that have no life and love behind them— *I will not hear.* We may be earnest and eloquent in our entreaties, but all they receive is God's deaf ear if *what we are* contradicts our intercessions.

In the narrative Isaiah said that Judah stood rebuked for her departure from God. Laden with iniquity, she tried to keep up religious appearances, sacrifices, and oblations. But such mock worship only earned God's disgust. "I will not accept them" (Isa. 1:13). One wonders what he thinks of modern worshipers who make "many prayers" but who are as hypocritical as those Isaiah depicted. Reporting a great religious gathering in Boston, a journalist described the opening prayer as "the very best ever offered a Boston audience."

The Blighted Oak Tree

"Ye shall be as an oak whose leaf fadeth." Isaiah 1:30, 31.

The mingled warning and promise of God which condemns the people for national idolatry forcibly reminds us of the fatal results of sin. So subtle are the inroads of iniquity that men do not realize how they are being deceived and how their character is being tragically changed. The figure of speech Isaiah used declares that *sin withers*. The massive oak is only a shadow of its former, majestic self. Blighted by unseen forces within and without, it is a pitiable sight. The prophet also used the figure of a garden not irrigated and therefore barren. Sin, operating in this way, causes all pure desires and innocent susceptibilities to die. All that is good and beneficial disappears, and life withers and becomes fruitless.

Further, *sin brings its own retribution*. "The strong shall be as tow." Sin persisted in means that the sinner easily catches fire at temptation. Conscience and memory are charged with explosives, and thus when a sinner meets his or her sin, whether here or hereafter, retribution begins. God cannot be blamed for the plight of the self-tormented sinner. Like Isaac he carries the wood and lays the pile for his own burning. Sin prepares the individual for destruction. Grace, however, can avail and restore the beauty and freshness of the blighted oak. The divine gardener is perfect at the task of transforming withered trees.

Peace for a Blood-soaked Earth

"They shall beat their swords into plowshares."
Isaiah 2:4.

Describing millennial days, the prophet envisaged the time when war drums will cease to beat and peace prevail throughout the world. For centuries now, people have been changing plowshares into swords and pruninghooks into spears. During World War II, in the constant drive for necessary metals, people were accustomed to see piles of farm and kitchen utensils deposited in public squares waiting to be taken to factories and transformed into engines of fearful destruction. War robs us of the necessities of life and destroys all that is peaceful and pastoral. But earth's travail is to cease with the appearance of the King of kings, who alone has the prerogative to make wars cease to the ends of the earth, break the bow, . . . and burn the chariot in the fire (Ps. 46:9).

Plowshares and pruninghooks depict the peacefulness of Christ's millennial reign. Surely our blood-soaked earth awaits such a conqueror. Think of it—for a thousand years all the anguish and horror of war will be missing from the world! When the prince of the kings of the earth appears, "nation shall not lift up a sword against nation, neither shall they learn war any more" (Mic. 4:3, 4). What a glorious era that will be! Let us pray for its hastening and likewise for peace in our time. Edward H. Bickersteth wrote, "The blood of Jesus whispers, Peace within."

God's Display Cabinet

"Him God raised up the third day,
and shewed him openly." *Acts 10:40.*

Jeremy Taylor, seventeenth-century English bishop, wrote of the believer as "a mysterious cabinet of the Trinity." How true is the figure of the Lord Jesus whom all heaven loves to display! After his resurrection from the dead, God let him be clearly seen. As a showcase of jewels in a jeweler's establishment indicates the goods that can be purchased, so, reverently, Jesus is heaven's showcase. God is not ashamed or afraid to expose his victorious Son to view. Proudly, he displayed him as the conqueror of Satan, sin, and sickness. The Father loved to draw attention to his Son who, raised from the grave by the power of God, could not be holden of death. Concerning the truths of the death and resurrection of Jesus, Paul reminded King Agrippa of the apostle who said, "This thing was not done in a corner" (Acts 26:26), or was no "hole-and-corner business." "God shewed him openly."

Are we found emulating the divine example? Paul was not ashamed to declare the gospel which the Saviour's death made possible but openly displayed him as the only mediator between God and men. Can it be that we hide him from the view of others, that we are ashamed to own our Lord? May grace be ours to exhibit his worth and wealth by our lips, life, and labor. Jesus could say, "He that hath seen me, hath seen the Father" (John 14:9). When others look at us, may they see the beauty of Jesus.

The Carpenter of Galilee

"Is not this the carpenter?" *Mark 6:3.*

What a descriptive cameo this is of Christ who came to mend a world broken by sin. If legend be true, Joseph died when Jesus was but a lad, and the burden of the carpenter's shop fell upon his young shoulders. For many years there at the bench we have the toil of divinity, revealing the divinity of toil. Jesus earned his own bread and possibly the bread of others in his humble home. Thus he was not removed from the toils and trials of life but touched life at every point. Incredulity is suggested by the question, "Is not this the carpenter?" as if to say, "Who ever heard of a young village benchhand manifesting superior wisdom and performing miracles?" Yet it was so!

It was most fitting that Jesus had wood and nails when he died, for as the carpenter he was used to them and loved to work with them. More than ever, this old broken world of ours needs the skillful hands of the carpenter of Galilee. If only we would allow his pierced hands to repair all that sin has damaged, what a different world would be ours.

Can it be that yours is a broken life or a broken home? Then do not despair. Call in the perfect carpenter to repair the damage and make you as good as new. Those pierced hands of his are skillful at remolding sin-misshapen lives.

10

The Noblest Work of God

"What is man . . .? . . . thou hast put all things under his feet." *Psalm 8:4, 6.*

In his *Essay on Man* Alexander Pope wrote that "An honest man's the noblest work of God." Years later Robert Burns used the same line in "The Cotter's Saturday Night." Without doubt, humankind is God's masterpiece in creation, but sin has robbed us of the pristine dominion David ascribed to us. Humanism exalts the individual as all-sufficient, requiring no assistance from God. Isaiah, who had some caustic things to say about pride and haughtiness, exhorted us to "cease from man, whose breath is in his nostrils" (Isa. 2:22). But the Lord can bring down the mightiest from their seats that he alone may be exalted. Those who are terrified by the threats of proud persons may be assured to know that the best of persons are only persons at the best whom God is able, in a moment of time, to wither up. The breath, even of arrogant, ruthless dictators, is in their nostrils and can be swiftly withdrawn by God.

We are guilty of misplaced trust when we depend upon what others may have. Often in church life and work the one with the fattest purse wields considerable influence and is feared because of what is given. "Cursed be the man that trusteth in man, and maketh flesh his arm" (Jer. 17:5). Is it not far better to trust in the Lord whose breath cannot be removed? The person after God's own heart is the new person in Christ Jesus, who alone is able to make the vilest one clean.

The Bondage of Ignorance

"My people are gone into captivity,
because they have no knowledge." *Isaiah 5:13.*

Educators never tire in reminding us that knowledge is power. In Isaiah's thinking and theology, knowledge also spells freedom. Did not a greater prophet say, "Ye shall know the truth, and the truth shall set you free" (John 8:32, 36; 14:6)? William Cowper wrote in "The Winter Morning Walk":

*He is the freeman whom the truth makes free
And all are slaves beside.*

Describing the willful ignorance of Israel, Hosea said, "My people are destroyed for lack of knowledge; because thou hast rejected knowledge, I will also reject thee" (Hos. 4:6). Lack of knowledge of God's omnipotence produces the bondage of doubt. Ignorance of God's protecting mercy and bountiful provision results in the bondage of fear. Want of knowledge of God's saving grace and mercy keeps the sinner in spiritual captivity. The romance of missionary enterprise is simply the knowledge of God breaking the shackles of heathenism.

Is yours the song of freedom because you have come to know him who is eternal life? Captive souls can only experience freedom from any kind of bondage as they come to discover God through his liberating Word and through Calvary's blood-bought emancipation. George Matheson, the blind poet, taught us to sing:

*Make me a captive, Lord,
And then I shall be free.*

Petitionary Grace

"The Lord standeth up to plead." *Isaiah 3:13.*

Tennyson wrote of

> *That petitionary grace*
> *Of Sweet Seventeen*

Isaiah had another feature of such grace in mind when he pictured the Lord as a petitioner pleading his case against the people with whom he had a controversy. John assured us that Jesus is our advocate in the court of heaven (1 John 2:1, 2). As our intercessor, he ever lives and pleads on our behalf. To quote from an unknown source:

> *Day and night our Jesus makes no pause,*
> *Pleads His own fulfilment of all laws,*
> *Veils with His perfectness mortal flaws,*
> *Clears the culprit, pleads the desperate cause,*
> *Plucks the dead from death's devouring jaws,*
> *And the worm that gnaws.*

After accomplishing his redemptive work, "He sat down on the right hand of the majesty on high" (Heb. 1:3). Luke, however, told of an occasion when Jesus could not keep his seat, namely, when he rose to welcome Stephen, the first martyr of the faith. As he died, Stephen looked up and saw Jesus *standing* on the right hand of God. The vital question is, Are we standing up for Jesus where he has placed us, assured that he is ever standing by us, and, as Paul experienced, standing to strengthen us (2 Tim. 4:17)?

Given to Strong Delusion

"Woe unto them that call evil good and good evil."
Isaiah 5:20.

We are indebted to Rudyard Kipling for the phrase from "The Islanders": "Given to strong delusion, wholly believing a lie." Paul forewarned that in the last days, "God shall send them strong delusion, that they should believe a lie" (2 Thess. 2:11). The softening terms invented for sin tend to hide its hideousness. The fall of Adam was a fall upward. Sin is a mistake, an error, an accident, an element in our spiritual education. Festering sores are covered with satins; guilt is veiled, and iniquity is garnished. We are loath to drag the serpent out and call it what it really is. We prefer to speak of that which is bitter as though it were sweet, of evil as if it were good. But condemnation faces those who are thus deluded. The same applies to those who call good, evil, which is as fatal as calling evil, good.

The way of holiness is pictured as rough, thorny, and perilous, and therefore undesirable. Trifling obstructions are magnified. Duty is looked upon as irksome. Satan delights in picturing the Christian life as something drab, unwelcome, and undesirable. Good is called evil. Camouflage is necessary for soldiers to deceive their foes, but to those who know the Word, and their own hearts, sin is always *sin*. The same agree with Robert Browning that "We've still our stage where truth calls spade a spade!"

Vacancy and Vision

"In the year that king Uzziah died I saw also the Lord."
Isaiah 6:1.

In his hour of personal grief over the passing of the king he revered, Isaiah learned how to look from a grave to glory. Vacancy of an earthly throne resulted in the vision of the heavenly king who cannot die. Often hearts and homes are emptied that they might be filled. Thus God never helps us better than when in the place of what he takes he gives us more of his abiding presence. Only when the leaves drop from forest trees do we see the blue sky that was hidden by dense foliage.

How slow we are to learn that when God empties our lives of a treasured love it is to fill them more completely with the greater treasure of himself. If he plunges us into a dark tunnel, it is that we might be brought out into a brighter, sunnier land. God loves to make our vacancies the channel of *the vision splendid*. When death came, Isaiah saw a grave but *also* the Lord who conquered death. Losses never leave us poorer, changes sadder, graves emptier, when we learn how to look up and see our king of glory on his throne.

To see him, even through our blinding tears which he preserves in his bottle, is to have all our fears, doubts, and despair transformed into joy, faith, and patient submission. To realize that he reigns is the Christian philosopher's stone, turning grief into gold. Tears will ever be ours, but we can make them our telescope enabling us to see more clearly the God of all comfort. George Matheson has taught us to sing of the "Joy, that seeketh us through pain" and of the rainbow through the rain.

All God's Children Have Wings

"Each one had six wings." *Isaiah 6:2.*

The designation of the section of the angelic hierarchy Isaiah described is significant. *Seraphim* means "the flaming or shining ones" and represents unearthly beings who flash with splendor, possess swift energy, and manifest fiery enthusiasm. These high creatural beings the prophet portrayed suggest that the nearer we are to God, who dwells in inaccessible light, the more we glow and burn. Nothing icily regular is found in his presence. The distinguishing feature of the Seraphim is that each one had six wings—two covering the face, two covering the feet, and the remaining two—for flying. Thus four wings were used for worship and only two for service.

Too often we use *all* our wings for flying, for we are ever on the go. Wings covering the face suggest *worship* and how we need to cultivate it. Our approach to God is far too careless and shallow. Wings covering our feet can stand for our *walk*. Arrogant steps hinder spiritual progress. Humility is not ours. But the more we walk with the Lord, the more we realize the need of clean and covered feet. Wings to fly with can represent our *work*. With face and feet wing-covered, ours will be a joyous, buoyant, unhindered motion. True worship regulates our walk and inspires our work.

May grace be ours to use all our wings aright. How tragic it is to watch a bird that cannot fly because of injured wings! Prayer preserves the motion of our wings, making them as the wings of a dove and enabling us to fly away from the cares of this life and to find rest in the Lord.

Soft Waters

"... the waters of Shiloah that go softly." *Isaiah 8:6.*

Alexander Maclaren, the Scottish preacher, wrote this helpful comment:

> The waters of Shiloah that go softly stand as an emblem
> of the Davidic monarchy as God meant it to be, since
> that monarchy was itself a prophecy. They therefore
> represent the Kingdom of God or the Messianic King ...
> The little brooklet slipping quietly along suggests the
> character of the King, the meek and lowly in heart. It
> suggests the manner of His rule, wielded in gentleness and
> exercising no compulsion but that of love.

The sorrow hinted at in the narrative was that "the waters strong and mighty" of the Euphrates, with all their turbulence and havoc, were allowed by God to overwhelm the refused gentle waters of Shiloah. The swift Euphrates constituted divine retribution upon Judah for forsaking God.

One is guilty of the worst kind of folly in refusing to pitch one's tent alongside the calm flow of those streams making glad the city of God and in choosing instead the raging torrents of sin, passion, and judgment. To quote Dr. Maclaren again, "The soul that rejects Christ's gentle sway is harried and laid waste by a mob of base-born tyrants. We have to make our choice—either Christ or these: Shiloah or Euphrates."

> *No earthly joy can lure my quiet soul from Thee;*
> *This deep delight, so pure, is Heaven to me.*

May we be delivered from the folly of rejecting the gentle flowing waters of Shiloah or the rest of soul Jesus promised when he invited us to appropriate his peace of heart.

Blessed Opposites

"Signs and wonders." *Isaiah 8:18.*

The evangelical prophet affirmed that the children of the Lord are for signs and wonders to those around—a kind of enigma to the world, or a bundle of contradictions. And paradoxes abound in our Christian life. The believer is made up of opposites. Polluted by sin, one is yet cleansed by blood. Fallen, one has been raised far above all principalities and powers. Mortal, one is yet immortal. Always rejoicing, one is yet sorrowful. In the world, one is not of it. Heart and brain move there; only the feet stay here.

Truly, the Lord and his redeemed children are signs and wonders! Satisfied, we yet hunger and thirst. Having a zest to live, we are yet glad to die. What throws us down and almost crushes us, lifts us higher. Our restrictions make for enlargements. Poor, we yet make many rich. The free gift we possess was bought without money and price.

The Lord we love and serve likewise presents us with intriguing paradoxes. He is God, yet man; priest, yet the lamb; the true vine, yet the branch. Sinless, he was made sin. The ancient of days, he yet became a child. The eternal king, he yet lived among men as a servant. Deathless, he yet died.

Thus the Savior and the saint are as signs and wonders to sinners who cannot understand the paradoxes of faith. The greatest wonder of all is that Jesus died to save poor, lost sinners and endow them with life evermore. Are you among the wonders of his grace?

Unwanted

"He came unto his own, but his own
received him not." *John 1:11.*

There is no experience comparable to that of being unwanted, undesired, or rejected by one's own kith and kin. Tragic, was it not, that the one who came from heaven, where chief honor was his, should be unwanted by earth? It is sorrowful enough to read that "the world knew him not," but it is heartbreaking to know that "his own—his very own—received him not." In the world he himself had created, he was treated as a stranger. He came to his own world, his own things, his own people, but there was no beauty in him that they should desire him. The nation of which he formed part would not recognize him. He came as the king of his own people, but they would not have him to reign over them, and they crucified him. As he moved among men, his lament was, "Ye will not come to me that ye might have life."

The intervening centuries have brought little change of attitude, for Jesus is still the undesired one in our godless world. He may be deemed a most admirable character in many ways; yet the world does not know him as the one who bled and died for its salvation. As for "his own," those who name his name, are not many of them guilty of affording him a partial reception? He is their Savior but not the sovereign of their lives. Their guilty past is under the blood, but their present experience is one of defeat. Jesus has not yet been sanctified in their hearts as Lord. Can we say that we have brought forth the royal diadem and crowned him as king over the empire of our lives?

Courage, the Highest Gift

"He shall not . . . be discouraged." *Isaiah 42:4.*

Joshua, at the outset of his leadership of Israel, received the solemn charge from God "to be strong and of a good courage; be not afraid or dismayed, for the Lord thy God is with thee" (Josh. 1:9).

The Bible has much to say about courage and also about *discouragement.* As Israel journeyed through the wilderness, the soul of the people was much discouraged. The spies, save Joshua and Caleb, discouraged the heart of the children of Israel, and the exhortation came, "Fear not, neither be discouraged" (Deut. 1:21). Isaiah portrayed one who is never discouraged but abounds in godly courage.

Slowly, yet surely, the predicted Messiah is reaching his goal to set judgment in the earth. Think of Jesus while among those of this world! He had more than enough to discourage his heart, but his courage never waned. Look at him as he set his face most courageously toward Jerusalem! No one and nothing could keep him from accomplishing his task. It would seem as if the present world is altogether out of his control, but he is not discouraged because he knows his day is coming. What an incentive he provides for our discouraged hearts. John Bunyan reminded us in "The Shepherd Boy's Song in the Valley of Humiliation":

> There's no discouragement,
>   Shall make him once relent
> His first avow'd intent,
>   To be a pilgrim.

If your heart is a discouraged heart, say right now, "Up and trudge another mile!"

When Ignorance Is Not Bliss

"We know not what we should pray for." *Romans 8:26.*

What is the use of praying if we do not know what to ask God for? But Paul would have us remember that left to ourselves we do not pray as we ought. Pray we may, but we receive not because ignorant of the divine will we ask amiss. At best we are, as Tennyson wrote in *In Memoriam,*

> *Infants crying in the night,*
> *With no language but a cry.*

Without the Holy Spirit, the indwelling intercessor, we cannot pray aright, for he, knowing the mind of God, can enable us to present our petitions in accordance with his will. John declared that this is the secret and condition of answered prayer (1 John 5:14, 15). The interceding Spirit takes our sighs, broken and imperfect utterances, and recasts them until they rise as sweet incense before God. As we approach the mercy seat where Jesus answers prayer, we are prone to forget that our heavenly Father ever responds to our prayers, not according to our intelligence, but according to his own. With his infinite wisdom he knows that many things we ask for would not be good for us and so withholds them. Thus we have great need to join the disciples, "Lord, teach us to pray."

It is essential to be instructed in such a holy art by the very one who invites us to approach him. Effectual prayer is dependent upon relationship. Born into the family of God and honoring him as Lord of our life is the basis of communion with him who is our heavenly Father and who is ever responsive to the petitions of his children.

Prison Prayers

"Epaphras, my fellow-prisoner . . . labouring fervently for you in prayers." *Philemon 23; Colossians 4:12.*

Paul experienced that "stone walls do not a prison make." Along with Silas in the dungeon at Philippi, Paul prayed, and God answered with an earthquake that destroyed all prison security. A collection of all the prayers prayed in prisons down the centuries would make a remarkable spiritual classic. Epaphras is conspicuous as an imprisoned prayer-warrior, a strenuous intercessor with an unceasing burden for the spiritual perfection of the children of God. Often commended by Paul, Epaphras must have been one of the finest Christians in the early church.

In the Scofield Reference Bible footnote to Colossians 4:12 reads, "A touching illustration of priestly service (see 1 Pet. 2:9, *note*) as distinguished from ministry of gift. Shut up in prison, no longer able to preach, Epaphras was still, equally with all believers, a priest. No prison could keep him from the throne of grace, so he gave himself wholly to the priestly work of intercession."

Paul urged the believers in Rome to *strive together* with him in their prayers to God for his ministry (Rom. 15:30). Praying without ceasing for sinners that they may be saved, and for the saved that they may be sanctified, is a most arduous task. Failing to persist in such intercession is a sin. For example, Samuel knew he would be guilty of such a sin if he failed to pray for the idolatrous multitude who would not obey God (1 Sam. 12:23). It is so true, as Tennyson wrote in *Idylls of the King*, that

> *More things are wrought by prayer,*
> *Than this world dreams of.*

Belief and Behavior

"Have faith in God." Mark 11:22.

It is often argued that it does not matter what one believes as long as one believes something. But such a premise is false since belief influences behavior. Because what we believe shapes our character and determines our eternal destiny, having the right object of faith is essential. A gangster believes that he should live by plundering others of their possessions, and such a faith makes him a menace to society.

Jesus gave us the perfect object of faith, "Have faith in *God.*" Have faith *in*—what follows *in* either enriches or impoverishes life. If it is *in* the omnipotent God, then ours can be the faith laughing at impossibilities. Abraham, under hopeless circumstances, hopefully believed. Strong in faith, the patriarch glorified God and was enabled to do exploits. Our forefathers used to say, "Act faith," which was what Abraham did as he believed God. General William Booth's slogan to his soldiers in the Salvation Army was, "Keep up with your repeated acts of faith." Another old Methodist preacher gave us practical wisdom when he wrote, "If the devil puts up a stone wall in front of us we are to believe right through it."

By faith we are saved. By repeated *acts* of faith we come to *act* faith, and when strong in faith we can make our way through barriers. Whether we think of faith as the bridge across the chasm between the soul and God, as the opening of a beggar's hand to receive the gold of heaven, or as active energy in devotion, such faith is ever the gift and the fruit of the Holy Spirit (Gal. 5:22). May he make us strong in faith.

The Insignia of Holiness

"Be ye holy, even as I am holy." 1 Peter 1:16.

The apostle bases his exhortation to holiness upon example. God who called you is holy, so be ye holy. But left to ourselves we cannot produce what God demands and desires. Wherein, then, is our hope? Paul has the assuring word, "Faithful is he that calleth you, who also will do it" (1 Thess. 5:24). God is not only the foundation and pattern of holiness; he is the source of it as well. Thus what he commands, he supplies. As Augustine put it, "Given what Thou commandest, and then command what Thou wilt."

The transmission of this divine holiness is the ministry of him who over one hundred times in Scripture is named the *Holy* Spirit. Paul names him the "spirit of holiness" (Rom. 1:4). A hymn by Harriet Auber has this verse:

> *And every virtue we possess,*
> *And every conquest won,*
> *And every thought of holiness,*
> *Are His alone.*

That such holiness should be at the center of our lives and travel out to the circumference is emphasized in so many ways in Scripture. Zechariah envisaged the time when *holiness* would be written upon the bells around horses' necks and *upon every pot* (Zech. 14:20, 21), implying that the holy one expects our commercial and social lives, as well as our personal lives, to bear the imprint of our allegiance to him. *Holiness upon every pot!* Your kitchen can become a sanctuary. Your sphere of labor should also wear the insignia of holiness.

A Lonesome Road

> "Every man went to his own home. Jesus went to the Mount of Olives." *John 7:53, 8:1.*

It was Coleridge who, in *The Ancient Mariner*, wrote of being

> *Like one, that on a lonesome road*
> *Doth walk in fear and dread.*

During his pilgrimage on earth, our Lord traveled over a lonesome road, but he never walked in fear and dread. His was indeed a lonesome road, but not lonely. He was never alone. Others could go home to family circles—he found serenity in the solitude of a mount.

Jesus knew what it was to be homeless although surrounded by a thousand homes. At night every man went to his own home, we read, but Jesus went to the Mount of Olives with darkness as the only blanket to cover him through the silent hours. Why did he not go to his own home in which he was born and lived for thirty years? The stark fact is that he was never *at home* when home. He once said, "A man's foes shall be they of his own household" (Matt. 10:36, 37).

A characteristic feature of our Lord's teaching is that it came out of the crucible of experience, and truth is ever effective when wrung out of one's own heart. Variance over allegiance to God on the part of some members within the home was something Jesus endured for many years as he lived out his life in Nazareth. At the early age of twelve, Jesus rebuked his parents for their failure to recognize his divine mission. His brothers and sisters did not believe in him. To them he was an alien and a stranger. His foes were of his own household, and the rejection of his claims by his own kith and kin was his deepest wound. Often this is also our price of discipleship. Our love and devotion for Jesus is not understood or shared by those dearest and nearest to us. The Man of Sorrows had a share in such grief and is ever near to console us when lonely.

Alice Pugh has taught us to sing:

> *Why should you be lonely,*
> *Why for friendship sigh,*
> *When the heart of Jesus,*
> *Has a full supply?*

25

When Gain Is Loss

"What is a man profited, if he shall gain the whole world, and lose his own soul?" *Matthew 16:26.*

The more of the world we gain, the more of us the world gains. How tragic it is when material gains result in spiritual loss, when temporal and worldly benefits are bartered for eternal treasures!

The very best the world can offer is only for a time and ends with the grave. The soul, however, is destined for eternity and should, therefore, have priority in our consideration. Loving this present world resulted in Demas' forsaking his close friend, Paul, who urged the saints to live godly lives in this present world. It is interesting to notice how the apostle contrasted *two loves* in his appeal to young Timothy as he set out on the Christian pilgrimage: "Love his appearing . . . loved this present world" (2 Tim. 4:8, 10). These are not similar loves but antagonistic in nature, for the one love ruins the other. We cannot entertain these two loves together. The one must yield to the other. If we love the glorious appearing of Jesus, then we will not strive to gain what a godless world can offer. The question of paramount importance each of us now must answer is, Which love dominates my heart? Is our gain *Christ* or the *world*? It *cannot* be Christ *and* the godless world.

There is a motto on the wall of a school in Germany which reads:

When wealth is lost, nothing is lost;
When health is lost, something is lost;
When character is lost, all is lost!

All Compact of Fire

"The light of Israel shall be for a fire,
and his holy one for a flame." *Isaiah 10:17*.

These expressive lines of Shakespeare in *Venus and Adonis* readily lend themselves to a spiritual application:

Love is a spirit all compact of fire,
Not gross to sink, but light, and will aspire.

Fire is a familiar figure of divine activity, as Isaiah's reference proves. Usually, the metaphor is associated with God's judicial operations. No one can read Old Testament history without feeling sorry for God who, in spite of all his goodness bestowed upon his people, had disappointment upon disappointment as his only reward. As children the Israelites had been nourished and brought up by God, but they rebelled against him. In the first chapter of his prophecy Isaiah indicated that man's neglect of divine benefits puts him below the animals that *know* the hand that feeds and governs them.

Constant rejection of grace results in divine judgment. God, as light with all its beneficial rays, becomes the fire-flame, consuming everything alien to his holy will. These opposite aspects of the divine character are spoken of as the goodness and severity of God. Jesus came as the light of the world, but the religious leaders of his day preferred their religious and moral darkness. What happened? Why, the light became a flame, for we read that Jesus looked upon his religious foes *with anger*, and such a fiery glance also carried a look of grief for their hardness of heart. Light, so gladsome to a healthy eye, is agony to a diseased one. The gospel, rejected as the source of life, becomes the herald of death.

A Quick Scent

"Of quick understanding in the fear of the Lord."
Isaiah 11:3.

Coming from royal stock, Christ received and retained the whole fullness of the Holy Spirit of God. There was no gauge checking the supply. Without measure, the sevenfold Spirit rested upon Jesus. Gifts—intellectual, moral, physical, and spiritual—were his in all their perfection. Among the double gifts Isaiah mentioned, the one gift of the Spirit arresting our attention is that of a "quick understanding," implying swiftness and clarity of intellectual and moral insight. The phrase speaks of one who is quick scented, enabling him or her to detect immediately the distinction between the true and the false.

What a gift such intuitiveness is! Jesus had this gift in abundance. He could sniff any crookedness in persons before he actually saw them. They could not deceive him, for he knew what was in them. In our physical make-up, the nose is just above the mouth so that we can smell food before we actually eat it. False cults would not thrive as they do if only religious people had spiritual noses. What a lamentable lack there is of spiritual discernment and insight; Satan is a past master at sugar-coating his poisonous pills. Would that all who name the name of Christ were more quick-scented, discovering immediately that which is antagonistic to his Word and will. When it comes to the many plausible doctrines today, have you a good smell, enabling you to discern truth as it is in Jesus and to reject all that is false?

Union of Hands and Hearts

"Mighty works are wrought by his hands." *Mark 6:2.*

In one of his sermons Jeremy Taylor spoke of marriage as "the union of hands and hearts." The Bible has much to say about the *hands* of the Lord, which are ever active dispensing the goodness of his heart. What is the use of hands, even though they bestow goods to feed the poor, if a heart of love does not prompt the giving? The hands of Jesus constantly wrought mighty works because hands and heart were in unison. His heart of compassion found expression in the miracles his hands performed.

Gertrude Bell wrote of Lawrence of Arabia, "Everything that he touches, flowers," a phrase equally descriptive of the impact of Christ's vivifying fingers. Oliver Goldsmith's monument in Westminster Abbey, London, bears the inscription, "He touched nothing which he did not adorn." Such a beautiful sentiment is truer of the hands of Jesus, whose touch has never lost its ancient power. Tolstoy described the ideal czar as one who kept an open house and a well-laden table for all comers. But guests had to face one condition. They had to show their hands before sitting down at the feast. Those with hands rough and gnarled through honest work were welcomed to the best the table provided; those with soft, white hands had to be content with crumbs and crusts.

Where there are hearts with the love of God shed abroad in them, there will be hands ready to serve the needy souls of men. Frances Ridley Havergal wrote:

> Take my hands, and let them move,
> At the impulse of Thy love.

Beforehand

"The Lord, he it is that doth go before thee."
Deuteronomy 31:8.

George Eliot in *Silas Marner* suggested, "Nothing is so good as it seems beforehand." Scripture often uses the promise of the Lord going before his people, and being in front implies many truths. First is the idea of leadership, and as our forerunner Jesus is ever present with his people in undying leadership. He has perfect knowledge of the road ahead and can guide accordingly. Second, the promise also suggests provision, for God went before his people to "seek out a resting place for them." Guidance, rest, and shelter were thus involved in the gracious leadership God offered his people.

The whole tenor of Scripture emphasizes that God is beforehand with our every need. This is seen in Creation when God prepared for man all he would require once fashioned out of the dust. Then the grace of God is ever *prevenient grace*, or grace that *goes before*. Is this not at the very root of the gospel of Christ? "While we were yet sinners, Christ died for us." Further, we have the preparation being made for the future of the redeemed, for among his parting words Jesus declared, "I go to *prepare a place* for you." Our heavenly home is being prepared beforehand. Jesus is our *Jehovah-Jireh*, the Lord providing beforehand all his saints require as they journey on to heaven and all they will require when ultimately they share heaven with their heavenly forerunner and provider.

Juvenile Obedience

"Jesus was subject unto them." *Luke 2:51.*

Modern juvenile delinquency presents parents and educators with many problems. Drugs, sex, and crime are afflicting our children at an early age; and parental discipline, authority, and influence are at a low ebb. The biblical injunction of children obeying their parents has been reversed.

What was Jesus like as a juvenile? The only glimpse we have of the first thirty silent years of his life was when he was twelve years old; yet this solitary reference is full of spiritual import. Reaching this tender age, Jesus accompanied his parents to Jerusalem to join in the annual Feast of the Passover. In the Temple he confounded the doctors by his understanding. Then, when rebuked by his mother for causing anxiety because of his failure to leave for home when she and Joseph did, although only a lad, he had a clear and definite conception of the God-given task he was in the world to perform. But Jesus went back to his Nazareth home and became subject to his parents. The only saying, however, Mary kept in her heart and came to understand as the years passed by was the question of her illustrious twelve-year-old son, "Wist ye not that I must be about my Father's business?"

Would that multitudes of children of the same age today could be found emulating the example of Jesus in putting God first in their young lives and in the desire to live in loving obedience with their parents until they become of age! The only effective solution to youth problems today is the winning of the young for the master. A deep experience of God's salvation is their only safeguard in a world of increasing sin.

Little Is Much If God Is in It

"A certain poor widow . . . threw in two mites,
which make a farthing." *Mark 12:42.*

When we talk about giving the widow's mite, we are apt to forget that her mite represented *all* the money she possessed at that time. The rich, who ostentatiously cast their gifts into the Temple treasury, gave what they could spare. Their offering was not tinged with personal sacrifice as was the widow's gift. What material for an artist there is in this incident of Jesus' watching the worshipers cast their gifts into the Temple box! Can you not picture him scrutinizing every giver as the offering was surrendered? With his omniscience he knew each one's worth, what each was able to give, and what was actually given. Although the rich man cast in much, he did not give according to his ability, and so his giving was not sacrificial.

Jesus judges our offering, not by the amount we give, but what is left after we have given. The widow had nothing left, for she gave *all* she had, believing that God would hear the scraping of her barrel and provide her with further money and food, for he is no one's debtor. Do we, like the widow Jesus commended, give and give until it hurts? He still sits over against the treasury, evaluating our giving. The needs of his Temple must be met and can only be met out of the money he has provided his own. Is mine a faithful stewardship? Can I truthfully sing with Frances Ridley Havergal, "Take my silver and my gold, not a mite would I withhold"?

Fame of a Nameless Small Ship

"Jesus spake to his disciples that a small ship should wait on him." Mark 3:9.

What a delightful touch Mark gives us of the need of Jesus at a time when the crowds were eager to hear him preach and teach! The disciples obtained an ordinary-looking little boat like many others used by those who earned their living by fishing. Its workmanship and fittings would be crude by standards today, but the day came when that little ship had its hour of opportunity. Its timbers were destroyed by decay centuries ago, and any name it may have had is unrecorded; yet the small vessel lives forever in the pages of God's record book because of the service it rendered the Master.

A great mass of people were eager to hear him, and the pressure of the crowd forced him to the edge of the Sea of Galilee. But Jesus performed no miracle to cope with the situation, as he could have done. He simply asked for a small ship which he could use as a pulpit to preach to the multitudes who had surged to the water's edge. This was a humble means to help him continue his self-sacrificing service.

Does not that small ship have a message for your heart and mine? We may be very ordinary, very frail, with nothing whatever to distinguish us from other little ships on the sea of life. Yet such is the condescension of Jesus that he asks us to be at his disposal, to wait upon him, ready should he need us. If we unreservedly place ourselves at his disposal, caring not what use he may make of us, conscious only of the honor that will be ours if he uses our ordinary ship, then one day his commendation will be ours: "Well done, good and faithful servant." Our small ship he used will bring eternal reward.

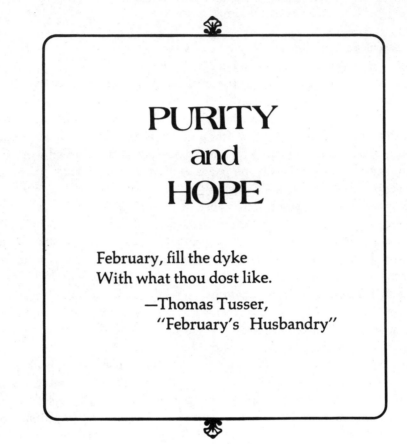

PURITY
and
HOPE

February, fill the dyke
With what thou dost like.

—Thomas Tusser,
"February's Husbandry"

Veils

"The veil that is spread over all nations." *Isaiah 25:7.*

In the "Rubáiyát of Omar Khayyám," translated by Edward Fitzgerald of the eighteenth century, is this interesting reference to veils: "There was the Veil through which I might not see." From first to last, the Bible has a good deal to say about veils. The veil that covered Moses' face hid from others the glory of the Lord upon whom Moses had gazed. The veil Isaiah mentioned was the emblem of national sin and unbelief. Humankind is blinded by the god of this world and cannot, therefore, see the God of another world. Sin always obscures God from our vision. Virtue is ever necessary to vision. "The pure in heart see God." Thus purity of heart means clarity of vision.

The smallest matter, alien to the holiness of God, can shut him out of the life. Individual sins may seem of small moment, but an opaque veil can be woven out of a very fine thread. To lose God from our sights is to commit self-murder, for he alone can completely fill our vision. Isaiah predicted the time when Israel's veil of unbelief is to be forever destroyed and the nation rejoice in the full-ordered vision of God. Through the rent veil of the Redeemer's flesh we can now behold all he made possible for our spiritual sight. The veil of sense hangs dark between his blessed face and ours, but before long this last covering of sense, the flesh, and time will be removed, and with nothing between we shall see him as he is and through seeing him be transformed into his likeness.

Prison Songs

"At midnight Paul and Silas . . . sang praises unto God:
and the prisoners heard them." *Acts 16:25.*

The power of song to charm the hearts of the most sullen is proverbial.
"Give me the making of the nation's songs, and I care not who makes
its laws" was the contention of someone who believed in the fascina-
tion of music. Hilaire Belloc, an English writer who died in 1953, would
have us know, "It is the best of all trades, to make songs, and the
second best to sing them." Songs have led crusades, won battles, and
molded the character of nations. The song Paul and Silas sang at the
midnight hour resulted in the manifestation of divine power and in the
transformation of lives. The prayers and praises of Paul and Silas must
be taken together, because, as an unknown author wrote,

Prayers and praises go together,
He hath praises that hath prayers.

What a charming influence that apostolic singing had—the prisoners
heard them. This trifling fact has a deeper meaning than a mere casual
hearing. In spite of their bleeding backs, confinement in a filthy prison,
and the late hour, Paul and Silas could sing, and their victorious gladness
in spite of adverse circumstances caused the other prisoners to listen
most attentively, for what they heard was the voice of God. It is quite
easy to be happy in pleasant circumstances when life is sunny and
bright, but to sing in a dungeon when all is bleak and dark is a miracle.
Sorrowful, yet always rejoicing is a special gift and grace of the Spirit.
General William Booth once said that God was so well pleased with the
praises of Paul and Silas that he said, "Amen! with a mighty earthquake." In the conversion of the jailer, the singing produced a spiritual
earthquake. Is yours the singing heart?

The Unknown, Unseen Audience

"And the prisoners were listening to them." *Acts 16:25*, RV.

When the earthquake rocked the prison, the jailer was afraid that all the prisoners had escaped, but Paul assured the Spirit-convicted man that all inmates were still present. Strange though it may seem, Paul and Silas escaped *from* prison while *in* prison because their faith in the Lord for whom they were suffering enabled them to be oblivious to adversity and superior to their surroundings. Singing praises to God after being soundly beaten and flung into prison, with feet locked in stocks, is an event of the most triumphant nature in the early annals of the church. When the two prisoners appeared to be hilarious, they were not thinking of fellow prisoners. They were unconscious of any audience, thinking only of God and his goodness and his unconquerable and all-providing love. The other prisoners, suffering the same fate and chafing under the same fetters, were not able to pray and sing, hence their desire to know the secret of that strange victorious thrill in the singing of Paul and Silas.

Our fault is our ignorance of the unseen audience watching us, noting our bearing, taking stock of our attitude when the trials, adversities, and sorrows of life overtake us. It has been said that consciously or unconsciously the one half of the world is playing eavesdropper to the other half. Do we personally realize that we have an unseen audience, that people take their view of Jesus from what they see in us? If they hear us sing in our prison rather than hear us moan when the dark and difficult overtake us, they will not be long in asking the secret of our glorying in tribulation.

37

Roses in the Desert

"The desert shall rejoice, and blossom as the Rose."
Isaiah 35:1.

Although the regathering of Israel and kingdom blessing were in the mind of Isaiah in the prophecy before us, there is a truth for our own hearts if ours is the solitariness and barrenness of a desert. Any personal desert blossoms as the rose when Jesus, the Rose of Sharon, passes through it. "For December God gives May," wrote Lord Byron. The desert of separation from all outward means of grace may be ours. Sickness may compel us to be deprived of the fellowship of the saints; yet Jesus can transform such a wilderness into a paradise. We may call those who never get out shut-ins; yet nothing can shut Jesus out of such isolation, for, wrote Charles J. Butler, "where Jesus is, 'tis Heaven there," and his presence makes the desert blossom as the rose.

In the desert of trials we may experience desolating afflictions, loss of health, possessions, and friends; yet if Jesus is our Savior and friend, he is able to transfigure all the barren experiences of life. His grace and power can transform the dreariest desert into a beautiful rose garden. Paradoxical though it may seem, Jesus was the saddest yet the gladdest man in the days of his flesh. True, he was the Man of Sorrows; yet his was the rapturous joy the Holy Spirit imparted.

Many shrink at the desert of death, recoiling from its approach. To leave a world they know and love and go out into an unknown, mysterious world makes death for them a king of terrors. But Jesus, because of his victory over the grave, can transform such a gloomy desert with the fragrant rose of a certain and glorious resurrection and bring us to the Father's home where the roses never fade.

A Face Like My Face

"The face of a man." Ezekiel 1:5, 10.

In his symbolism of the living creatures Ezekiel commences with the likeness of a man, which is as it should be since God made humankind the head of all things material (Ps. 8:6). The human face, as the Creator meant it to be, signifies conscience, intellect, sympathy, love, and all the best in humanity. The face is the window of the soul. The more completely we put on the new person, the more completely do we wear the face of a true person. These lines from "Thrice-Blessed Spirit" by James Montgomery are recollected:

> *Then with the gift of holiness within me;*
> *We're not less human, but made more divine;*
> *Our lives replete with Heaven's supernal beauty,*
> *Ever declare that beauty, Lord, is Thine.*

The world is ever quick in responding to the magnetism of a sanctified humaneness. This is why the woman of Samaria, after meeting Jesus, said to her friends, "Come see a man." Strength, holiness of character, and sympathy of heart were written upon his countenance. A man approved of God, Jesus ever remained the best of persons. Do you recall Robert Browning's moving reference to the face of Jesus in his poem "Saul"?

> *Saul, it shall be*
> *A Face, like my face that receives thee, a Man like to me,*
> *Thou shalt love and be loved for ever, A Hand like this hand*
> *Shall throw open the gates of new life to thee! See the Christ stand!*

As someone wrote, his is

> *That one Face, far from varied, rather grows,*
> *Or decomposes but to recompose.*
> *Become my universe that feels and knows.*

Saints Who Wear Aprons

"Clothe (apron) yourselves . . . with humility."
1 Peter 5:5, Amplified Bible.

The translation of Peter's exhortation given by the New English Bible reads, "All of you should wrap yourselves in the garment of humility towards each other." Phillips' New Testament in Modern English has, "All of you should defer to one another and wear the 'overall' of humility in serving each other." William Cowper wrote the line, "Humility may clothe an English dean," but such a virtue should grace everyone naming the name of him who was "meek and lowly in heart" and who "humbled himself." Growth in holiness depends upon our determination to cherish the biblical view of our own littleness and insignificance, of our vileness and unworthiness, and of our own absolute and constant dependence on the mercy and holiness of God. The possession of a meek and quiet spirit is, in the sight of God, of great price. It begets humility under cross providences, and makes us content with our lot or with such things as we have.

A Spirit-begotten humility is the best and most attractive garment for a justified sinner to wear, for God has said he will look to and dwell with the humble and grant them all necessary grace. Further, we have the promise that "he that humbleth himself shall be exalted" (Luke 14:11). It is very hard for us, though, to learn that the only way *up* is *down*. How we need to pray for the removal of a proud heart with its bane of self-adoring love! We also need to be delivered from a mock humility or from pride in being humble. Charles Dickens' Micawber prided himself on being "ever so 'umble." Both Samuel Coleridge and Robert Southey referred to one dwelling in "a cottage of gentility," whose "darling sin was to pride that apes humility." May the Lord deliver us who are made of dust from such a sin.

The Voice of the Lord

"The voice of him that crieth." *Isaiah 40:3.*

Although the possessor of this authoritative yet gracious voice is not named by the prophet, John the Baptist had no difficulty in relating Isaiah's prophecy to his own ministry as a forerunner of Jesus Christ (John 1:23). With characteristic and immovable humility John declared that in himself he was nothing. He was only a *voice*, and voices are heard not seen. He never courted prominence but wanted Jesus to be all—"He must increase, I must decrease" (John 3:30).

As a *vassal* John was harnessed to the divine chariot until his noble head was severed from his desert-tempered body. As a *vessel* he realized that his was the joy and privilege of conveying to thirsty souls the water of life, as well as baptizing those who repented of their sins in Jordan's waters. As a *voice* John wanted his tones and utterances to sound forth the praises of Jesus, whose way the Baptist prepared.

Has it dawned on us, if we are the Lord's, that we are voices, only voices? With such a recognition we must see that our voices are distinct and individual. A ventriloquist's dummy has a voice which is not its own and has no clear accent of its own. As the saints of God we are no mere echoes, like parrots that can only repeat what they pick up from our speech. Ours must be a personal, definite, and unmistakable accent. "My King has his secrets for me, for me apart from my brother and sister in the family," said an unknown writer of a past generation, "and these secrets should give their distinctive aroma and perfume to the gospel I speak." Are our ears tuned to hear "the voice of the Lord" from the excellent glory (Gen. 1:6)?

41

A Mixture of Liquids

"Come ye to the waters . . . come, buy wine and milk."
Isaiah 55:1.

Because of the abundance of divine provision for our needy hearts, the Bible multiplies metaphors to describe the variety of blessings God waits to bestow. All our thirsty souls require has been bountifully secured and can be had without money and without price. In God's uttermost salvation there is no deficiency or disappointment.

Think of it—*there is water!* As sinners, dying of spiritual thirst, we have but to stoop and drink and live. In Jesus we discover the well of water springing up into eternal life. Tragic, is it not, that countless numbers die of thirst when the unfailing well is close at hand. Then *there is milk*—even the milk of the Word, with all its spiritual nourishment. Life begotten by the Spirit of God must be sustained by the Word of God. Left to ourselves we are so frail and helpless, but milk, plenty of it, is at our disposal in the divine promises that we might be strong and grow thereby.

Further, *there is wine* in God's cup of salvation, and how gracious it is of him to provide us with the wine of spiritual joy! Such wine not only makes our faces to shine, but counteracts all restlessness and begets a deep and abiding peace—a joy unspeakable and full of glory. Full of the new wine of the Spirit, ours is a spiritual merriment independent of all circumstances. A person, drunk with manmade wine, has been guilty of excess drinking, but there is no excess when it comes to the infilling of the Spirit, for we can never have too much of him, or he of us (Eph. 5:18–20). Let us come often to God's market and buy from him the water, milk, and wine he freely and fully offers.

My Gross Flesh Sinks Downward

"They that are in the flesh cannot please God."
Romans 8:8.

A good deal of biblical truth can be found in Shakespeare's couplet in *King Richard II*:

Mount, mount, my soul! thy seat is up on high;
Whilst my gross flesh sinks downward, here to die.

Doubtless the famous bard only had the body in mind when he wrote of "gross flesh"; yet is it not true that what we know as the flesh sinks downward and that those controlled by it cannot please God? But what exactly is the flesh which, if we live after, shall die?

Dr. C. I. Scofield wrote in his reference Bible that " 'Flesh,' in the ethical sense, is the whole unregenerate man, spirit, soul, and body, as centered upon self, prone to sin, and opposed to God. . . . The regenerate man is not 'in [the sphere of] the flesh, but in [the sphere of] the Spirit' . . . ; but the flesh is still in him, and he may, according to his choice, 'walk after the flesh' or 'in the Spirit' . . . . Victory over the flesh will be the habitual experience of the believer who walks in the Spirit" (see note, Jude 23).

Paul warned us against making a "fair shew in the flesh" and "living after the flesh." Then the apostle also enumerated the evil offspring the flesh produces (Gal. 5:19). It is far better to bear "the fruit of the Spirit." We read that in the days of Gideon "Fire out of the rock . . . consumed the flesh" (Judg. 6:21). *Fire* is a symbol of the Holy Spirit, and "the smitten rock" is a type of Christ. Had there been no smitten rock at Calvary, there would have been no fire at Pentecost. Our sinful flesh cannot abide the blood of a rock and the fire of the Spirit.

My Feeble Arms Entwine Thy Stem

"Without me ye can do nothing." John 15:5.

This authoritative assertion must be interpreted in the light of our Lord's metaphor of himself as the "true vine." As branches are entirely dependent upon the main stem for life-giving sap, enabling them to bear fruit, so apart from him, in whom we live, move, and have our being, we can do nothing, have nothing, and are nothing. We are not, and can never be, sufficient of ourselves, and it is utter folly to attempt to do anything without reliance upon him who is our wisdom and strength. A conscious and constant sense of weakness and utter inability makes us sensibly dependent upon the Lord as our hidden source of every precious thing.

In him alone is our help found. Only in union with him can we receive from him all that is necessary for us to glorify him, adorn our profession, enjoy our blood-bought privilege, and obey all the holy precepts of his gospel. As we come up out of the wilderness leaning on him who is our beloved, we shall not perish by the way. Is he not the life-giving head, the fountain from which we can draw our supplies, the friend to whom we can carry all our cares, and our never-failing treasury filled with boundless stores of grace?

As branches, then, we cannot bear fruit of ourselves. Around him, as the all-supporting vine, our feeble arms must twine, and as we abide in him, he works in and through us to do of his own good pleasure. We sing the words from "I Hunger and I Thirst" by J. S. B. Monsell:

> *Thou true life-giving Vine,*
> *Let me Thy sweetness prove;*
> *Renew my life with Thine,*
> *Refresh my soul with love.*

Here We Stand!

"Our God . . . is able to deliver us . . . .
But if not . . . we will not serve thy gods." *Daniel 3:16–18.*

Without doubt, the three Hebrew youths who defied the edict of a heathen king were the forebears of the courageous Mr. Standfast, whom John Bunyan depicted. His head was so steady and his heart like "a glowing coal while he stood and talked in the middle of the giddy stream," and he is our inspiration to "stand fast in the Lord." With their backs to the wall, the three youths assumed a stand of faith which no threats could shake. They scorned any compromise in the choice they were called upon to make. The foundation of the faith of Daniel's companions was the unshakable belief that God would see them through since he knew how to checkmate all plans of evil. The prospect of a burning fiery furnace did not frighten those three brave, godly youths, for they knew that wrong cannot heat a furnace which God cannot put out.

But their faith did not rest in God's ability to deliver them from the furnace. What if he did permit his stalwart followers to perish in the flames? This brings us to one of the most blessed *buts* of the Bible— "But if not, be it known unto thee, O king, that we will not serve thy gods." Was this not the same spirit actuating Martin Luther when, declaring his opposition to heresy, he exclaimed, "Here I stand, I can do no other"? God responded to such faith as the three youths and Luther displayed; he always does. In the furnace (Dan. 3:25), one "like the Son of God" assured their hearts that as they were standing up for him he was present, standing up for them, delivering them from the very smell of fire.

Going Round in Circles

"It is he that sitteth upon the circle of the earth."
Isaiah 40:22.

Although this is the only reference to the term *circle* in the Bible, and applies to the sphericity of the earth, a fact frequently mentioned, the kindred term *circuit* occurs more often. The word *compass*, meaning to go round about, to surround, encircle, occurring over ninety times, has the similar connotation as *circle* or *circuit*. Disraeli once wrote, "We all of us live too much in a circle." But there are some circles we cannot live too much in as a perusal of the God-breathed pages of the Bible reveal.

There is the *circle of divine providence*: "Thou *compassest* my path and lying down" (Ps. 139:3). Blessed to know that we have a God of love encircling us at all times! An ancient saying of unknown origin reads, "The nature of God is a circle of which the center is everywhere and the circumference is nowhere." Our activity and resting are within the sweep of such a circle of divine favor and provision (Ps. 5:12). All saved by grace are within the gleaming circle of Jehovah's approval.

Then the psalmist desired to live in the *circle of worship*: "So will I compass thine altar, O Lord" (Ps. 26:6). Compassing the altar means continuous, watchful, and enthusiastic worship. Further, our spiritual witness may bring us into the *circle of enmity*: "My deadly enemies compass me about" (Ps. 17:9). When God permits such a formidable circle to be drawn around his children, he is ever within the circle with them for their protection and deliverance, even when compassed about with iniquity (Ps. 49:5).

He promises the *circle of a joyful deliverance*: "Thou shalt compass me about with songs of deliverance" (Ps. 32:7). *Infirmity* may be a tragic circle hemming us all in, but ere long our presence will be in the glittering circle of the glorified (Heb. 5:2, 12:1). Till then, let us rest in the circle of his love.

The Bubbling Wellspring

"Therefore with joy shall ye draw water
out of the wells of salvation." *Isaiah 12:3.*

George Meredith was a nineteenth-century English writer. In "Love in the Valley," one of his beautiful descriptions of nature, he bade us ever remember her loveliness and provision and then said to his own heart:

So were it with me if forgetting could be willed.
Tell the grassy hollow that holds the bubbling well-spring,
Tell it to forget the source that keeps it filled.

The wells of water springing up into everlasting life have their source in Jesus, as the woman at the well of Sychar came to learn. Isaiah's reference to wells was colored by the service of the priests who, during the days of the Feast of Tabernacles and amid the blare of trumpets and clash of cymbals, would draw with the golden vases the cool, sparkling water from the pool of Siloam, while the people exchanged the words quoted above.

The source of our salvation is no mere, small reservoir, but *wells*, for the springs of grace is the Trinity—the Father, the Son, the Holy Spirit. All three combine to emancipate the soul from sin and hell. The *drawing* process is equivalent to the sinner's personal appropriation of the Savior. As the sinner comes to experience the gladness of forgiveness of sin and a quieted conscience, there is received the joy of a conscious fellowship with the Savior and a bright hope of an inheritance incorruptible. This joy renders the sinner independent of all circumstances. Why die of thirst with such bubbling wellsprings at hand?

The Greatness of Little Things

"Behold how great a matter a little fire kindleth."
James 3:5.

The ancient question, "Who hath despised the day of small things?" reminds us of our tendency to look with suspicion and even contempt upon that which is outwardly insignificant. But past history and present experience prove the folly of underrating the value of little things. The fall of an apple led to the discovery of the law of gravitation, just as steam from a kettle inspired the invention of the steam engine.

Little things often result in great spiritual changes. The mere "look" of Jesus produced a great transformation in Peter. *Little things reveal human character.* Adam was tested by an apple. Those who are faithful over a few things, even giving a cup of cold water in Christ's name, earned his reward. Often we are presently judged by how we act in reference to little things, therefore, we should never be off our guard, acting unconscious of observation. *Little things will be judged in the high court of heaven.* Often a trifling occurrence forms damning evidence against a convicted person. We may think words to be little things of no consequence, but Jesus said that we are to account for every idle word spoken.

Let us then beware of looking with doubt or contempt on little things. The great Protestant Reformation under Martin Luther may be traced to the hour when he discovered an old Bible in the Erfut Monastery.

Jehovah of the Thunders

"I answered thee in the secret place of thunder."
Psalm 81:7.

Rudyard Kipling in his "Hymn before Action" described God as

Jehovah of the Thunders,
Lord God of Battles, aid!

From the psalmist's mystical avowal Israel was reminded that their cry had penetrated the divine dwelling place, "the secret place of thunder," out of which "the voice of his thunder" is heard (Ps. 104:7). God always recalls and answers those prayers in harmony with his will, but such answers come out of "the secret place of thunder." Bishop John Perowne called it "the secret place of *the* thunder." Thomas Macaulay asserted that "God made the thunder, but the lightning made itself."

Thunder is secret if not silent. How awed we are by all-shaking, mysterious thunder! The electric collisions by which science explains thunder do not fully account for its reverberating peals. The psalmist would have us know that this is God's shrine of mystery. He ever abides in "the secret place of thunder." God is loving and merciful; yet he is a great and terrible God. His grace is environed with secrecies and awfulness, but behind his thunderous terribleness is his love.

A tender heart is ever at the source of things. Thunder may affright us, but ineffable sympathy causes us to lose our fear in a great delight. "Behind a frowning Providence, He hides a smiling face," wrote William Cowper. God answers prayer from his secret place of thunder. Although the thunderclouds surrounding him may be very dark, they cannot deaden the voice of believing prayer. Triumph is ours when we have prayer answered from God's awesome abode.

The Instrument of Words

"I have put my words in thy mouth." *Jeremiah 1:9.*

We all know that there can be "a barren superfluity of words," as Sir Samuel Garth, who died in 1719, wrote in "The Dispensary," but the words Jeremiah mentioned are wonderful words of life and are therefore to be treasured. If a friend anticipates and articulates what we are to say, our common expression is, "Why, you took the words right out of my mouth!" But here is one who puts words into our mouths to utter.

Among those believing in divine inspiration are two schools of thought. The *plenary* inspiration of Scripture means that God gave us thoughts but left us to express these revealed thoughts in language of our own choice. Those who believe in *verbal* inspiration hold that God gave us both the thoughts and the words with which to clothe them. God affirms such verbal inspiration in his mandate, "I have put my words in thy mouth."

We cannot have thoughts apart from words. Any thoughts coming into our mind are a collection of words. It is utterly impossible for a thought to be naked of words. When God compiled his Word, he put his thoughts into the minds of men and his words into their mouths, and then they wrote and spoke as they were moved by his Spirit. The truth of God shapes our testimony, for when his Word dwells richly in us with all wisdom, there is no difficulty about a correct and effective utterance. The words of our mouth coming out of the meditation of the heart are ever acceptable in God's sight and fruitful in accomplishing his redemptive purpose. When a watch is set upon our lips, the words leaving them honor God.

Unbelieving Believers

"If I had called, and he had answered me; yet I would not believe that he had hearkened unto my voice." *Job 9:16.*

Is not this honest admission of Job's a strange one? The patriarch certainly believed God heard and answered prayer, but on this occasion he was evidently an unbelieving believer. He would have been amazed if God had hearkened to his request.

Is this lack of faith strikingly illustrated for us in the early history of the church? Because of his loyal witness, Peter was thrown into prison, and fellow believers, with no reservations about God's ability to deliver his faithful servant, met to pray for his release. As their prayers became intense, Rhoda heard a knock on the door and, recognizing Peter's voice, was too overwhelmed to open the door and let him in. She hurried back to the praying band who were still pleading to God for Peter's liberation. When Rhoda raised her voice and said that the miracle *had* happened and that Peter was at the door, the intercessors said to her, "Thou art mad." But she constantly affirmed that it was so and was told, "It must be Peter's angel." The knocking continued, however, and when the intercessors opened the door and saw the answer to their prayers, they were astonished.

Are we not also guilty of praying without faith in God's ability to respond immediately? An unknown author declared:

> *God tries us by His long delays,*
> *And then our faith surprises;*
> *While we in unbelief deplore*
> *And wonder at His staying,*
> *He stands already at the door*
> *To interrupt our praying.*

Here's Double Health to Thee

"Thy saving health among all nations." Psalm 67:2.

Often we salute each other's health, as Lord Byron did in his salutation to Thomas Moore: "Here's a double health to thee!" Such a custom recognizes the importance of health, emphasized by Izaak Walton of the seventeenth century, who gave us the remarkable work on fishing, *The Compleat Angler.* "Look to your health; and if you have it, praise God, and value it next to a good conscience; for health is the second blessing that we mortals are capable of; a blessing that money cannot buy."

The Bible has much to say about our health and about the secrets of its continuance. God declares himself the source of health when he extols himself as the saving health of nations (Ps. 67:2; Rev. 22:2). Our prospect of paradise includes being perfectly healthy because then we shall be perfectly holy. Presently, God offers himself as "the health of our countenance" (Ps. 42:11, 43:5).

Those who want to look healthily beautiful should tarry longer in God's beauty parlor. Cosmetics may produce an artificial healthy look, but a shower of rain can soon remove a temporary glow on the cheeks. Clear eyes, ruddy cheeks, and a well-nourished face depend upon pure blood for their healthiness. Good food, good living, good books, and good company all share in creating those streams responsible for a fresh-looking countenance. Twice over God offers himself as "the health of our countenance," which means that he is the unfailing source of both our physical and spiritual health.

What God Hath Joined Together

"A just God and a Saviour." *Isaiah 45:21.*

There is a great deal more than meets the eye in this double designation of the Almighty one—God and Savior—the evangelical prophet exalted. The former appellation represents justice, and the latter, grace. God is also the source of love, but he cannot part with his justice even to gratify his love. The marvel of the gospel of redemption is that his justice shines equally with his grace in the present and eternal salvation of the repentant and believing sinner.

The message of Calvary is that God gave his Son as the substitute for sinners appointing him to be his surety, punishing him in the sinner's stead. Though guiltless, God justly condemned his Son to die because the sin of humankind was imputed to him. Then God justly raised Jesus from the dead because sin had been expiated by him. Thus, as a just God, he will never exact the same debt of the sinner, which was paid by his surety, or condemn the sinner for that which his or her substitute atoned. As the result of the cross God is still just, yet the justifier of all those who believe in him who died on it (Rom. 3:26).

Divine justice will ever sparkle as a jewel in our eternal acquittal and be eternally honored in our endless salvation. In a past eternity God conceived the plan of salvation and sent his Son to execute it. He then gave the Holy Spirit, who brings us into possession of all purest grace has provided. To quote from an unknown writer:

Here His justice He displays,
While He saves my soul by grace.

53

Earth's Greatest Traveler

"Went not mine heart with thee?" 2 *Kings 5:26.*

In these days of speedy air travel we are able to reach far distances in no time and can journey around the world quickly and repeatedly. Still more staggering to the mind is that the heart is able to undertake pilgrimages and excursions. In reply to Elisha's question as to where he went, Gehazi answered, "Thy servant went no whither" (II Kings 5:25). Then the prophet uttered a reply which must have humiliated his evil servant. The pursuing heart of Elisha, because it was godly, was capable of traveling to remoter reaches than the hearts of many can attain.

There is a sense in which all hearts can, and do, travel swiftly and widely. In a moment of time our thoughts and imaginations can be with a dear one thousands of miles away. But the travels of consecrated hearts are more wonderful still, even though we may never journey physically from our own homes.

The penetrating word of Elisha can be given several applications. As the heart of Elisha followed Gehazi every step of his wicked way, so the heart of God ever follows the sinner on his evil course, striving to arrest the sinner and save him. As those who love God we too should travel out to the lost in prayer, love, hope, and compassion. Further, when Spirit-led Christians set forth as God's emissaries to preach the gospel in any part of the world, does not the heart go with them? And the hearts of those who tarry by the staff at home should travel to the regions beyond in intercession and sacrificial giving. Have we much-traveled hearts of sympathy? When dear ones leave us for glory, do our hearts journey heavenward? Do we have "mystic sweet communion with those whose rest is won," as Samuel J. Stone wrote? A greater than Elisha says to us all, "Went not mine heart with thee?" Did he not say, "Whither canst thou flee from my presence?" (Ps. 139:7)?

Rosemary, That's for Remembrance

"Thus saith the Lord, I remember thee." *Jeremiah 2:2.*

Shakespeare in *Hamlet* chose the fragrant shrub Rosemary as an emblem of fidelity and undying remembrance, and "Pansies, that's for thoughts." As the lover of our souls, God never forgets the kindness of our spiritual youth. He ever remembers our first love, and if such has declined, he strives to bring back the joy and blessedness of our espousals. By his Spirit and through his Word and providential dealings God seeks to restore the joy and grace of a day that seems to be dead. In various ways he endeavors to wean us from a disappointing present and return us to a much-blessed past. Spiritual decline can overtake us in many ways. Love must be fed, but we forget to nourish our affection for the Master and for his Word. If love for him is to be kept fresh and warm and ever-deepening, then unbroken, intimate fellowship with the Lord must be daily cultivated.

Possibly the root cause of spiritual coldness is the failure to exercise our love for the divine lover and remembrancer. Love failed to busy itself laboring for the beloved. Self-pleasing overcame sacrifice. Preoccupation gradually misplaced our energies, and love waned. In the chilly, hostile atmosphere of the world, love for spiritual things quickly withers if we fail to shield such a love. Fleshy appetites and carelessness can also produce the little rift within the lover's lute. Is it not blessed to know that God's love is ever the same, that nothing can change his attitude toward us, that if we forget him, he will never forget us? Divine remembrance is a paradise from which we cannot be driven. Clasp this blessed truth to your heart and sing with William Cowper: "I will ever remember thee."

A Trinity of Evil

"Iniquity . . . sinned . . . transgressed." *Jeremiah 33:8.*

Because of the enormity of sin the Bible has many ways of describing its nature and works. Jeremiah, the weeping prophet, sadly depicted Judah's sin in the triad of terms above, all three of which refer to the same ugly sore afflicting, not only those to whom Jeremiah preached, but also ourselves. First, the word *iniquity* carries the idea of something that is warped, bent, twisted. The word *right* suggests that which is straight and direct, while *wrong*, associated with "wrung," indicates something forcibly diverted or wrung, from a right line. From Eve down, Satan has diverted humanity from its original, proper course. Born with a twist in the wrong direction, man is not "straight." A sinner by birth, he becomes a sinner by practice.

The second word *sin* carries the hiss of the serpent in its pronunciation and has the idea of an archer "missing the mark." We read in the *Shorter Catechism* that "man's chief end is to glorify God, and to enjoy him for ever," but such an objective has been missed, for all have sinned and come short of the glory of God, as Paul affirmed. The miss becomes a *mess* in life and character.

Transgression, an oft-repeated biblical description of sin, signifies "rebellion" or sinning against authority. We are accustomed to seeing the notice over some forbidden area, Trespassers Will Be Prosecuted. A sinner then is one who has trespassed, entered forbidden grounds, thereby rebelling against God's commands. But the glory of the gospel is that our *iniquities* can be removed, our *transgressions* forgiven, and our *sins* covered, all because of Calvary.

Author of Peace, Lover of Concord

"Until Shiloh come." *Genesis 49:10.*

The above title is part of a Collect for Peace found in the Book of Common Prayer: "The Author of peace and Lover of concord, in knowledge of whom standeth our eternal life, whose service is perfect freedom." The promise and prophecy of Shiloh is primarily related to Israel. The name means "Peace-bringer" and forecasts the mission of the coming Messiah to bring peace to those who walk in darkness and also to the blood-soaked, war-scarred world. Until Shiloh comes, there will be distress among nations with perplexity, and men's hearts will fail them for fear. May he, as the Prince of Peace, hasten his coming as the lover of concord!

The present question is, As Shiloh, has Jesus come to our hearts? Possibly he is our Savior, but not our Shiloh. We have his pardon for the past but not his peace of heart for the present. We deny him, the lover of our souls, full control of our lives. Yet he who is our peace and our Shiloh is the only safeguard against fear, worry, and unbelieving anxiety. When he takes the throne and conquers every harassing foe, a peace passing all understanding is ours. Beset then by trials and temptations though you may be, a blessed tranquillity becomes yours when Shiloh comes to reign over the empire of your heart. "My peace I give unto you" (John 14:27).

Glittering Like a Morning Star

"There shall come a Star out of Jacob." Numbers 24:17.

Edmund Burke, the eighteenth-century British statesman, wrote of the then queen of France in flattering terms. Among other similes, he described her as "glittering like the morning star, full of life, and splendour, and joy." Alas, however, Burke lived to see such a star extinguished. But in Jesus we have a star whose life and splendor and joy can never be extinguished, for external brilliance is his.

Balaam's messianic prophecy provides us with a most expressive picture of Christ's mission. At his birth a brilliant star called "his star" guided the wise men to his feet. Balaam, however, looked upon the Messiah who was to come as *the* star himself, which agrees with Jesus' own description of himself as the "Bright and Morning Star." Christ came as prophesied, not only to guide his people Israel, but with undimmed light and radiance to provide direction for all who follow him. Like the morning star, he is the promise of a better, brighter day, not only for Israel, but for the world at large.

Emerson advised us in "Civilization" to "hitch our wagon to a star." We never lose our way if the wagon of life is hitched to him who is our star out of Jacob. Ours is a dark age, but to the believer Christ is the bright pole star of hope, for in him alone is there the prospect of a life without sin and a world without tears. John S. B. Monsell wrote in "Fight of Faith":

> *Run the straight race through God's good grace,*
> *Lift up thine eyes, and seek His Face;*
> *Life with its ways before us lies,*
> *Christ is the path, and Christ the prize.*

Unto His Captain, Christ

"As captain of the host of the Lord am I now come."
Joshua 5:14.

In *King Richard II* Shakespeare wrote the following lines:

And there, at Venice, gave
His body to that pleasant country's earth
And his pure soul unto his captain, Christ,
Under whose colours he had fought so long.

The mysterious man Joshua saw declared himself to be the captain of the Lord's host, who was indeed the "captain Christ" in theophanic form. Immediately, Joshua recognized the superior command of the one who had intercepted him and wisely accepted his divine leadership. The hosts of Israel stood before the gateway of the Promised Land. No swords were drawn for their own defense and conquest; yet Jericho and all the giants of the land were forced to submit as Israel went forth under the colors of their invincible captain. Israel was no longer master of its own fate or captain of its own soul.

In the Gospel era Christ was presented as "the captain of our salvation" (Heb. 2:10). Bishop William Walsham How described him: "Thou, Lord, their Captain in the well-fought fight." Valiantly, he met the satanic foe, triumphed gloriously over him, and now seeks to lead all who are sin-bound into liberty. Is he our "Captain Christ" under whose colors we march? If so, then his orders must be obeyed and his plans gladly executed. We repeat with Charles Wesley:

Captain of the hosts of God,
In the path where Thou hast trod,
Bows my soul in humble awe,
Take command. Thy word is law.

Thou Great Good Husband

"Thy Maker is thine husband." Isaiah 54:5.

In his poem "The Ant" Richard Lovelace, of the seventeenth century, said, "Forbear, thou great good husband, little ant." I have no hesitation in lifting the poet's description out of context, however, and applying it to him whose husbandhood is frequently mentioned in Scripture. Isaiah's statement provides us with a twofold description of our Lord. First, he is our *maker*. We often speak of those who achieve success in business as being self-made, but actually there are no self-made individuals, for the Lord is the Maker of us all. All were made by him (John 1:3). Would that all men knew how to bow before their marvelous Maker!

Next, this maker is our *husband*, a love relationship applicable to Israel who is often called the wife of Jehovah (Hos. 2:1–23). But as a wife Israel was unfaithful, and God, as her husband, constantly endeavored to win back his whorish wife and forgive her for all her adultery (Isa. 54:5–10).

Another aspect of God's husbandhood, so comforting, is that of "a father to the fatherless, and a judge of the widows" (Ps. 68:5). God is often portrayed as husband of the widow and protector of her fatherless children (Hos. 14:3). If death has robbed you of a loving, good, and provident husband, leaving heart and home vacant, is it not consoling to know that he who offers to fill your dear one's place is near and can be more to you than ever a human husband could be? He can soothe your sorrows and heal your wounds since he is your "Shepherd, Husband, Friend," as John Newton would have you sing. Before long his church will be adorned as a bride to meet him as her husband.

Each to His Great Father Bends

"Our Father which art in heaven." *Matthew 6:9.*

Do you not love Samuel Coleridge's *Rime of the Ancient Mariner,* especially that section in which he described a goodly company who walk together to the kirk (Scottish for *church*)?

> *And all together pray,*
> *While each to his great Father bends,*
> *Old men, and babes, and loving friends*
> *And youths and maidens gay!*

Having considered God as husband, we now think of him as a great Father. Often a husband remains a husband, being denied fatherhood, but God is before us both as *husband* and *Father*, the latter being one of his most precious portraits. His tenderness as a Father carried him to great lengths to extricate his wayward children out of trouble. All strength, wisdom, love, and provision are his as the Father of the fatherless.

While, in the sense of creation, God is the Father of all, we cannot look up into his face and call him our heavenly Father unless his beloved Son is our personal Savior. Such a relationship is based upon regeneration in which we receive the Spirit of adoption whereby we are privileged to cry, "Abba, Father." Far too many are living without the Father's compassion displayed in the gift of his Son for a sinful race. Further, in the trials of life how consoled we are if we can sing from the heart, "I know my heavenly Father knows." We have his promise that "like as a father pitieth his children, so the Lord pitieth those who fear him" (Ps. 103:13). Are you resting in your Father's love and care?

A Rejoicing Bridegroom

"As the bridegroom rejoiceth over his bride, so shall
thy God rejoice over thee." *Isaiah 62:5.*

Jesus himself spoke of a friend rejoicing on hearing the bridegroom's
voice (John 3:29), but Isaiah reminded us of the divine bridegroom's
own joy. Such a frequent metaphor gives us another glimpse into the
tender heart of our Lord. How does a bridegroom rejoice over his bride?
First, a joyful union is the consummation of love, and the church is the
bride, for by the Spirit believers are joined to Christ in a blessed union
death cannot break. As the bridegroom claims his bride at the altar, so
Christ by his cross has possessed us forever. As the bridegroom promises
to endow the bride with all his worldly goods, so Christ makes his own
the sharers of all he possesses. "Mine are thine" (John 17:10). For his
church, the joyful marriage of the lamb is not far away, when the bride
will not gaze at her garment but on her dear bridegroom's face. How
he will rejoice over his bride when he returns for her future bliss! With
his own around him Jesus will see the travail of his soul and be satisfied.

Do we realize that we are the objects of Jehovah's delight, as Isaiah
indicates in his use of the simile of the rejoicing bridegroom? If redeemed by the blood of the Son of his love, we are the objects of his
highest love, the subjects of his sweetest thoughts, and his joyful portion
forevermore. What a source of comfort, love, and holiness the incomparable privilege of having Jesus as our bridegroom should be! We have
more cause for gratitude than the angels who cannot know him as their
bridegroom.

The Days May Come, the Days May Go

"I am with you all the days, even unto the end
of the world." *Matthew 28:20,* RV, *margin.*

We do not know the kind of days before us. Will they be full of
flowers or full of thorns, or flowers and thorns mixed together? Will
the weather be the blackest winter or glorious summer, or a mixture of
both? What we do know, however, with certainty is that the unchanging
Christ will be with us *all our days,* irrespective of nature, meeting our
every need as we seek to make each day count for him. Every day and
all the days he will be our abiding companion, to the end and through
and beyond the end to the glorious eternity where a daily calendar
is unknown.

Until the end, almost every day will include temptation, whether at
home or in business, in loneliness or with a crowd, but Jesus will be
with us to make us more than conquerors. Many days of monotony
may cause us to sigh for experiences more unusual and romantic than
unnoticed toil at home or at work. But drudgery can bring us a love-
message in disguise in the thought that he who lived among carpenter's
tools and among peasant people in his village home is with us to grace
the ordinary with his extraordinary grace. Further, as sure as tomorrow's
sun will rise, days of trial, sorrow, and loss will be ours in the future,
but he will be near us as our consoler, soothing our troubled hearts. One
of the days will be our last day; yet even then he will not leave us but
with his everlasting arms will carry us through the flood to the celestial
city where no eyes are ever wet with tears and where it is eternal day.

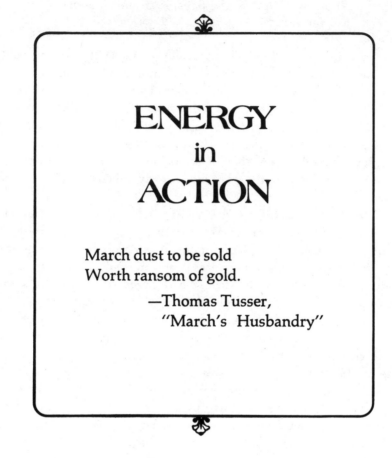

ENERGY
in
ACTION

March dust to be sold
Worth ransom of gold.

　　　　—Thomas Tusser,
　　　　　"March's Husbandry"

Here Will I Dwell

"Dwell deep . . . dwell without care . . . dwell alone."
Jeremiah 49:30–33.

The title of this meditation is taken from "Faustus," a sixteenth-century poem by Christopher Marlowe. In it Marlowe extolled Helen whose "face launched a thousand ships" and of whom Mephistopheles said, "Here will I dwell, for heaven be in these lips." We know, however, that ours is the assurance of dwelling in heaven because of the promise from Jesus' lips. Here and now we have the superb dwelling place Jeremiah spoke of, a sphere where we can "dwell without care." The villagers of Hazor were urged to flee to a city where they could "dwell without care." Jerusalem is described as a place where the inhabitants "are at rest, that dwell safely [confidently], . . . dwelling without walls" (Ezek. 38:11; Zech. 2:3–5). Haste was necessary, for Hazor was to become "a dwelling place for dragons, and a desolation for ever" (Jer. 49:33).

The Lord would have us live without carping care, but such a care-free life is only ours as we "dwell deep" in him in whom there is nothing but peace. Having such an impregnable dwelling place deep in his heart, we are safe from calamities that would overtake us (Jer. 49:8). There must also be the determination to "dwell alone" if we would "dwell without care." Our error is that we live too much with the world and are so laden with its cares and anxieties. Alone with him who would have us live "without carefulness," we are guarded against finding ourselves in "a dwelling for dragons"—the dragons of fear, worry, and remorse. How blessed we are when we can truthfully sing with Anna L. Waring:

> *My heart is resting, O my God,*
> *My heart is in Thy care;*
> *I hear the voice of joy and health*
> *Resounding everywhere.*

Much in Our Vows

"Jacob vowed a vow saying, If God will be with me . . .
then shall the Lord be my God." *Genesis 28:20, 21.*

In Shakespeare's *Twelfth Night* Viola says:

*for still we prove
Much in our vows but little in our love.*

There was much in the vow Jacob made when he found himself a solitary, friendless exile. Forced from home through his deceit, he was heavyhearted and sorrowful, and the way before him was dark and uncertain. At the close of his first day's journey, weary and sad and having the cold earth for his bed and a stone for his pillow, he wisely entered into covenant with God as to his vow if divine protection and provision were forthcoming. Jacob was not "little in his love" when he made such a vow although he was "little" in his wishes. What he humbly asked for was "to be kept in the way" and "to have bread to eat and raiment to put on."

As we know, the ensuing experiences of the sojourner prove how graciously and generously God responded to the vow Jacob made. Twenty years later when, richly laden, he returned to his "father's house in peace," he fulfilled his vow and for the rest of his days honored the Lord as *the* God whom he loved.

Have we covenanted with God and dedicated ourselves to him to honor him in the unknown path ahead? How tragic it is to set out as a traveler through the desert of the world without a guide, without a friend to "keep us in the way" and to give us bread to eat and raiment to put on! All who honor him are honored by him. He never fails. Because of all he is, he cannot fail.

A Divine Decree

"While the earth remaineth, seedtime and harvest, and
cold and heat, and summer and winter, and day and
night shall not cease." *Genesis 8:22.*

In his poem "Sleep and Poetry" John Keats referred to ten years of
overwhelming himself in poetry and then continued:

> *so I may do the deed*
> *That my own soul has to itself decreed.*

God decreed to himself that, having made the heavens and the earth, he
would guide and govern all things concerning the universe according to
his will and pleasure. Seasons return in their order as he promised they
would.

This divine decree proves *the faithfulness of God*, for he has never
failed to give us all things richly to enjoy. Every returning harvest in
every passing year reminds us of his own declaration, "I will not break,
nor alter the thing that has gone out of my lips" (Ps. 89:34).

The decree is likewise an evident manifestation of *the infinite power
of God*. Humankind may alter the surface of the earth, sow and plant
and reap, but with all its genius and science it cannot clothe the field
with golden corn or fashion one leaf of a great tree. God retains his
power of creation. His glory he cannot give to another.

Further, the decree magnifies *the goodness of God*. There are those
who try to banish him from his own creation as the atheistic philosophy
of communism does; yet God continues to shower down his blessings
even upon the communists, for he is "the Father of mercies." Over four
millenniums have elapsed since God gave his decree to Noah, and
through succeeding generations the returning seasons and harvests testify
to the fact that what God decrees, he does, and what he promises, he
performs.

An Awful Rainbow Once in Heaven

"The bow shall be in the cloud, and I will look upon it."
Genesis 9:16.

What a magnificent sight is a rainbow encircling the heavens with its belt of golden hues! Sir Walter Scott in "Marmion" praised it as being beyond man to reproduce:

> *What skilful limner o'er would choose*
> *To paint the rainbow's varying hues,*
> *Unless to mortal it were given*
> *To dip his brush in dyes of heaven?*

The rainbow God promised Noah is the one John Keats described in "Lamia" as:

> *An awful rainbow once in heaven:*
> *We know her woof, her texture; she is given*
> *In all the dull catalogue of things.*

Originally given to inspire grateful emotions in the heart of man, the rainbow God called Noah to look upon after the flood testified of God's promise never to deluge the earth again. Every rainbow that appears after a heavy shower of rain is a fresh evidence that "the water shall no more destroy all flesh." God himself, looking upon "the bow in the cloud," remembers his everlasting covenant.

But a rainbow is a striking type of spiritual blessing, as well as temporal ones. Jesus is our "bow in the cloud" of heaven's wrath, assuring us who have been saved from it that fiercer storms than any that have devastated the world have passed forever. As we see Jesus with the eye of faith appearing in the spiritual firmament, all fear is dispelled, for he is our hope of eternity's calm brightness, the reality of God's faithfulness and love—our rainbow around the throne.

When the Roundabout Way Is Best

"He led them about." *Deuteronomy 32:10.*
"God led the people about." *Exodus 13:18.*

When ultimately Pharaoh let Israel leave her bondage in Egypt, God did not allow the people to take the shortest route out of the land but led them by a roundabout way through a wilderness to the Red Sea. Thus for them the longest way out of their travail was the best way. God does not always take us by the hand and guide us over the shortest way out of trials. Had Israel taken the nearest route through Philistine country, there would have been war. The God directing them was one of deliverances even though he led his people by the most circuitous route possible. There were two ways from Egypt to the promised Canaan. One was a shortcut from the north of Egypt to the south of Canaan, a four or five days' journey. But the other way was much farther, through the wilderness, and as God was to be the guide of his people, this was the way he chose to lead Israel.

It is so hard for us to learn that if God is not directing us over the nearest way that he has not chosen the best way. What the Israelites seemed to forget was that their spirits had been broken by the prolonged slavery under Pharaoh and that if God had guided them by the quickest way to the Red Sea it would have meant such formidable enemies as the Philistines. This would have been tragic for the Israelites who were raw recruits as far as war was concerned. May grace be ours to rest in the fact that God ever does his best for those who leave the choice with him and that he has no shortcuts to his best!

Where Thou Art Guide, No Ill Can Come

"He found him in a desert land . . . he led him about, he instructed him, he kept him as the apple of his eye."
Deuteronomy 32:10.

The nineteenth-century hymnist James Edmeston wrote the following couplet in one of his sacred lyrics:

Guard us, guide us, keep us, feed us,
For we have no help but thee.

Describing most accurately God's care of his people, Moses reminded us that the eye of God's love was fixed upon them in a fourfold way: "He *found* him"; "He *led* him"; "He *instructed* him"; "He *kept* him."

What a blessed quartet of divine operations for our own hearts to dwell upon! Can you not see an emblem of yourself in Israel? Where did God *find* you? Was it not in a desert land of sin, is a waste-howling wilderness where there was no refuge for your soul? "I was lost, but Jesus found me." Then, once found, there came divine guidance and protection, for the phrase "He led him" can be translated "He compassed or encircled him about," even as the walls are roundabout Jerusalem.

Next, there is divine *instruction*: "He instructed him." Lessons are ours in God's love, faithfulness, and goodness. He teaches us about our own weakness and his all-sufficiency, about our frailty and his constancy, about our lack of fidelity and his unwavering faithfulness to his Word. Last, "He kept him as the apple of his eye." Here we have God's watchful guardianship over his saints, his unceasing vigilance even of the most obscure, unknown child of his. Not for a solitary instant does God forget or overlook any believer—a blessing no earthly monarch can bestow. May we be found resting in the joy of all God is in himself.

Lord, Contentment Still I Crave

"Better is little with the fear of the Lord than great
treasures and trouble therewith." *Proverbs 15:16.*

That such godly contentment is of great gain was emphasized by John
Bunyan in "The Shepherd Boy's Song in the Valley of Humiliation":

> *I am content with what I have,*
> *Little beit, or much:*
> *And, Lord, contentment still I crave,*
> *Because Thou savest such . . .*
> *Here little, and hereafter bliss,*
> *Is best from age to age.*

The verdict of the world, daily hastening to become rich, is different.
It forgets the wise prayer of Agur: "Give me neither poverty nor
riches; feed me with food convenient for me." We are not forbidden to
acquire riches through honest industry. What we have to guard against
is the *danger* in our fullness and the danger of forgetting that we
are but stewards under obligation to devote our substance to God's glory
through the furtherance of his cause throughout the earth. If our means
are restricted and we have to look at every penny, then "the fear of the
Lord" will keep us from repining and fill our hearts with a sweet contentment. Whatever our lot may be, we must regard it as the appoint-
ment of our heavenly Father, who knows what things we have need of.
May heavenly grace be ours to be content in whatever state God may
appoint, for such godly contentment results in great gain.

Diligence, the Mother of Good Fortune

"The thoughts of the diligent tend only to plenteousness."
Proverbs 21:5.

It is somewhat remarkable to find that the Bible has much to say about the virtue of diligence. A saying in *Don Quixote* by Cervantes was, "Diligence is the mother of good fortune, and idleness, its opposite, never brought a man to the goal of any of his best wishes." Such an observance is in agreement with Scripture: "He that tilleth his land shall have plenty of bread: but he that followeth after vain persons shall have poverty enough" (Prov. 28:19).

The term *diligence* and its cognates are found thirty-seven times in the Bible, and from these references a most enlightening exposition of all the facets of such an attribute can be developed. We are exhorted to give diligence to make our calling and election sure, to be diligent that we may be found of him in peace, without spot and blameless. "Whatsoever thy hand findeth to do, do it with thy might" (Eccles. 9:10). God does not require us to attempt what we are not able to accomplish but to serve him diligently and faithfully. "She hath done what she could" (Mark 14:8).

Because the end is drawing near, time for rescuing the perishing is running out. How can we be idle when each moment's delay may take a pearl from his crown? This is not the time to sit with folded hands, for multitudes are dying in sin, and dying thus are lost forevermore. The day is fast approaching when the Master, who commanded us to work in his vineyard, will reward those who served him faithfully and with all diligence. May his benediction be ours.

A Daily Beauty in His Life

"As thy days, so shall thy strength be."
Deuteronomy 33:25.

In *Othello* Shakespeare wrote two lines so true of the believer's daily life when he is in harmony with him of whom it is said, "O Jesus, Thou the beauty art" (Bernard of Clairvaux):

> *He hath a daily beauty in his life*
> *That makes me ugly.*

When our days are under divine protection and in receipt of divine provision, there is about them the beauty of holiness which throws into relief the ugliness of those whose days are completely destitute of divine grace and graces. Believers are pilgrims traveling through a dreary wilderness, and their days often require great strength, energy, and patience because of their differing nature.

But no matter what kind of day they face, there is always a sufficiency of strength to meet the hour of trial. The emphasis then in the promise vouched to Asher—and to your heart and mine—is on the little words *as* and *so. As* our day, no matter how it may turn out, *so* shall come the supply of sufficient grace. The promise does not pledge that we shall *not* feel the burden of the day or that we shall *not* feel the weight of our responsibilities and trials. The promise pledges that necessary grace will be imparted equal to the kind of day we experience. Strength will be provided when the tempest rises and rages, just as strength will be imparted to grapple when the last enemy comes forth to meet us. We may not know what a day may bring forth, even if ours is, as Wordsworth wrote, "the dreary intercourse of daily life," but God knows what each day holds for us. If need for grace arises, there will be grace for the need.

Forward and Onward

"The path of the just is as the shining light that shineth
more and more unto the perfect day." *Proverbs 4:18.*

George Meredith wrote of "the rapture of the forward view." Was this
not the rapture flooding the soul of Paul when he urged the saints to
"press toward the mark for the prize of the high calling of God in
Christ Jesus" (Phil. 3:14)? As pilgrims we must make progress and never
pause in our heavenly journey. We can never be static, for we are either
advancing or going backward. Not until we reach "the perfect day" can
we pause and say, "Here will I rest." Grasping with firmness the banner
of the conquering cross, we must affirm the motto, "Forward and
Onward." Our path, if we are among those justified by the blood, is a
"shining light." In spite of any obscurity or gloom that may cloud our
path, God's marvelous light is ever enabling us to see ahead and make
progress. Jesus is always with us as "a light to lighten our darkness."

Our light is also progressive, shining "more and more." Even as the
dawn of morn creeps gradually on to midday splendor, so we journey on
from the first dawn of spiritual light to the warmer rays of "the Sun
of Righteousness" who ever compasseth our path. Further, that first
dawn is the undeviating precursor of the perfect day of glory, for "Love
perfecteth all that it begins." How often we are exhorted to advance at
all times, never weary in our well-doing and holy living, knowing that
"we shall reap, if we faint not"! May grace and power be ours to finish
our course in triumphant joy.

Worn with Life's Cares

"But I would have you without carefulness."
1 Corinthians 7:32.

The wish of Paul for the saints at Corinth can be grouped with the Savior's injunction, "Take therefore no thought for the morrow: for the morrow shall take thought for the things of itself. Sufficient unto the day is the evil thereof" (Matt. 6:34). Both passages emphasize the same truth and indicate the same line of Christian conduct. Often the words of the Savior and the apostle are misunderstood. Such a dual exhortation does not imply that we are to be "without carefulness" in regard to our highest and eternal interests. What is meant by "carefulness" and "take no thought" is not prudent attention to the affairs of life, not the suppression of forethought, but freedom from *anxious, corroding, and carping care.*

That Jesus commended forethought is seen in the verse preceding the one above where he urged his own to "Seek first the kingdom of God, and his righteousness." Both verses, thus, refer to the carefulness of overanxiety, but not to the carefulness of prudence. Godly care in all matters is praiseworthy, but Scripture forbids distrustful care and a restless apprehension as to what may happen since such an attitude robs us of peace of heart. William Henry Davies wrote in "Leisure":

What is this life if, full of care,
We have no time to stand and stare?

Faith leaves all obstacles and events in the hands of him who holds the balances in which are weighed grace and trial and who stands ready to make good the promise, "My God shall supply *all* your need" (Phil. 4:19). Why worry then about the morrow? Worry is the enemy of trust.

I Am a Stranger Here

"I am a stranger in the earth." *Psalm 119:19.*

The Israelites were bidden to remember that they were not only strangers but strangers in a strange land (Exod. 2:22). Yet they had the assurance of the presence and provision of one who could say, "I am a stranger with thee" (Ps. 39:12). Enlarging upon their sojourning in the wilderness, the writer to the Hebrews described them as being both "strangers and pilgrims on the earth" (Heb. 11:13). Is there any difference between a *stranger* and a *pilgrim*? We think there is, for a stranger is *away from home* and a pilgrim is *on his way home.* As believers we are both. In this meditation I am concerned with the *stranger* aspect of our pilgrimage.

Our roots are not in earth. We have no fixed and final residence here, for like those of old we seek "a better country that is an heavenly." This world, "the City of Destruction," as John Bunyan described it, is but a stop on the way to our heavenly home. Like Israel, we are in a "land wherein thou art a stranger" (Gen. 17:8). The inhabitants of this land who are very much at home in it and are loath to leave it may think us strange as we live detached from the ways of the world, but this is part of the price we must pay for being followers of him who had nowhere to lay his head and who said, "They are not of the world, even as I am not of the world" (John 17:14). In "The King's Business" Dr. E. T. Cassel wrote:

> *I am a stranger here within a foreign land,*
> *My home is far away upon a golden strand;*
> *Ambassador to be of realms beyond the sea,*
> *I'm here on business for my King.*

An Early Riser

"I sent unto you all my servants the prophets, rising early, and sending them." *Jeremiah 44:4*.

Early birds catch more than worms as the psalmist proved when early in the morning he sought the Lord and as Mary Magdalene discovered when early in the morning, while it was yet dark, she came to the grave of Jesus (John 20:1). The continuing message of the Bible is of God's tender and unwearied efforts to wean persons from their sin, and the revelation of Jesus "rising early" to accomplish such an objective indicates his persistent labors in wooing and winning the sinful.

God is ever first when it comes to the rescue of the perishing. His is ever the first advance in the salvation of a soul. Unwearingly, God strives to charm persons from their sins and earnestly pleads with them not to do those abominable things he hates. The sorrow is that all his pressing claims are met with stubborn opposition. The unyielding resistance of the Jewish nation to whom Jeremiah was sent, and of sinners of all ages, is summed up in the phrase "They hearkened not." When it came to the redemption of a lost world, God rose early. Ultimately he sent his beloved Son who, like the prophets of old, was despised and rejected; yet the Son was offered up in a past eternity. Calvary was no late afterthought of God. Provision was made for sin before the sinner's creation.

Are you among God's sent messengers whose compassionate pleadings are scorned? Then with the psalmist say, "I myself will awake right early." Have a date with God early in the morning, not only for your own spiritual culture, but for intercession that those you are eager to win for Christ may be brought under deep conviction of sin. You will discover that he responds to those who seek him early. "They that seek me early shall find me."

Mercy Every Way Is Infinite

"He delighteth in mercy." *Micah 7:18.*

Scripture abounds in confirmation of Robert Browning's declaration of the infinity of divine mercy. Prophets, psalmists, and apostles combine to extol the Almighty as the God of mercy. Sin rendered the individual as a miserable sinner, and misery is the proper object of mercy. God has revealed himself as being rich in mercy and as one who delights in pardoning our sins, saving our souls, and relieving us of our necessities. The Father of mercies has pleasure in forgiving sinners who repent and turn to the Savior in faith.

If any would obtain mercy, all they have to do is to draw near the mercy seat without any doubt as to his pity, kindness, or grace. Only thus can they know how consoling and precious it is to be an infinite debtor to his eternal mercy. Has God been merciful to you as a sinner? Then believe in his mercy as an undoubted truth, plead it as a powerful argument in prayer, and daily rejoice in such a divine virtue. Ascribe all to mercy which is its due, and ever be active spreading abroad the good and glad news that God delights in unmerited favor, even toward the vilest of sinners. Sing with John Stocker:

> *Thy mercy in Jesus exempts me from hell;*
> *Its glories I'll sing, and its wonders I'll tell,*
> *'Twas Jesus, my Friend, when He hung on the tree,*
> *That opened the channel of mercy for me.*

Hope, Like the Gleaming Taper's Light

"Every man that hath this hope." 1 John 3:3.

The lines from "The Captivity" by Oliver Goldsmith take on a spiritual significance when applied to what the Bible calls the "blessed hope":

> *Hope, like the gleaming taper's light,*
> *Adorns and cheers our way;*
> *And still, as darker grows the night,*
> *Admits a brighter ray.*

The glorious appearing of the Savior as he returns to receive his true church unto himself is a hope we can rejoice in even though we may not have many possessions here on earth to rejoice over. The final installment of our redemption, namely, the redemption of the body, is the hope laid up for us in heaven.

The second coming of Jesus, plainly promised and certain of fulfillment, not only excites desire, produces courage, and prevents despondency as darker grows the night, but it also is a hope, acting as the anchor of the soul, sure and steadfast. As those who shall so soon be made partakers of such a hope, we dare not yield to gloomy feelings or to distressing forebodings over the condition of things around. The darker the night, the brighter the ray the hope of his coming emits. John reminded us that holding such a hope should make for holiness in life. "Every man that hath this hope in him, purifieth himself, even as Christ is pure." E. May Grimes declared:

> *"Upheld by hope," in darkest days*
> *Faith can the light descry.*
> *The deepening glory in the east*
> *Proclaims deliverance nigh.*

Among the Faithless, Faithful Only He

"God is faithful." 1 Corinthians 10:13.

John Milton's glowing tribute to seraph Abdiel in *Paradise Lost* is far truer of God, of whom it is said, "Great is thy faithfulness" (Lam. 3:23):

> *So spake the seraph Abdiel, faithful found,*
> *Among the faithless faithful only he:*
> *Among innumerable false unmov'd,*
> *Unshaken, unseduc'd, unterrify'd*
> *His loyalty he kept, his love, his zeal.*

It is interesting to note that the American Revised Version translates "Verily thou shalt be fed" as "Feed upon His faithfulness" (Ps. 37:3). What a bountiful feast is ours as we feed upon divine faithfulness, running like a golden thread through the Bible! Among the faithless, faithful only *he*. We are so fickle, spasmodic, and disloyal, but there has never been the least flicker in the lamp of divine loyalty. Because "he is faithful and true," he is effective as our "shield and buckler" (Ps. 91:4; Rev. 19:11).

No promise of his has ever failed and cannot fail because of his honor. He is not a man that he should lie. Whether his promises are related to time or eternity, to our physical life or spiritual welfare, God will realize them to the full. "Faithful is he who promised." Because of all he is in himself, he cannot go back upon his Word. Ours should be the desire to claim his promises by faith. T. O. Chisholm's words are inspiring:

> *Great is Thy faithfulness, O God, my Father,*
> *There is no shadow of turning with Thee.*

Sceptre and Crown Must Tumble Down

"The crown is fallen from our head." *Lamentations 5:16.*

James Shirley, poet of the early sixteenth century, wrote in "The Contention of Ajax and Ulysses":

> *Death lays his icy hands on kings:*
> *Sceptre and crown*
> *Must tumble down,*
> *And in the dust be equal made,*
> *With the poor crooked scythe and spade.*

How true is the saying in Shakespeare's *2 Henry IV*, "Uneasy lies the head that wears a crown." Describing vanished pomp and royalty, Jeremiah spoke of those brought up in scarlet, being forced to embrace dunghills (Lam. 4:5). Does not history, biblical and secular, provide us with tragic illustrations of the humiliation of royalty? In our lifetime many crowns have fallen. The past glory of the crowned heads of Europe has almost vanished in our revolutionary age.

But are there not pointed applications one can make in Jeremiah's lament, "The crown is fallen from our head"? Humankind was made in the image of God and given dominion over all things, but through sin, it lost its crown—a fact that the prophet stresses in his lament. "The crown is fallen from our head: woe unto us, that we have sinned!" "The throned monarch" is no longer "better than his crown." Yet divine grace can restore "the likeness of a kingly crown," and thus many crowns are offered to sinners saved by grace. Some, alas, will be crownless at the judgment seat of Christ. Although saved, theirs was a lost life, and a crown they could have had for diligence, loyalty, and service will not diadem their heads. If ours is the crowned life now, our victory and faithfulness will earn us the crown of life from him upon whose head there are many crowns.

Words, Words, Words

"Take with you words, and turn unto the Lord."
Hosea 14:2.

Shakespeare's Polonius asks, "What do you read, my lord?" and Hamlet answers, "Words, words, words." Job reminded Eliphaz that "vain words have an end" and that he was able to "heap up words" against Eliphaz's troublesome words. Philip Massinger, poet of the early seventeenth century, wrote in "The Instrument of Words" of those who were:

All words
And no performance!

Robert Louis Stevenson, however, in "Songs of Travel," would have us know that:

Bright is the ring of words
When the right man rings them.

What a power there is in words, whether they be those of the Savior or of Satan, of saints or of sinners! We read that "the words of the men of Judah were fiercer than the words of the men of Israel" (2 Sam. 19:43; 20:1). Angry words create anger, and there is often a man of Belial close at hand to cause mischief. Thomas Gray in "The Progress of Poesy" wrote, "Thoughts that breathe, and words that burn." How the words of Jesus scorched the consciences of the Pharisees! Through the prophets God could say of those who had turned from him, "I have slain them by the words of my mouth" (Hos. 6:5). Yet the Father and the Son were "coiners of sweet words." May the words of our mouths ever be acceptable to God. From an unknown source we learn that:

Words are things of little cost, quickly spoken, quickly lost.
Oh! how often ours have been idle words and words of sin!
We forget them, but they stand witnesses at God's right hand.

Follow The Gleam

"Walk in the light, as he is in the light." *1 John 1:7.*

A visitor to the great annual flower exhibition in London related an unusual experience. He saw that one of the prizes was taken by a magnificent bloom of geranium in an old tin can, brought to be exhibited by a small child from a tenement building which had no garden. Being interviewed by one of the judges as to the success of her flower, the little girl simply related how a lady had given her a slip from a geranium plant. Retrieving an old can from a trash barrel, she scraped off the dirt, without and within, and planted the slip in it. "Then," said the wee girl, "in the morning I put it in the east window, and in the afternoon I removed it to the west window, and, please sir, I just keep it in the sun."

Is this not a good illustration of the fruitful and fragrant life of those who strive to "walk in the light" or "to follow the gleam," as Tennyson put it? Jude exhorts us to "Keep ourselves in the love of God." He is ever in the light, for he is the light, and by following him we are made radiant. Again we recall Horatius Bonar's great hymn, in which he told us how to keep our little tin can ever in the sun:

> *I heard the voice of Jesus say,*
> *   "I am this dark world's light;*
> *Look unto Me: thy morn shall rise,*
> *   And all thy day be bright."*
> *I looked to Jesus and I found*
> *   In Him my star, my sun;*
> *And in that light of life I'll walk*
> *   Till traveling days are done.*

The Grace of Gratitude

"What shall I render unto the Lord for all his benefits?"
Psalm 116:12.

A precious aspect of the psalmist's question is that he answered it himself in a most unexpected way. He said in effect, "I have received so much from the Lord; to show my gratitude to him, I'll hold my hand out for more"—"I will take the cup of salvation" (Ps. 116:13). His gratitude for divine benefits found expression in a yearning for a deeper experience of God's grace in his heart and life.

What is our response to the load of benefits we daily receive? In his description of Gentile-world apostasy Paul said that one characteristic feature of the godless is, "Neither were they thankful" (Rom. 1:21). Surely Wordsworth had such thanklessness in mind when he wrote in "Simon Lee":

> *Alas! the gratitude of men*
> *Hath oftener left me mourning.*

If, as the redeemed of the Lord, we would have our gratitude to him increase more and more till like a holy flame it burns within us, then we must cherish the ever-increasing thankfulness to God. Let us consider his manifold spiritual mercies and realize that the best return we can make for these is a deeper love for him from whom all mercies flow. Then there are also family mercies, physical mercies, and material mercies for which to bless and thank the Lord. If we are truly grateful to God, then we will honor him with our love and trust and endeavor to walk before him in the land of the living, expressing our gratitude by our lives as well as by our lips. Gratitude for all his benefits also tends to increase our delight in his service. It becometh well the just to be thankful.

84

The Prayers of Saints

"Golden vials full of odours, which are the prayers of saints." *Revelation 5:8.*

Tennyson in "St. Simeon Stylites" could write of "battering the gates of Heaven with storms of prayer." Such aggressive prayers, along with those less forceful like the ones Tennyson had in mind when in *In Memoriam* he said of a saint, "Her eyes were homes of silent prayer," fill up those golden vials. Because prayer is the Christian's vital breath and native air, it is essential to "pray with all prayer and supplication in the Spirit" (Eph. 6:18), who is the mighty intercessor within the heart of every child of God. Promises, assuring those who pray that God answers believing prayers, abound in Scripture. Amid numerous needs, fears, and anxieties, believers are sustained as they turn in faith to him who hears and responds to cries of the heart, even though language may appear too weak to express what is desired. Comforting to know, is it not, that when needs seem too big for utterance the Holy Spirit interprets the thoughts and reads the language of desire, and makes intercession for the praying one? Are we not invited to take everything to God in prayer, which is our holy privilege?

It is prayer that keeps every grace of the spirit in active, holy, and healthy exercise. It is the stream, so to speak, that supplies refreshing vigor and nourishment in all the plants of grace,—it is the sacred channel, through which the Savior supplies all the needs of his pilgrim followers. When our voices are upraised in sincere prayer, they are speaking in the ears of the living God, for "his ears are open unto their cry." May grace be ours to live in the spirit of prayer and ever to pray in the Spirit.

The Guidebook of Pilgrims

"Lead me in thy truth, and teach me." *Psalm 25:5.*

As pilgrims to the celestial city we have, not only a perfect guidebook in the Bible, but one who is ever with us to explain and interpret all its information and instructions. The psalmist said that, first of all, God must lead us into his truth or beget, and continually deepen within us, a desire to search his guidebook. Such is a necessary requirement if we seek to be taught of the Lord. Loving him and his Word, we come to pray, "Open thou mine eyes, that I may behold wondrous things out of thy law" (Ps. 119:18). *Out of* implies that the wondrous things have always been in the guidebook, but we have failed to discern them and are now desirous of discovering them. This is what we call *revelation* and what we seek when we pray, "Open mine eyes, illumine me, Spirit divine!"

Truth is revealed, not by the mere perusal of the words of Scripture, but by God's Holy Spirit whom Jesus promised to send as the divine interpreter, well qualified to lead and guide us into all truth. Are we humble enough to confess our ignorance and to pray, "Lord, teach me"? The first result of such divine tuition will be a discovery of our own need of cleansing and sanctification, so evident in Job's prayer, "That which I see not teach thou me: if I have done iniquity, I will do no more" (Job 34:32). Thus the guidebook makes us better pilgrims as we journey on to the land of pure delight where joys immortal await us.

We Live in Deeds, Not Years

"Be thou faithful unto death, and I will give thee a crown of life." *Revelation 2:10.*

While the whole of humanity is in the funeral march to the grave, death does not come to all at the same age or period in life. Many reach the close of their journey when, to all human appearance, it has scarcely begun. We have a saying that "the good die young," which may be true in some cases, but untold numbers of those who are good live on until they are ripe for glory. But whether our days are many or few matters little. The question of all-importance is, How have we lived our days? for life is not always to be reckoned by the number of its days. It is not the length of the life that counts but the quality of it. It is possible for the longest to be really briefer than the shortest, for, as Philip J. Bailey wrote in "Festus":

> We live in deeds, not years; in thoughts, not breaths;
> In feelings, not in figures on a dial.
> We should count time by heart-throbs. He most lives
> Who thinks most, feels the noblest, acts the best.

Whether then we die young or old, we act the best when, by the grace of the Spirit, we are faithful unto death. No matter how short or long the journey, the conflict with sin and Satan will never cease, being one *until* death parts us. As faithful soldiers of Christ Jesus, clad with the whole armor of God, we must never relax our vigilance, but keeping near to our divine captain we must remain faithful and true. Seeing him who is invisible, we will endure in the secret of faithfulness to him in every realm of life. At the end of the day, that will bring us his "Well done!"

The Proclamation and the Presence

"Go ye into all the world . . . . Lo, I am with you always."
Mark 16:15; Matthew 28:19–20.

The two little key words in our Lord's commission are *go* and *lo*. With the proclamation there was the promise of the presence of him who made it. "My presence shall go with thee." That the apostles acted upon the Master's instructions is seen in Acts where we read that "they went forth, and preached everywhere, the Lord working *with them*." The *lo* was linked with the *go*.

Sir Robert Stopford, who commanded one of the ships under Lord Nelson, wrote in his diary: "We are half starved and otherwise inconvenienced by being so long out of port, but our reward is that *we are with Nelson*." Those gallant seamen felt they could endure anything as long as their brave commander was with them. Is it not so with ourselves as we go forth, not only *for* Christ, but *with* him? Along with Enoch, we share the privilege of walking and working for God. The promise, "I am with you always," is a balm to wounded spirits and a source of inspiration as we witness for him who is the friend sticking closer than a brother. We may not always feel him near our side, but we must not mistake feelings for the fact that he will never leave us. There are times, however, when ours is a joyful consciousness of his presence. Henry F. Lyte wrote:

> *I need Thy presence every passing hour;*
> *What but Thy grace can foil the tempter's power?*
> *Who, like Thyself, my guide and stay can be?*
> *Through cloud and sunshine, Lord, abide with me.*

Who Doth Not Crave for Rest?

"I will give thee rest." *Exodus 33:14; Matthew 11:28.*

What God offered Israel, Jesus promised his church, namely, the gift of *rest*. Frederick W. Faber said that the "rest" all persons crave is paradise:

> *Rest comes at length; though life be long and dreary,*
> *The day must dawn, and darksome night be passed.*

But the *rest* that Jesus spoke of to his own was not eternal rest but a present rest, a resting in himself, the ever-present companion. Shakespeare's Romeo says, "So sweet to rest." It is blessed to know that "there *remaineth* a rest for the people of God," but what they crave here and now is the sweet rest of heart amid the tribulation of the world, a foretaste of the calmness of the heavenly rest awaiting them.

Jesus offers an *inward* quiet in spite of *outward* trials. Rough winds may ruffle the surface of a lake, but far down in its depth there is perfect calm. Can I say that this rest of a forgiven soul, and the quiet of a loved, confiding child, is mine? The rest Jesus gives does not imply inactivity but the peace of congenial activity, unwearied yet joyful employment in the service of God. Labor is rest to the loving spirit. Even in heaven, where the redeemed rest from their earthly labors, they "rest *not* day nor night." With Evans H. Hopkins we sing:

> *My Saviour, Thou hast offered rest:*
> *Oh, give it then to me;*
> *The rest of ceasing from myself,*
> *To find my all in Thee.*

Letters—Soft Interpreters of Love

"Hezekiah received the letter . . . and spread it before
the Lord." *Isaiah 37:14.*

Letters are not always like those Matthew Prior, poet of the early
eighteenth century, described in these lines from "Henry and Emma":

And oft the pangs of absence to remove
By letters, soft interpreters of love.

The Bible has much to say about letters and letter writing, and the letter
Hezekiah received was by no means "a soft interpreter of love." It was
a threatening letter from Rabshakeh about God being unable to deliver
his people. What did the prophet do with this distasteful letter? Sit
down and in the heat of the moment draft a stinging reply? No, Hezekiah
read the letter, then went into the house of the Lord, and spread it
before the Lord.

Praying and sleeping over an answer to unwelcome letters enables us
to answer them in a Christlike way. We know from the letters found in
Scripture that letter writing can be a very blessed ministry indeed.
Epistle means "letter," and the Epistles are letters sent by the apostles to
individual saints or to a group of saints. Those written by Paul are
called "weighty and powerful letters." Then we have the marvelous
letters Jesus sent to the seven churches (Rev. 2, 3). Is yours a sanctified
pen? Here is an anonymous prayer-motto to have before you when
you write your letters:

Be present at this desk, O Lord;
Be here and everywhere adored.
Each letter bless—O may it be
A little messenger from Thee.

Take Arms against a Sea of Troubles

"The Lord . . . delivers them out of all their troubles."
Psalm 34:6, 17.

During World War I we were accustomed to both soldiers and civilians singing the catchy chorus, credited to George Asaf:

What's the use of worrying? It never was worth while,
So, pack up your troubles in your old kit bag,
And smile, smile, smile!

But if our troubles are still in our kit bag, our smile is very unreal. Shakespeare's advice in *Hamlet* on how to get rid of trouble is just as unsatisfactory:

To take arms against a sea of troubles,
And by opposing end them.

Experience teaches us, however, that the sea is not so easily calmed. Then there is the doggerel with a good deal of truth in it: "Never trouble trouble, till trouble troubles you."

In a time of tremendous crisis Jesus asked his disciples, "Why are ye troubled?" (Luke 24:38). If we claim to be redeemed, then why should we charge our souls with anxious care? If troubles, like a sea, dash against us, it is folly to take up arms and fight them when the Lord has promised to deliver us out of *all* our troubles. What troubles *you*? Is it sin? Then he will pardon and destroy it. Is it Satan? Jesus has triumphed over him and calls you to share his victory. Are your troubles the cares and needs of life? "Let not your heart be troubled," says one from whom all blessings flow. "Goodness and mercy shall follow you all the days of your life." So when in trouble, *trust*. Leave all to him who offers to calm your troubled sea.

91

Sphere-born Harmonious Sisters

"Martha served . . . Mary . . . anointed the feet of Jesus."
John 12:2, 3.

Admirers of John Milton will know that the particular sisters he mentioned in "At a Solemn Music" were not human persons, but human possessions:

> *Blest pair of Sirens, pledges of Heaven's joy,*
> *Sphere-born harmonious sisters, Voice and Verse.*

I have borrowed his phrase to describe Martha and Mary who were "harmonious sisters" in many ways and likewise "pledges of Heaven's joy." Both sisters loved the Lord and, along with Lazarus their brother, were equally loved by him. While there were marked differences between the two sisters, "Martha, practical, business-like, and thoughtful of all that could affect the comfort and well-being of those she loved—Mary, clinging, spiritual, gifted with all a woman's delicacy of insight and tender sympathy," theirs was a harmony of devotion to Jesus. Martha welcomed Jesus into her home, and Mary sat at his feet in the home. We must not forget that Jesus did not find fault with Martha for serving, which was necessary. He lovingly corrected her for being *cumbered*, or "worried and bothered about so many things" (Luke 10:38–42). As for Mary, she was commended by Jesus for putting first things first. Thus Martha, who represents *work*, and Mary, who suggests *worship*, are reconciled. Sitting at his feet in adoration should always have precedence over sitting at a table to be fed. An unknown writer proclaimed:

> *Mechanic soul, thou must not only do*
> *With Martha, but with Mary ponder, too;*
> *Happy's the house where these far sisters vary;*
> *But most, when Martha's reconciled to Mary.*

Vocation and Vision

"Under their wings . . . were human hands."
Ezekiel 1:8, ASB.

In his great prophecy Ezekiel followed the method of symbol and vision also characteristic of Daniel and John. In his highly figurative description of the Cherubim, Ezekiel emphasized an interesting feature which expressed similar, spiritual contrasts to those we considered in the preceding meditation. All living creatures had "the hands of a man under their wings."

Wings and hands! What opposites are here combined like "harmonious sisters." Wings represent *worship*—hands, *work*; wings, *vision*—hands, *vocation*; wings, *flight*—hands, *fight*. With wings we soar *from* the earth; with hands we serve *on* the earth. Alas! Some visionary souls are all wings and live in the clouds, and thus their dreaming is divorced from their doing. Such persons are too heavenly minded to be of any earthly use. Others are all hands and never leave the earth. Activity is theirs, but not spirituality. But God expects work and worship to be happily balanced, or to have Martha and Mary in happy fellowship.

Ezekiel observed that the *wings* covered the *hands*; vision controlled vocation. Hands under wings surely suggests that the work of our hands should be governed and influenced by the worship of the Lord in the beauty of holiness. Service, no matter its nature and diligence, is fruitless if it is not constantly inspired by unbroken fellowship with him we seek to serve. William Longstaff wrote:

> *Take time to be holy . . .*
> *Forgetting in nothing His blessing to seek.*

If Winter Comes, Can Spring Be Far Behind?

"The time of the singing of birds is come."
Song of Solomon 2:12.

Springtime has been a favorite theme of poets from Solomon down the ages. There is the great verse of Robert Browning, "The year's at the spring." With all nature awakening into new life,

> *God's in his heaven—*
> *All's right with the world!*

George Herbert wrote of "sweet spring, full of sweet days and roses." Edmund Spenser agreed with Solomon's description of such a season:

> *Fresh spring the herald of love's mighty king,*
> *In whose coat armour richly are display'd*
> *All sorts of flowers the which on earth do spring*
> *In goodly colours gloriously array'd.*

Flowers appear and birds sing to welcome spring. The cuckoo is the foremost herald. Wordsworth wrote of the cuckoo, "Thrice welcome, darling of the Spring." Spenser also referred to "the merry cuckoo, messenger of Spring."

All of us welcome the passing of the gloom of winter and the coming season of resurrection. Yet without the winter hardening and consolidating the resources of trees and plants, spring would very soon sap them of all their energy. The circle is complete, not only in God's year, but in our spiritual experience. Everything is beautiful in its season. We cannot have spring without winter, or summer without spring, or autumn without summer. God does not permit us to live in a perennial spring or an unceasing summer. "Because they have no changes, they fear not God" (Ps. 55:19). Spring is the season that awakens hope, revives deadened sensibilities, and gives us a new sense of life. Has yours been a hard, spiritual winter because of a crushing sorrow or some chilling doubt? The creator of the seasons of the year is at hand to bring a new springtime in your soul and the promise of a summer of rich fruitfulness.

PART II

Resurrection and Glory

The leading month of the second quarter of the year's circle is truly nature's debutant, coming to us with all the beautiful garments which poets have vied one another to describe. April, the womb of nature, opens with life as trees break their buds to bear golden leaves. Resurrection is seen in the carpet of primroses, violets, and spring flowers covering the earth. April's lady comes forth with all her glory to praise the Creator who furnished her. What a fitting time of the year this is to illustrate the victory of the Rose of Sharon who rose again, alive forevermore.

The poet Keats spoke of the merriment of May because of the mirthful singing of the birds, the livery of green, and the beauty of the gardens. Loveliness and vitality are implied by Shakespeare as he spoke of May's new-fangled mirth. How fascinating also it is to watch the economy of growth. The silent agencies of nature seek to perfect the fruits and flowers of the earth—a lesson for our hearts to learn in growing, not only to grace but to graciousness.

When we reach the closing month of the second quarter of the year, the green woods laugh with the voice of joy completing the circle of spring. There is a gaiety in the hearts of all true lovers of nature when June comes around. Every prospect seems to please, and only human-kind is vile. "Rejoice, and again I say, rejoice" is the injunction of Scripture.

RESURRECTION

O, how this spring of love
  resembleth
The uncertain glory of an
  April day.

  —William Shakespeare,
   The Two Gentlemen of Verona

Each to His Great Father Bends

"Our Father which art in heaven." *Matthew 6:9.*

The Bible abounds in illustrations of the tenderheartedness of God. We know of his loving, kind, and understanding nature as our heavenly Father, whose gentleness makes him great. Jesus not only exhibited fatherly tenderness and forgiveness when, as he died, he prayed for his enemies. Isaiah depicted him as the everlasting Father, or Father of eternity. *Father!* What a precious portrait of the Lord this is, manifested in his love, carrying him to great lengths to extricate his wayward children out of trouble. All strength, wisdom, and provision are his as the Father of the fatherless.

While, in the sense of creation, he is the Father of us all, we cannot look up into his face and speak to him as our Father in heaven unless his beloved Son is our personal Savior. The privileged relationship of sonship is based upon regeneration (John 1:11–13). Only by the spirit of adoption can we cry, "Abba, Father!"

Are you certain that God is *your* Father through faith in his Son? If he is your heavenly Father, then rest in his fatherly pity and provision, singing at all times, "I know my heavenly Father knows." He can never forget his own, neglect their concerns, or turn a deaf ear to the needs and requests of his beloved, blood-bought children. His fatherly love is infinite and will remain fixed on us forever. Having loved us out of our sin to himself, he will love us unto the end. May we be found sharing the Father's compassion, displayed in the gift of his Son, for a sinful and sinning race.

In Mystery Our Soul Abides

"Now we see through a glass, darkly," 1 Corinthians 13:12.

We can couple with Matthew Arnold's phrase, used above as the title of our meditation, the line of Shakespeare in *King Lear*, "And take upon 's the mystery of things." Paul reminded us that with our finite minds we cannot fully understand the significance of so many things our infinite God permits. "Now we see in a mirror dimly—or in a middle" (1 Cor. 13:12, RV).

Scientists used to write about the "Riddle of the Universe," but are there not a good many riddles in the little universe of your life and mine? Jesus said to Peter, "What I do you do not realize now; but you shall understand hereafter" (John 13:7). Often we are at a loss to account for many of the tears and trials in our Lord's dealings with us. Yet amid "the mystery of things" we must rest in the Lord's promise that we shall know hereafter. We must take comfort from the fact that heaven will explain the mysteries—"Then face to face." Said Paul of the paradise of Revelation, "Then shall we know."

When we see him who never makes a mistake or takes a wrong turning, then problems will be solved and all the trying dispensations of divine providences accounted for. Meantime, let us acknowledge the right of our all-wise Father to conceal the cause of his working until he has fully accomplished his designs. An unknown writer said:

> *I cannot read His future plans; but this I know:*
> *I have the smiling of His face, and all the refuge*
> *   of His grace,*
> *While here below.*

100

As Sentinels to Warn the Immortal Souls

"Give them warning from me." Ezekiel 3:17–19.

Although the *sentinels* Christopher Marlowe referred to are "the angels on the walls of heaven," those of us who are the Lord's should ever function as heaven-sent sentinels, warning immortal souls of their peril if they persist and die in sin. There are no more solemn words in the whole of Scripture than those in which Ezekiel is given his commission to warn the godless of the judgment awaiting them. The prophet was to stand before them in God's stead and tell the wicked of the dire consequences of their iniquity. If as a watchman he failed in his grim task, then the blood of the godless would be upon his own soul. Out he must go and watch for souls as one that must give an account of his stewardship. Only thus could the sentinel deliver himself (Ezek. 3:19).

We often read of the prophets being laden with a *burden*, the nature of which was the perfect fulfillment of a divine commission. Have we a burden for the lost around us? As God's representatives, are we warning sinners to flee from the wrath to come? Does the eternal hopelessness of the sinner apart from Christ constrain us to give ourselves, unceasingly, to the unpleasant task of warning the wicked of their doom? Are we beseeching them in God's stead to be reconciled to him?

If only ours could be a passionate passion for souls. How terrible it is to realize that they may be souls in hell who might have been delivered from such eternal condemnation and despair if only we had been more faithful in warning the immortal of their fate in their final rejection of Christ! Tell some perishing soul *today* that Jesus died to save from sin and hell.

His Commands Are Enablings

"Faithful is He who calls you, and He will also bring
it to Pass." *1 Thessalonians 5:24,* ASB.

One of the most attractive aspects of the divine character is that whatever God commands he is able to supply. What he asks for, he gives, for his commands are his enablings. Paul reminded the Thessalonians that God desired their entire sanctification in the light of Christ's return—a state of soul absolutely impossible if left to themselves to produce it. So there came hope in the assertion that the one demanding such holiness would bring it to pass.

Augustine said, "Give what Thou commandest then command what Thou wilt!" To Israel of old came the command of the Lord, "Keep my judgments and do them." But power to obey came from him who said, "I am the Lord your God" (Ezek. 20:19). In such a relationship we have all necessary resources to fulfill what God requires of us. The order to walk in his statutes and keep his judgments would fill us with despair if we were left to our own ability to obey it. But when we remember that the Lord is our God and that he is the one who "worketh in us, both to will and do of his good pleasure," then we do not faint or give way to discouragement.

When we are wholly yielded to the Lord, he accomplishes in us, for us, and through us all he requires of us. How blessed we are when we discover that what God orders, he offers! Who among us could fill the order, "Be ye holy," if left to ourselves to manufacture such holiness? But what God seeks, he supplies—"For I am holy" (I Peter 1:16). Thus the holiness which is *to* the Lord is a holiness which is first *from* the Lord who is "the hidden source of every precious thing."

102

Plain Living and High Thinking

"Let them give us pulse to eat and water to drink."
Daniel 1:12.

Four lines from Wordsworth's "In London" are worthy of notice:

Plain living and high thinking are no more:
The homely beauty of the good old cause
Is gone; our peace, our fearful innocence,
And pure religion breathing household laws.

An unknown Englishman of a bygone century wrote, "I should be spare of sleep, sparer of diet, and sparest of time, that when the days of eating, drinking, clothing and sleeping shall be no more, I may eat of my Saviour's hidden manna, drink of the new wine in my Father's Kingdom, and inherit that rest which remaineth for the people of my God for ever and ever."

Plain living aids the body as well as the mind. With Daniel and his three friends, plain living resulted, not only in high thinking, but in a physical beauty and fitness surpassing those who dined off the rich fare of the king's table. Seasons of fasting, not only from food but from bodily pleasures that would ensnare us, are good for body and soul. Often when the apostles prayed, they fasted. Paul was *in fastings often.* Spiritual giants down the ages set themselves against the undue indulgence of the body in eating and drinking. They knew that nothing was more certain to befog and darken and blunt the mind. Thus abstinence fitted them for the lofty and sublime delights of fellowship with heaven.

Let us beware of overmuch restfulness and ease in sleep. Let us guard ourselves against the sloth and spiritual darkness engendered by over-indulgence. It is better to eat to live than to live to eat. *High living* is a decided barrier to *living on high.*

When from Earth the Fourth Descended

"The form of the fourth is like the Son of God."
Daniel 3:25.

In the early part of the nineteenth century W. Savage Landor wrote about the *fourth* dignitary, meaning the sovereign, George IV, with whom, Landor said, "God be praised, the George is ended!" But the *fourth* seen by the three Hebrew youths was a heavenly king whose reign will never end. Those courageous young men came to learn that there is no fire so fierce that the king of glory himself will not bear the heat and glow by their side. To Shadrach, Meshach, and Abed-nego, being near the furnace meant being near the Lord. When the fire was at its fiercest, he was there as their protector.

In our time science magnifies physical power and talks much about the survival of the fittest. But the fiery furnace proves that often the weakest in the eyes of the world have the secret of true survival. Christ has all power in heaven and on earth to rescue and deliver his persecuted, despised children. One of the old divines said that "every Christian is a Christ-enclosed one." How true this is! "When thou walkest through the fire, thou shalt not be burned" (Isa. 43:2). Christ bears the heat of the furnace flames every time.

Whether our furnace is sickness, poverty, temptation, misapprehension by others, or spiritual desolation, "the fourth . . . like the Son of God" is in it to protect and provide. When those three Hebrew youths were thrust into the furnace, the *fourth* was already there, waiting to welcome and console his valiant yet despised witnesses. Our blessed assurance is that whatever our lot, the mystic fourth is ever at our side as companion and deliverer.

104

Short Weight

"Thou are weighed in the balances, and art found wanting."
Daniel 5:27.

Scales are everywhere. We meet them in drugstores, restaurants, and fruit and candy shops, and almost every bathroom has a miniature scale to tell if we are keeping our weight down. In fact, our weight has become a matter of great concern, and all kinds of exercises and diets are prescribed to remove those extra pounds. Inspectors visit businesses and warehouses where scales are used to check whether the weights and measures are correct. Often heavy fines are imposed on salesmen guilty of selling food at short weight.

Evidently God is the heavenly inspector who has his standard measure to check whether any come short of his glory. Few, however, are willing to be weighed in God's balances. Belshazzar stepped on the scales and was found wanting. In our day the scales of accepted human morality are more popular, but the standards by which our hearts and lives are to be judged fall short of divine standards. A life may be moral, according to the highest earthly estimation, yet be sadly wanting—underweight —when weighed in the balance of the sanctuary. God's message to Belshazzar was, "The God in whose hand thy breath is, and whose are all thy ways, hast thou not glorified" (Dan. 5:23). Here then is the correct and only standard by which our hearts are to be weighed.

In his great sermon "Weighed in the Balances" the famous evangelist Dwight L. Moody used the Ten Commandments as weights by which to test ourselves. These and the various commands of the Lord Jesus are scales by which we are to try our weight if we want to know whether we are giving God good measure. As "the children of men are deceitful upon weights" (see Ps. 62:9), may our standards be true.

Surety Secure

"Jesus has become the guarantee of a better covenant."
Hebrews 7:22, ASV.

What a deep truth there is in Shakespeare's *Troilus and Cressida*:

> ... *The wound of peace is surety,*
> *Surety secure.*

The wounds of the Prince of Peace secured a perfect surety for all who believe. If a sizable loan is required from a bank, those negotiating the loan want to know what security or collateral can be offered. Some guarantee equivalent of the value of the loan required must be available.

Is it not blessed to know that Jesus placed himself as our collateral, surety, bondsman? Is it not wonderful that, having no security of our own to offer, we can yet draw as much as we like on heaven's bank as long as we present our surety's name and merits? Did he not pledge himself as our security when he said, "Whatsoever ye shall ask in my name, that will I do" (John 14:13)?

With such infinite resources at our disposal there is no need whatever for spiritual impoverishment. Yet when needs arise, we lack the assurance that our heavenly collateral is more than sufficient. We are not altogether confident that the one who declared that "the silver and the gold are mine" (Hag. 2:8) is able to foot our bill. So we struggle on with so little, living too often as spiritual paupers, with such wealth at our disposal. Then, to think of it, what we draw on the bank of heaven is never a loan! Coming, in all our need to our surety, he willingly grants us an outright gift, all we ask of him.

Everything from A to Z

"I am Alpha and the Omega, the beginning and the end, the
first and the last." *Revelation 22:13 (see also 1:8, 21:6).*

I remember seeing over the window of a store trading in all kinds of
merchandise the sign, "We sell everything from A to Z." Three times
over Jesus referred to himself as Alpha and Omega in describing his
all-sufficiency. These two titles constitute the first and last letters of the
Greek alphabet, hence our Lord's application, "I am the first and the
last." But he is not only our *A* and *Z*; he is also everything in between.
Whether we think of creation, revelation, redemption, or personal experience, Jesus is "the beginning and the end." None is before him as *A*,
and none can follow as *Z*.

Can we truthfully confess that he is everything from *A* to *Z* in our
daily lives? When it comes to our desires, plans, and ambitions, is he
the beginning and the end? Is everything inspired by his Spirit and
undertaken for his glory? "In the beginning, God." "Man's chief end is
to glorify God" (*Shorter Catechism*). What tranquillity is ours, and how
life is made radiant with his provision when Jesus is all and in all to us!
To have him answer to the whole of the alphabet of life is to spell out
the language of heaven. How expressive of him as our *A* to *Z* are these
lines of the English poet F. W. H. Myers in "St. Paul":

> *Yea, through life, death, through sorrow*
> *and through sinning,*
> *Christ shall suffice me, for He hath sufficed.*
> *Christ is the end, for Christ was the beginning*
> *Christ the beginning, for the end is Christ.*

Paul makes it clear that Jesus, who is before all things and in whom
all things hold together, must have the first and last place in everything
(Col. 1:15–19). He must be sanctified as Lord in the heart.

The Only Free Men Are the Only Slaves

"Paul, a servant of Jesus Christ." *Romans 1:1.*

The word Paul used for *servant* is given as "bond servant" and literally means "slave." In the apostle's day slaves abounded throughout the Roman Empire, slavery being countenanced in a most despotic and cruel form. But Paul took the term and ennobled it and would have us know that the saints are, or should be, the slaves of Jesus Christ. Thus William Cowper's phrase is apt, for the believer, freed from the penalty and dominion, is free and as such is bonded to the deliverer. He wrote in "The Winter Evening":

> He is the freeman whom the truth sets free,
> And all are slaves beside.

But they are slaves in the wrong sense.

Jesus was sold for thirty pieces of silver, the price paid for a common slave. But he came as the love-slave of heaven. While on earth he was subservient to the Father in all things. "Not my will but thine be done" (Luke 22:42). Like his Master, Paul looked upon himself as being harnessed to the chariot of the Lord and thus spoke of himself as a slave and a prisoner of the Master he dearly loved and so loyally served. Proudly he could boast, in the words of an unknown author:

> A prisoner of Jesus Christ,
> Love's handcuffs neither cut nor chafe.
> I am the freest man in Rome
> All sins forgiven, for ever safe.

The question you must answer is, Am I Christ's slave or the slave of sin? You cannot be the slave of both at the same time.

God . . . Ordains for Each One Spot

"He which was ordained of God." Acts 10:42.

The one spot Rudyard Kipling felt God had ordained for him was his beloved Sussex. Although "God gives all men the earth to love" and "for each one spot" and "each to his choice," which for the poet was "Sussex by the sea," God ordains not only *where* we live but *how* we live. Jesus speaks of ordaining his own to function in the world as fruit-bearers (John 15:16).

In our basic verse Peter spoke of Jesus as one ordained of God for a specific mission. When do you think he received his divine ordination? Was it not in a past eternity when he gladly offered himself as the Savior of the world? Peter called attention to the twofold obligation of the ordained Christ, namely, to be the judge of the living and the dead and to give remission of sins.

No wonder that as Peter spoke thus of Jesus, the Holy Spirit fell with a marked effect on those hearing such a message. The Christ-honoring spirit ever blesses the full testimony of the sent one of God who realized to the full his ordination vows. Usually we limit the term *ordination* to those entering the ministry or some church office, but Jesus says of all believers, "I have ordained you." The tragedy is that there are those ordained of men who were never divinely ordained. Are you the Lord's? Although you are not among the number wearing clerical garb —a symbol of religious ordination—yours is the ordination of the pierced hands of him who has saved you and set you aside to serve him fruitfully.

From Whom All Good Counsels Do Proceed

"His name shall be called . . . Counsellor." Isaiah 9:6.

Many collects of the Anglican church are rich in spiritual significance. An evening one from which I have taken the title of this meditation reads, "From whom all holy desires, all good counsels, and all just works do proceed."

In English law a QC is a Queen's Counsellor and represents high legal knowledge and authority. Isaiah declared that we are privileged to have the heavenly king himself as our counsellor. The first two names, *Wonderful* and *Counsellor*, are sometimes linked together and read, "The wonder of a Counsellor." And truly the Lord is "wonderful in counsel" (Isa 28:29). Such is his perfection in this realm that it is said of him, "Who hath been his counsellor?" (Isa. 40:13; Rom. 11:34). Court counsellors sometimes err or change their decisions, but our kingly counsellor gives verdicts that stand forever (Prov. 19:21).

When a case comes up in law courts, there are opposing counsellors, one defends the accused, and another prosecutes him. There is no counsel, however, against the Lord, for his case against those he accuses can never be refuted (Prov. 21:30). He is ever just and right in his decisions and judgments. Would that we could always accept the immutable, strong counsel of him who cannot err! (Jer. 32:19; Heb. 6:17). With James G. Small let us ever follow the advice of:

> *So wise a counsellor and guide,*
> *So mighty a Defender!*

Is it not encouraging to know that our heavenly counsellor has never lost a case?

An Ever-welcome Visitor

"What is man . . . that thou visitest him?" *Psalm 8:4.*

Some visitors are always welcome, and once with us we wish they would prolong their stay. Others are not so welcome, and the sooner they leave, the better, for they bore us by their company and conversation. Have you ever thought of the Lord as a visitor whose visits are most gratefully appreciated by those who love him? But there are others to whom his visits are unwanted, not because he is not the best of company, but because of their hatred for what he has to say. When in the hour of your salvation Jesus knocked at the door of your heart and asked, "May I come in?" he did not enter as a visitor, but as one who wanted to live with you or, to use his own phrase, "make his abode with you." Presently, your heart is his home, and when you reach the end of the road, you will be at home with him in heaven.

It is somewhat surprising how much the Bible has to say about the visits the Lord and his angels have paid to humans here on the earth. When he visited the sin of his people upon them, they were not pleased. Yet how warmly was his visit received when he came down to deliver them (Exod. 13:19). We Gentiles would have been of all men most miserable had he not visited us (Acts 15:14). A dreadful day of visitation awaits a godless world. Do we welcome the privilege of opening the door to him every morning, as Job 7:18 says we should? Once the door is opened to receive him, he closes the door behind him and becomes the abiding companion, promising never to leave us. We reflect on an unknown writer's words:

> Come, not to find, but make this troubled heart
> A dwelling worthy of Thee as Thou art.

It Is the Lord's Passover

"Christ our passover is sacrificed for us." *1 Corinthians 5:7*.

The Passover, although still observed by the Jews, is no longer a *feast* but a *figure*, even Christ himself. The origin of the Passover is typical of Christ in many ways.

For instance, the lamb had to be without blemish; Christ was holy. The lamb had to be slain; Christ died for us. The blood had to be applied; Christ must be appropriated by faith. The blood instituted a perfect protection from judgment; Christ, by his finished work, affords eternal security for all who are blood-washed. Further, the feast itself answers to Christ as the Bread of Life. The Jews had the Passover; the church has the Lord's Supper.

What a great phrase that is—When I see the blood, I will pass over you! Is Christ your Passover in this respect? Is his blood upon you and your children? Paul enforced his appeal for separation from sin and sinners by using the illustration of Christ, sacrificed as our Passover. The Jews kept the feast with unleavened bread; so must we, not only for seven days, but for all our days. The whole life of a Christian must be a Feast of unleavened bread. The old leaven must be purged out. As those redeemed by Christ's precious blood we must be without guilt in our conduct toward God and humankind. The willing sacrifice of God's lamb at Calvary is the strongest argument for purity and sincerity.

The solemn question for each heart is, Am I sheltered by his blood? Critics and cynics may scoff at the necessity of being washed in blood, but apart from the covering his ruby blood offers, we have no hope of salvation here or in heaven hereafter.

When the Prince of Glory Died

"Ye killed the Prince of life." *Acts 3:15*.

Every lover of the Bible knows that apparent contradictions abound. I say *apparent*, for truth cannot contradict itself. The text before us is a case in point. They *killed* the Prince of *life*, but life is indestructible. Because Jesus came as the *Prince* of life, how could he, the eternal one, be put to death? Yet such is the mystery of the cross that he who said "I am . . . the life" died in agony and shame. Peter in his sermon contrasts the death of the Prince of life with Barabbas, the murderer who took life. Jesus, who came that men might have life, was the bestower of life; Barabbas was the destroyer of life. As the Prince of life Jesus' own life was so princely. With his disregard for life there was no nobility about the character of Barabbas.

Now alive forevermore, the crucified Prince proclaims that we can have life and have it more abundantly. Apart from him there is no life. If he who is our life is not within the heart as Savior and Lord, then spiritual death reigns. The tragedy is that multitudes prefer such a state of death, resulting ultimately in a condition of eternal death, to living evermore with Christ. Thrice happy are those who have received from heaven's Prince his gift of a life that death itself can never destroy. If we are among the number who have received him as our life, is it not our solemn obligation to introduce our Prince to those who are dead in their trespasses and sins? Does not the hymn say, "If Jesus has found you, tell others the story"?

A Glory That Transfigures You and Me

"Instead of the thorn shall come up the fir tree."
Isaiah 55:13.

Isaiah's prophecy of national and personal transformation in which thorns give way to fir trees is poetically emphasized in the lines of Julia Ward Howe's famous "Battle Hymn of the Republic":

In the beauty of the lilies, Christ was born, across the sea,
With a glory in His bosom that transfigures you and me;
As He died to make men holy, let us die to make men free.

If Christ were born among the lilies, he died with thorns encircling his brow, thereby making possible for us the fir trees of holiness and freedom. Eastern farmers in Isaiah's day had to cultivate open land which, in the early spring, was covered with weeds and overrun with thorns so closely woven together that it was impossible to dig them up. Fire was the only remedy, and when kindled, weeds and thorns burned like paper. Thereafter, it was easy to dig up the old roots and prepare the land for the planting of fir trees.

The lesson all this enforces is that our hearts and minds are like the soil; they can be ruined by neglect or improved by cultivation. In his parable of the sower Jesus described how seed falling among thorns is quickly choked. If the seed is to bring forth fruit, it must fall into good or cultivated ground. It is said that soil grows weeds more readily than seeds, and that, according to an unknown source, "the soil is mother to the weeds, but she is only stepmother to the good seeds." The divine gardener knows how to destroy the weeds and thorns in the soil of the heart, enrich the soil, and cultivate useful trees. Those reclaimed by the Lord are referred to as stately trees. Planted by him, they are ever full of sap and honor him as trees of righteousness. May we allow this gardener to root up any thorn that may be in our heart and in its place plant a beneficial fir tree.

Great Minds—Such Should Govern

"Bethlehem . . . out of thee shall come a Governor."
Matthew 2:6.

In "The Prophetess" John Fletcher, quaint poet of the early seventeenth century, reminded us that:

'Tis virtue, and not birth that makes us noble:
Great actions speak great minds, and such should govern.

The nobility of his birth, his virtue, his great actions, and his great mind qualify Jesus to govern. Among his birth-cameos, none is more prophetic and suggestive than that of Governor, by which he is directly related to Israel and to a government having no end (Isa. 9:6–7).

The word Matthew used for *Governor* means one who goes first, leads the way, chief in war, and Jesus fulfills all these requirements of triumphant governorship. But as a Governor he is not a hard despot. He rules by love. Some governors who have risen from low positions become officious and unsympathetic. Not so with him who is ever our *fellow* and who sways our souls by his scars. Triumph is his because of the tree. And if we would govern in life, we too must go to a tree. Death of self leads to a diadem.

While universal government will yet be his, the present question of paramount importance is, Are we giving him more territory? Is his government of our life daily increasing? We can be certain that Satan will contest every inch of ground we yield to our heavenly Governor. But we have nothing to fear, for he is likewise our defender. Philip Massinger of the seventeenth century wrote in "The Bondman":

He that would govern others, first should be
The master of himself.

115

Great Heir of Fame

"Whom he hath appointed heir of all things." Hebrews 1:2.

In his "Epitaph on Shakespeare" John Milton wrote of the famous Bard as "Dear son of memory, great heir of fame." But is not the Savior a greater heir of fame? Paul described him as "the heir of God" (Rom. 8:17).

Jesus had this personal prerogative in mind when, in the parable of the householder, he said, "This is the heir; come, let us kill him" (Matt. 21:38), which they did at Calvary. But he rose again, ascended on high, and became the recipient as God's heir of a great domain in glory. To be an heir means that sooner or later one enters into possessions willed by someone. "God hath appointed Jesus heir of all things" (Heb. 1:2), and what vast possessions are to be his! Already he has received part of the treasure in his church. The possession of his full inheritance is still future when he will come into his own and every knee will bend before him.

The marvel of grace is that we are joint-heirs with him, that is, if we are the children of God through the regenerating ministry of the Holy Spirit. "If children, then heirs; heirs of God, and joint-heirs with Christ" (Rom. 8:16, 17). When the kingdoms of this world become his world kingdom, Jesus will make us co-rulers, for we are to reign with him. If only we could be more worthy of sharing all the coming honor and treasure of God's appointed heir and daily live as those who are joint-heirs with Christ! May he teach us how to possess our possessions here and now as heirs of salvation, the purchase of God.

At Their Hearts the Fire's Center

"They came to him from every quarter." *Mark 1:45.*

The verse from "I Think Continually of Those" by Stephen Spender, a modern poet, is worthy of attention:

I think continually of those who were truly great.

. . . .

The names of those who in their lives fought for life,
Who wore at their hearts the fire's center.

If we would be truly great in fighting the good fight of faith, Jesus must be in the fire center of our hearts. Longfellow would have us know that "every arrow that flies feels the attraction of earth." As arrows in the hands of the Almighty we must ever feel the attraction of Jesus to whom men came from every quarter. They found themselves drawn to him as filings to a magnet. Because of his unusual personality, unique teachings, and marvelous works, those in all walks of life were compelled to tread the pathway leading to his feet. All kinds of persons were drawn to him who is the center and circumference of all things.

And they are still coming to him from every quarter of the globe because there is none other to whom the needy of earth can go. He alone has the word of eternal life and is the unfailing source of all the best the heart craves. They are coming to him out of all nations, out of all conditions of life, and out of all ages, for young and old alike have found in him their heart's true center. The question is, Have we come to him from the quarter of our need and found in him your never-failing treasure, full with boundless stores of grace?

The Invincible Knights of God

"The people that do know their God shall be strong and do exploits." *Daniel 11:32*.

Throughout the Bible God is found making a strong appeal to the heroic in his own. He would have them function as his noble knights and, to adapt Shakespeare's phrase in *I Henry IV*, never "usurp the sacred name of knight." Quaint Chaucer could write of one who was "a very perfect, gentle knight." Garibaldi, the Italian patriot, has been described as a "gentle hero."

God calls us to action and summons us to aggressive service; as his happy warriors we are not to be daunted by difficulties. The gospel is brought to us in terms of battle—the sword, the shield, the armor, the soldier, the enemy, the fight. It is God who teaches our fingers to war. From the literature of courage the Bible furnishes, we have sufficient to support the fighting spirit of our faith. As soldiers of the cross we must manifest a militant spirit. We must dare to be a Daniel. Sir Walter Scott felt that a fitting epitaph on "Marmion's lowly tomb" would be:

> *He died a gallant knight,*
> *With sword in hand, for England's right.*

It is thus that God's gallant knights should live and die defending his right. As "every morning brings a noble chance," so every chance should bring out "a noble knight." In these days of spiritual delusion, abounding iniquity, and actions hostile to God and truth, we have need to pray for more iron in our blood, more courage in our piety, more of the bracing north in our personal witness. Tennyson's verse in *Idylls of the King* provides us with a challenging example to follow:

> *And indeed he seems to me*
> *Scarce other than my own ideal knight,*
> *"Who reverenced his conscience as his king;*
> *Whose glory was, redressing human wrong;*
> *Who spake no slander, no, nor listened to it."*

The Red Gods Shall Call Us Out

"He shall honour the god of forces." Daniel 11:38.

Rudyard Kipling's expressive phrase "The red gods call us out and we must go" refers to the gods whose hands are red with the blood of those slain in war and are thus the gods of forces or of munitions about which Daniel wrote. The New American Standard Bible translates, "He will honour a god of fortresses, a god whom his fathers did not know . . . a foreign god." Antiochus, whose blasphemous pride he shared with Alexander the Great (Dan. 8:4, 11:3), called himself "King Antiochus, God Manifest." The god of fortresses he worshiped was probably Zeus for whom Antiochus built a temple near Antioch. This fearsome person, called "the little horn," is the forerunner of "the man of sin," the coming Antichrist who will magnify himself above every god.

World War II, the bloodiest war in all history, plunged the world into unparalleled misery because one man worshiped the god of munitions. Since then the reliance of nations upon such a red god has become more evident, and astronomical sums are being spent on nuclear bombs, other dreadful engines of destruction, and national defense. Although the Bible declares that no king can be saved by the multitude of a host or by his trust in tanks, planes, and bombs, the rulers of nations prefer to depend on their red gods rather than upon the God who with a breath destroyed 185,000 godless, God-defying Assyrians. Bless him. He is high over all.

119

Be a Star in Someone's Sky

"Shine . . . as the stars for ever and ever." Daniel 12:3.

Movie centers of the world speak of their top-ranking performers as *stars* and *starlets*. What a degradation of terms! The majority of those whose names are emblazoned as stars have no more real brilliance about them than a can of boot polish. Further, although advertised and applauded as stars, their appearance is but for a little. Many of them end up putting out their own light in suicidal death.

Star names quickly disappear from print, and new so-called stars appear. But Daniel would have us know that soul-winners are to shine as stars forever. Permanent brilliance is to be theirs. Having turned many to righteousness, they are to shine as the brightness of the firmament. Those who were wise followed a star to the feet of Jesus.

Are you a star in someone's sky? We often sing with Eliza Hewitt, "Will there be any stars, any stars in my crown?" Too many of us will face Jesus at reward day with a saved soul but a lost life—no souls to our credit. May yours be the honor of eternal radiance of the star that led many to Jesus who himself is to appear as the "Bright and Morning Star." He is indeed "Star of our might, and hope of every nation." Emerson urged us to "hitch our wagon to a star." If the wagon of our life is eternally hitched to him who is our "Star and Sun," then he in turn will endow us with all necessary wisdom to lighten the way of those lost in the darkness of sin and come to find in the Savior the one able to transform them into his marvelous light. A final word—we read of "wandering stars." God forbid that we should be in such a galaxy.

Thou Art Absolute Sole Lord

"A Saviour, who is Christ the Lord." *Luke 2:11.*

That spiritually quaint poet of the early seventeenth century, Richard Crashaw, in a hymn to St. Theresa of Avila wrote:

> *Love, thou art absolute sole Lord*
> *Of life and death.*

Since Jesus came as the personification of divine love and sacrificed his life for a lost world, he has every right to reign as our "absolute sole Lord." Luke's account of him suggests authority and dominion as Messiah and Lord accruing from his death at Calvary. Shortly after his ascension the apostles could preach that "God hath made that same Jesus . . . both Lord and Christ" (Acts 2:36). Once despised, he will yet reign as the "absolute sole Lord," as Lord of all. He is Lord of our life and the Lord of death, since "the keys of Death and Hell" dangle from his girdle.

Hudson Taylor, founder of the China Inland Mission, used to say that if Jesus is not "Lord of all, he is not Lord at all." We may believe him to be the Lord of hosts, able to deal with any or all circumstances and to carry out his will in spite of demons and people, yet we may not crown him as the sole Lord of our life. We have allowed other lords to have dominion over us and have failed to sanctify the Savior in our hearts as Lord. Life has been lived independently of him whose lordship ever makes for the spiritual enrichment of those who lovingly give him his rightful place of sovereignty. If we call him Lord, may we be found doing the things he says.

The Invisible Citadel

"My son, give Me thine heart." *Proverbs 23:26.*

Our heart is not something we wear on our sleeve for all and sundry to see, but, as Peter expresses it when referring to outward adornments, easily conspicuous "the hidden man of the heart" (I Peter 3:4). Yet, although unseen, like the covered mainspring of a watch, it is the most important part of our human mechanism. In his own captivating, Scottish style, Robert Burns wrote of the *heart* of man as being the part that makes him right or wrong. The marvel is that the One whose workmanship the heart is, asks for it to occupy as his throne from which to rule our whole life.

Having fashioned it by his power, God now wants to reign from it by his grace, for he knows that if he has the heart, he has all, for out of it are the issues of life. If the heart is God's undisputed habitation, then the outer life will be resplendent with his holiness. The secret of godlikeness is to commence each new day with a fresh surrender of our inner citadel to God to sanctify by his grace, engrave upon it his own image, and preserve by his power from the corrupt influences without that would change the heart into a stable of sin. Only the pure in heart is qualified to see God. Such a "vision splendid" is the privilege of all who seek to perfect holiness in the fear of the Lord. Was it not the Master himself who described himself as being "meek and lowly in heart," and that if we emulate his humility we too can find an inner peace and rest and nothing in a turbulent world can disturb or destroy (Matt. 11:28–30).

As Robert Burns says in his "Epistle to Davie":

> The heart aye's the part aye
> That makes us right or wrong.

Heaven's Matchless King

"Where is he that is born King?" Matthew 2:2.

In his religious masterpiece *Paradise Lost* John Milton graphically described those evil forces "warring in Heaven against Heaven's matchless King" who, being "matchless," conquers all his foes. The question of the wise men is of great import. *Born King!* It is very rare indeed for one of royal blood to be born a king. Born a prince, yes, but only becoming king when his father either abdicates or dies. But Jesus was *born* King, implying that he was a King before he was born. Paul could write of him as "the King eternal" (1 Tim. 1:17).

That Christ was a truer King than Herod who sought his life is evident from the capital *K* given to Jesus and the small *k* to the Roman ruler. All kings are small before our matchless King. The world has yet to see him as the King of kings. But strange insignia of royalty awaited the King born in Bethlehem. A stable was his palace; his courtiers, the lowly shepherds; his throne, a mother's knee; his robe, the swaddling clothes; his diadem, a crown of thorns.

Valiant knights said of King Arthur, "We never saw his like; there lives no greater leader." The glory of Arthur, however, pales into nothingness alongside the richer glory of Christ our King. It is thus we sing, "Hail Jesus, King of my days and nights." When he comes as King and ushers in his millennial reign, his kingdom will stretch from shore to shore. Is he King of our lives, exercising his sovereign rights over all we are and have? If so, then it will be evident to all we contact that being his children we resemble him as King (Judg. 8:18, 19). With loving obedience let us serve our King of glory.

Two Visitors from Heaven

"There talked with Jesus two men . . . Moses and Elijah."
Luke 9:30.

What a remarkable episode is the Gospel story of the manifestation of glory on Mt. Hermon! We could devote our meditation solely to the glorious transfiguration of Jesus when the deity within him sprang to the light of day and the three disciples were overawed as they beheld his glory. As Jesus prayed, the fashion of his countenance was changed, and prayer can secure for us a radiant transfiguration.

We are, however, concerned here with the two men who came down from heaven for the express purpose of having a talk with Jesus about his death at Jerusalem. On Mt. Nebo Moses was kissed to sleep by the angels, and God buried him in a secret grave—the only man to have had God as his undertaker! Elijah, however, never died, for like Enoch before him he was raptured, caught up in a whirlwind, to heaven. Yet both famous figures returned to earth and were immediately recognized by Peter, proving that they had not lost their identity and that they also were alive.

How consoling is the truth that our loved ones who departed in Christ are not mantled in a dreamless sleep but like Moses and Elijah are in full possession of their faculties with their gracious Lord who is "the God of the living." The bodies of the godly dead sleep but await a glorious resurrection. "I believe in the resurrection of the body." But the Christian dead themselves have been raised already and sit together with Christ. None can awaken what is awake or bring to life what never ceased to live. The appearance then of Moses and Elijah on the mount assures our hearts that those who leave us and whose bodies are left to lie like fallen trees, like the Lord they are with, are alive forevermore.

The Umpire Between Us

"Jesus the mediator of a better covenant." *Hebrews 12:24.*

The word Job uses for *daysman* is equivalent to the New Testament *mediator* and implies an *umpire* or a person chosen to decide a question. Job's lament (9:33), which the cross banishes, was:

> *There is no umpire between us,*
> *Who may lay his hand upon us both.*

This idea of mediation, of God dealing with the person, or the person with God, not directly, but through the interposition of another, is a prominent Scripture truth. The marvelous Epistle to the Hebrews has much to say about Jesus as the mediator or umpire between God and humankind, and surely there is no more expressive word of our Lord's sacrificial work on our behalf.

In these days of widespread industrial strife the word and office of mediator are often used. Capital and labor cannot agree; differences keep them apart, and an arbitrator is secured to bring both sides together to effect an amicable settlement. The Savior accomplished this by his cross. He laid his hand upon a holy and just God and a vile, lost sinner and reconciled them. Apart from his mediatorial work, we are helpless and homeless, and to reject him as the umpire means certain doom. "No man cometh unto the Father, *but by me*" (John 14:6).

Jesus is the only daysman between God and the person. Laying one hand on God and the other on the sinner, he makes them eternally one. The only way to an offended God then is through the pierced side of Jesus by which we can know what it is to be at peace with God. Would that sinners would heed his invitation, "Come, let us reason together. Though your sins are as scarlet, they will be white as snow" (Isa. 1:18).

The Hound of Heaven

"I will search Jerusalem with candles." *Zephaniah 1:12.*

It is not without reason that God was described by Francis Thompson as the Hound of Heaven, for unceasingly he tracks down sin to destroy it. Zephaniah, the prophet, was raised up to prophesy against the idolatrous practices and religious degeneracy of the people around him, and thus he declared that the Lord's search of their lives would be minute and thorough. He would search the corners of every life with a candle, even as the woman in the parable, with the aid of a candle, sought diligently for her lost piece of silver until she found it. David prayed for God to search the innermost recesses of his being. He wanted every nook and cranny scrutinized and so prayed, "Search me, know my thoughts . . . see if there be any wicked way *in* me" (Ps. 139:23, 24).

The Highlanders in Scotland use the more drastic word *ransack* for "search." "Ransack or turn me inside out, O God." Are we willing for the divine searcher, whose eyes are a flame of fire, to scan the very wounds shame would hide? Is it not folly to try to keep anything secret from him when he is the omniscient one? Does he not know us altogether? If the heavenly Hound is on our track, we have nothing to fear, for what the light of his candles reveal, his precious blood can cleanse. The primary object of his search is our sanctification. Are we prepared to pray, then, along with F. Bottome,

> *Search, till Thy fiery glance has cast*
> *Its holy light through all,*
> *And I, by grace, am brought at last,*
> *Before Thy face to fall.*

With Healing in His Wings

"He healed many who were ill with various diseases."
Mark 1:34.

During his public ministry Jesus gathered universal acclaim as the physician who never lost a case, and his miracles of healing established his deity and his mission as the sent one of God. "No man can do these miracles that thou doest, except God be with him" (John 3:2). His conquest over all manner of diseases, mental, physical, and demonic, proved him to be the Son of God with power and Lord over all. It must have been a great sight to watch him moving among the sick, afflicted, and distressed, relieving them of all affliction. An unidentified writer reflected:

Oh, in what divers pain they met!
Oh, with what joy they went away!

There were times, however, when the unbelief of people limited the manifestation of his miraculous power. He could have healed multitudes more, but unbelief, causing him to marvel, curbed his power to relieve the needy. Is it not blessed to know that his touch has still its ancient power? A remarkable saying of his was that his own would be able to accomplish greater works than even his miracles (John 14:12). It was indeed wonderful for him to impart physical healing, but when we lead a sin-sick soul to him and spiritual restoration is received, that is a greater miracle still. It was indeed wonderful to raise the dead, yet those quickened by his power died again. Our greater work is to bring those who are dead in their sin into the realization of life forevermore. Are *you* doing these greater works for your miracle-working Lord, whose touch has still its ancient power?

Give to a Gracious Message, a Host of Tongues

"Behold, I am going to send my messenger." *Malachi 3:1.*

The prophet Malachi mentions two messengers in the verse before us. "My messenger" refers to John the Baptist who came to declare the divine message of redemption and also to prepare the way for the redeemer himself who came as the "messenger of the covenant." His ministry as the heavenly messenger covers both of his returns, with special reference to the events following his coming. The function of a messenger is to deliver a message from one person to another. A post office messenger is only an intermediary and has nothing to do with the composition or content of the message, whether glad or sad. In *Antony and Cleopatra* Shakespeare declared that:

> *Though it be honest, it is never good*
> *To bring bad news. Give to a gracious message*
> *An host of tongues, but let ill tidings tell*
> *Themselves when they be felt.*

But a host of tongues in the Bible, including those of John the Baptist and of Jesus, sounded forth bad news as well as good. Jesus could say, "I have given them the words which thou gavest me." He did not originate the message he proclaimed, but receiving it from God, he declared it whether its content were heaven or hell. Would that all preachers were such messengers! Who and what is a messenger? He comes from the throne with a God-given message, and whether it pleases or pains, encourages or enrages, delivers it without apology or compromise. Are you a true messenger of the covenant of grace?

128

THE QUEEN

Blow trumpet, for the world is
white with May.

—Alfred Tennyson,
Idylls of the King

He Goes before Them and Commands Them All

"Behold, I have made him . . . a leader and commander."
Isaiah 55:4.

History provides us with thrilling stories of renowned commanders, like Napoleon, whose ability to lead and whose daring compelled multitudes to follow him, sometimes to disaster and death. In *Love's Labour's Lost* Shakespeare cited another notable leader and commander:

When in the world I liv'd, I was the world's commander;
By east, west, north, and south I spread my conquering might;
My scutcheon plain declares that I am Alisander.

But in Jesus we have one given by God to command his people, and beside him the bravest and the best pale into insignificance. Think of the uncounted myriads who, at his command, left all and followed him even unto death! In the hour of his nation's travail Winston Churchill could offer nothing but "blood, sweat, and tears." And such a call electrified millions into sacrifice. With heaven's commander, sacrifice is ever the order of the day. All who follow him must take up a cross and deny themselves. There are many who drop out by the way. They find complete obedience to his commands too hard. For them there must be an easier round to travel. A picnic, not a battlefield, suits them better.

Our heavenly commander is incomparable in that he was the first to fall in the battle against Satan and his evil hordes. In his supreme victory all his followers are secure and by his death gather inspiration and strength to fight the good fight beneath his blood-red banner. An anonymous writer advised:

Thy Commander speaks: His word obey;
So shall thy strength be as thy day.

Continual Comfort in a Face

"I will not leave you comfortless: I will come to you."
John 14:18.

In the portion of this wonderful chapter where Jesus spoke of his coming ascension we find him promising, "I will pray the Father, and he shall give you another comforter" (John 14:16). The language Jesus used implies that while among his own he was their comforter with sweet comfort ever in his face, but since he was about to leave his followers, he would send another consoler to take his place. In the original the word *another* means two things. First, another of the *same* kind; second, another of a *different* kind. Which word do you think Jesus used? Why, the first—another of the same kind. Thus as he breathed his tender, last farewell, he bequeathed the Holy Spirit to them as one who would continue in his capacity as comforter, another like unto himself.

After Christ's ascension the disciples Jesus had left behind were found walking in "the comfort of the Spirit" (Acts 9:31). Scripture has much to say of the God of all comfort, as you will find by tracing the word *comfort* with the aid of a concordance. Paul would have us remember that God comforts us in all our tribulation that in turn we may comfort those who are in any trouble (2 Cor. 1:4).

As the result of our own heartaches, sorrows, and trials, have we been fashioned into missionaries of consolation to those who are now sitting where we sat? Are we being used to assure those who are passing through any dark valley that there is one known as the "Man of Sorrows" who can comfort their stricken hearts? Our own griefs will not be lost if they mold us into a Barnabas, a son of consolation, who refreshes the distressed and outworn saints along the way.

131

No Divinity Is Absent If Prudence Is Present

"Behold, my servant shall deal prudently." *Isaiah 52:13.*

As Isaiah was portraying Jesus, the coming Messiah, he certainly illustrated the proverb of the Roman poet Juvenal in the title above, for as the divine servant, the virtue of *prudence* was always evident in his dealings with men. The prophet's portrait was fulfilled abundantly in the carefulness, wisdom, and discretion of the incarnate one. Have you ever meditated upon the prudence of Jesus? We think of Jesus' heroism and willing self-sacrifice, and rightly so, but seldom think of him as one exhibiting the attractive grace of prudence. The word *prudent* as used by Isaiah is two-sided, carrying the ideas of prudence and prosperity. He shall deal prudently, so that prosperity shall be the result. Often prudence on our part fails, but the Master's ever succeeded and conquered hearts by sagacity.

Paul spoke of Jesus abounding "in all wisdom and prudence." Thus the apostle thought of Jesus' life as the manifestation of godlike prudence. Cunning men sought to kill him before his time, but he knew how to evade a premature death. Jesus prized life, not excessively, but moderately, and his dealings with all men and women were ever prudent. With adroitness he could meet all questions and face all difficult situations with an inborn discreteness. As servants of the Lord, have we learned that prudence is essential to ultimate and permanent results in his service? His prudence was not the brand of many so-called prudent people, which is but the instinct of self-preservation acutely developed. His self-sacrifice was the highest prudence—an example we must emulate.

132

His Identity Presses upon Me

"But he could not be hid." *Mark 7:24.*

The New American Standard Bible translates Mark's item in his biography of Jesus as "when He had entered a house, He wanted no one to know *of it*, yet He could not escape notice." What an ageless truth there is in this historical fact! How could a personality like his be hid? As Matthew Henry commented, "A candle may be put under a bushel, the sun cannot." Did he not come as "*the* Light of the world," and was it not therefore impossible to hide such a glorious Orbit? A potent personality cannot be inconspicuous, and thus the solar presence of the Lord irradiated every region in which it tarried. He was the ever-evident Christ.

Lesser figures in Scripture may be shrouded in obscurity, but the glory of such an orb as Christ must attest himself everywhere. "He could not escape notice." It is affirmed that he hides himself and his purposes from us. "Verily, Thou art a God that hideth Thyself" (Isa. 45:15). He is certainly hid from the lost who have been blinded by the god of this world. None are so blind as those who won't see.

But can we who know him as the revealed one say that ours is the Christlike life revealing him to others? In a consecrated life he cannot be hid. A truly surrendered life forces Christ upon the gaze of the world. If we adorn his teachings in all things, then ours will be the witness showing forth his beauty. The perfume of holiness cannot be hid. *We* may escape notice, but that matters nothing so long as men see Jesus. "His identity," to quote and adapt John Keats, "presses upon me," and through me upon others.

Where Ignorance Is Bliss

"Moses wist not that the skin of his face shone while he talked with him." *Exodus 34:29.*

We cannot altogether agree with Christopher Marlowe that "there is no sin but ignorance." Rather do we believe as Thomas Gray of the eighteenth century expressed it in "Prospect of Eton College" "Where ignorance is bliss, 'Tis folly to be wise." In the chapter before us we find Moses, of "the shining face," miraculously sustained for forty days on the mount, then returning to earth with the best treasure in his hands, the two tables of the law, and adorned with the best beauty, for the skin of his face shone. Thus he carried the credential of his commission in his very countenance. Moses was oblivious of his transfigured face, and as Alexander Smellie, early twentieth-century Scottish minister, expressed it, "That is truest sainthood that never dreams of the beauty with which it is invested. Any self-consciousness detracts from the graciousness of a devout character, and lowers the disciple to lower levels."

The facial radiance of Moses was the effect of his sight of God, and when we have been on the mount with him, our light should shine before men as they take knowledge of us that we have been with Jesus. A devoted son wrote of his mother, "I read her face as one who reads a true and holy book." It is thus we read the supreme face of Jesus and how those around should read our faces as those who walk in the light with him.

Moses was ignorant of his shining face, and whatever beauty God puts upon us should fill us with a humble sense of our own unworthiness and cause us to forget that which makes our faces shine. Moses put a veil upon his face when he became conscious it shone. But when he went before the Lord, he put off the veil, and with open face he beheld the glory of the Lord. May we be saved from the fatal ignorance of Samson who did not know that the Lord had departed from him.

Closer Is He Than Breathing

"The Lord is near." Philippians 4:5.

An old divine said of Paul's pregnant phrase: "It is even more compacted as Paul uttered it. What he literally said was—*The Lord near.* Three words! No verb was used, for none was needed. It is abrupt to the point of dramatism. It is a bolt of benediction."

Is it not comforting to know that Jesus is ever accessible and available and that he is not far removed from any one of us? "Closer is he than breathing, and nearer than hands and feet," Tennyson reminded us in "The Higher Pantheism." Through the darkest night and over the roughest road he is near as a friend sticking closer than a brother. How different life would be if only we could realize his presence at all times and under all circumstances! May grace be ours to rest in his abiding nearness.

Others, so near and dear to us, have left us and are no longer at hand to soothe and sympathize, but Jesus is ever at our side, even within our heart to undertake for us under all circumstances. While it is true that ills have no weight and tears no bitterness when Jesus is at hand to bless, we can make another application of Paul's affirmation. The chaotic condition of the world would seem to indicate that the return of the Lord is at hand. He is certainly nearer his second coming than when we first believed. Here is the only hope for a broken world: "The Lord is near." In the gloom of this midnight hour, his trumpet may sound and his glory blaze upon us. Can we say that we are ready to hail him? Are we living near to him who is ever near us? If so, we shall not be surprised when he appears for the final installment of our redemption.

Comparisons Are Odorous

"What is your beloved more than another beloved?"
Song of Solomon 5:9.

There are occasions when comparisons are *odious* and not *odorous*, as Shakespeare said many comparisons are. There is a fragrancy about Solomon's figure of the bride extolling her lover above all other lovers. To her he was dazzling and ruddy and outstanding among ten thousands who also knew how to love. To the spiritual mind Solomon's Song is strikingly typical of the union existing between Christ and his church. As our beloved, he is beyond the best of earth altogether. He is incomparable, peerless, without an equal.

Often Jesus is compared with great religious leaders, but he is beyond compare. But does he ravish our hearts as he ought to? Is he precious beyond all preciousness, even as the one whose price is above rubies? The bride in Solomon's Idyll was so captivated by her beloved that she sang his praises everywhere. She was so intoxicated with love for him that she could not be silent as to his adorable person and virtues. Is this our attitude toward him who is the fairest of all the earth besides? Silence where his worth is concerned is treachery. May grace be ours to declare in glad tones our heavenly beloved's charms! If we deem him "the chiefest among ten thousand" and the one "altogether lovely," then let our lips publish his love and loveliness abroad so that others can see his beauty and come to desire him. Charles W. Fry shared his discovery:

> *I have found a friend in Jesus, he's everything to me,*
> *He's the fairest of ten thousand to my soul;*
> *The Lily of the Valley, in him alone I see*
> *All I need to cleanse and make me fully whole.*

Here Is My Throne

"Christ in you, the hope of glory." *Colossians 1:27*.

The root of Christ's teaching in the Gospels reaches a rich fruitage in the Epistles. He often spoke to his own about being *in* them, and it was given to Paul fully to expound the glorious truth of Christ's indwelling our hearts by faith (Eph. 3:17). Then for the Colossians was the mystic truth, *Christ in you*. What a precious gem this is from the casket of pearls found in the first chapter of this Christ-exalting epistle! Spurgeon said of verse 27, "The words read like a whole body of divinity condensed in a line."

At Calvary it was Christ *for* us, but since Pentecost it is Christ *in* us by his Spirit. He died for us that he might be in us. Such then is the mystery of our faith that although Christ is in heaven, throned in glory everlasting, he yet indwells you and me. Thus he has two thrones: one above, glorious beyond compare; the other, a saved and trustful heart. Paul reminded us that Christ dwells in our heart *by faith*—the little unimposing door by which he enters human personalities.

Further, he himself declared, "Greater is he that is in you than he that is in the world," and being within, he is the sanctifying principle of life. Indwelling us, he ever seeks to transform us into his image. Then is not his indwelling the hope of the glorious life to come? His presence within us is the basis of "that blessed hope," about which Paul reminded Titus. Does not the constant remembrance of indwelling deity keep such a hope of glory vivid and vital in our present life? May we know him increasingly both as the indweller and as the friend sticking closer than a brother.

To Err Is Human, to Forgive, Divine

"Thy sins are forgiven thee." Luke 5:20.

Jesus preached and practiced forgiveness. He urged his disciples to forgive until seventy times seven and to forgive their enemies. At Calvary he prayed God to forgive his murderers. Christ's forgiveness of the palsied man raised the ire of the unforgiving Pharisees. Condemning Christ with blasphemy, they said, "Who can forgive sins, but God alone?" This was true. God alone can forgive. What they forgot, however, was that God was in Christ, who was therefore qualified to forgive. Further, the revelation is that when he forgives he forgets, remembering our sins no more against us.

Are we forgiven? Have we proved that there is forgiveness with him that he may be feared? How blessed we are if "ransomed, healed, restored, forgiven"! And if God, for Christ's sake, has forgiven us, then it is our responsibility to emulate the divine example and be found "tenderhearted, forgiving one another." On the basis of a divinely bestowed forgiveness we must manifest the Christlike virtue toward others.

Is there someone you should forgive, but is your attitude one of reluctance? How often we hear one say, "I can never forgive them for what they have done." How would we fare if this were God's attitude toward us who have sinned exceedingly? We manifest the virtue of divinity when we forgive, even as we have been forgiven by God in virtue of Calvary. Have we personally experienced the blessedness of the man whose sin has been forgiven? Then our obligation is to manifest such a divine action in dealing with others.

His Mind, His Kingdom, His Will Is Law

"Lord, if thou wilt . . . I will: be thou clean." *Luke 5:12, 13.*

Can you not hear the chiming of wedding bells in the miracle Jesus performed the day he cleansed the leper of his foul disease? The marriage vows read, "Wilt thou take this man?" and the answer is, "I will." The diseased man said to Jesus, "If thou wilt?" and Jesus replied, "I will." Truly a marriage took place as the two met face-to-face, for the Lord and the one-time leper became one.

No one can read the Gospels without being impressed with Christ's willingness to heal and cleanse, to forgive and save. At all times he was ready and willing to relieve the distressed; in fact, he was more willing to bless than the needy were to be blessed. Did he not have to say, "Ye will not come to me, that ye might have life" (John 5:40)?

Jesus is not willing that any should perish, but, alas, multitudes willingly go to hell. He waits to heal all of their moral leprosy, but he cannot exercise his power to cleanse and deliver unless his will and the human will harmonize. A sinner is halfway saved when he is willing for Jesus to say to him, "Be thou clean!" If a man wills to know Jesus' will, he comes to experience all the healer can accomplish in his heart and life. We learn from a hymn translated by John Mason Neale:

> If I ask Him to receive me
>   Will He say me, Nay?
> Not till Earth, and not till Heaven
>   Pass away.

The Kingly Crowned Head

> "The first man is of the earth, earthy: the second man
> is the Lord from heaven." *1 Corinthians 15:47*.

In many ways Christ, our federal head, is a contrasting type of Adam. As the first man, Adam was fashioned out of dust; Jesus was conceived by the Holy Spirit. Adam was created innocent; Jesus came as the holy, perfect one. Adam became a sinner; Jesus knew no sin. Through Adam we have physical life; through Christ we have life forevermore. Adam was of the earth; Jesus came from heaven. In Adam we bear the image of earthly things; in Jesus we bear the image of heavenly things. Adam was the natural head of the human race; Jesus is the head of a new creation (Luke 3:38; Rom. 5:14). In Adam we die; in Jesus we are made alive. By his sin Adam brought ruin to mankind; by his obedience Jesus brings blessing to all who, although the sinning sons of Adam's race, receive him as savior. In a garden Adam succumbed to the wiles of Satan; in another garden Jesus overcame the enemy of humankind. The first Adam derived his life from another; Jesus came as the life and as the life-giving spirit, or as the fountain of life, able to impart life to others, whether physical, spiritual, or eternal.

As the whole of humanity can be separated under two heads, namely, Adam or Jesus, in which are you to be found? You must be in one or the other, either in sin or in grace, either saved from the guilt and penalty of sin or lost in sin and in danger of being lost eternally. Is Christ your head, directing all that concerns your life? If found in him, then walking in the light with him counteracts the wiles of the old Adamic nature.

Powerful Preacher and Tenderest Teacher

"From that time Jesus began to preach." *Matthew 4:17.*

Although it was Father O'Flynn of "ould Donegal" that the poet Augustus P. Gardner had in mind as the "powerful preacher," I recall the description used of a still more powerful preacher. Now and again some eloquent pulpiteer, like Charles H. Spurgeon, is referred to as "a prince of preachers." But there has only been one princely preacher, and there will never be his like again. "Never man spake like this man" (John 7:46). If only we could have listened to the discourses that made him the greatest preacher the world has ever known. As the master preacher he knew how to "open his mouth" (Matt. 5:2). He opened it because he knew what to preach about, and he preached it simply, clearly, and distinctly. Beautiful indeed were his feet as he journeyed here and there preaching peace.

To Jonah came the command, "Preach the preaching that I bid thee," and Jesus appeared as a God-sent, Spirit-inspired preacher preaching nothing but a God-given message. "I have given unto them the words which thou gavest me" (John 17:8). That he practiced what he preached is evident from a study of the Gospels. With him, lips and life were in complete harmony. His influence as a preacher did not bring high, bestowed honors but a cross of agony and shame. And now the kind of preaching he always blesses is the preaching of that cross as the only remedy for sin. The world sadly needs more preaching that will cause sinners to flee to Jesus from the wrath to come.

Fairest of All the Earth Beside

"He is altogether lovely." *Song of Solomon 5:16.*

We read that Saul and Jonathan were lovely and pleasant in their lives, but Jesus is preeminent among men for his loveliness and pleasantness. Are you not amazed as you meditate upon the extent and variety of descriptions and designations, definite and implied, setting forth the excellencies of God's beloved Son? And it takes them all to set forth his perfections, including his tender relation with his own and as the center of God's counsels. Those who are taught of the Spirit cannot fail to see Jesus in Solomon's matchless Song. There are so many naturally beautiful things in the world, and because he fashioned them all, how lovely he must be. His beauty must be beyond compare. Not only is he lovely in form and feature, but in every word and wish. Everything about him bears the imprint of his exquisite attractiveness. No wonder Zechariah cried, "How great is thy beauty!" (Zech. 9:17).

Can we say that the beauty of the Lord is upon us and that we are sharing his loveliness? Whether we have beauty of countenance or not makes little difference. Behind the plainest-looking face may be one of the loveliest of characters because of the indwelling of him who is "altogether lovely." Beholding the beauty of the Lord should result in the beauty of holiness in your life and mine. A proverb has it, "Handsome is as handsome does." We petition with Mrs. H. Bradley:

> *I ask this gift of Thee,*
> *A life all lily-fair,*
> *And fragrant as the place*
> *Where seraphs are.*

142

In Goodly Colors Gloriously Arrayed

"Blue, and purple, and scarlet, and fine linen." *Exodus 25:4.*

Dear old Edmund Spenser of the sixteenth century had all sorts of spring flowers in mind when he conceived the line in the above title. I like to use it to describe the beautiful colors employed in the tabernacle that Moses set up in the wilderness. Although the tents in which the Israelites lived were ordinary and commonplace, the sanctuary in the midst of them was resplendent with its scarlet roof, golden furniture, and gay-colored curtains. That God is a lover of the artistic is proven, not only by the blue, scarlet, white, and purple used in the tablernacle, but in the gorgeous, unmatched colors of the rainbow—his pledge that he will not flood the earth again.

The costly and beautiful tabernacle occupies a most important place in the story of redemption, hence, the space devoted to it in Scripture. At most, Moses devoted only two chapters to the creation of the world; but his record of the tabernacle and the consecration of its priests spread itself into thirteen chapters.

The royal colors mentioned are symbolic. *Blue* is the color of the sky and suggests heavenly peace—"as it were the body of heaven in his clearness" (Exod. 24:10). The deep blue of the firmament leads us to think of the sweet peace of God, the most real and precious of blessings. *Purple* is the royal and imperial color and carries first the thought of sovereignty, then of grace, grace being the most attractive form in which sovereignty manifests itself.

Scarlet is both the sin and sacrifice color. Though our sins are as scarlet, the sacrifice at Calvary provides a full cleansing and deliverance. *White* consists of the union of the seven prismatic colors forming the rainbow, and in the tabernacle white was the background of all, the ground on which the lovely hues were wrought. White is the color of holiness and purity, and in heaven the bride of the lamb will be arrayed in fine linen, clean and white. Blue, purple, and scarlet are ours in the "grace, mercy, and peace" from God; and white is our purity of heart and life in response to all we have from God.

143

A Traveler between Life and Death

"A certain householder . . . went into a far country."
Matthew 21:33.

The traveler between life and death that Wordsworth depicted in "She Was a Phantom of Delight" was a virgin with "reason firm, the temperate will, . . . a perfect Woman, nobly planned." But in his Olivet discourse, under the guise of a householder making all arrangements about his possessions before traveling into a far country, Jesus painted a precious portrait of himself. In this parable, so full of spiritual teaching, Jesus described his departure from the earth and the committal of responsibilities to his servants he was to leave behind. At his ascension he was the glorified man traveling from a world where death reigned into the far country of heaven with its life, eternal in nature.

During his absence he expects his own to be faithful in their stewardship. With the coming of his Spirit at Pentacost, gifts were imparted for service, some being more gifted than others. As all of us have a gift of some sort or another, the question is, Are we using our Christ-bestowed talents to the full? During the absence of the traveling man, are we trading with and multiplying our talents?

Having taken his journey, he left us behind to take his goods and distribute them among the needy. He does not expect five talents more from the one who has only two talents. Whether we have five, two, or one makes little difference. Reward can only be ours when he returns from the far country if we have used to the limit what he gave us to serve him with. What folly it was for the man with the one talent to bury it in a handkerchief. He should have used to it wipe the sweat from his brow as he used his talent unceasingly.

144

None Invincible As They

"If God be for us, who can be against us?" *Romans 8:31.*

Cowper was poetically describing the forces of the British warrior queen, Boadicea, as they faced Caesar's proud legions, when he wrote, "None invincible as they." But Paul, who also knew something of the might and cruelty of Rome, assured us that the soldiers of the heavenly warrior King have a far greater invincibility than that experienced by Boadicea's brave fighters. Hence the apostle's challenge, "If [or *since*] God is for us, who can be against us?" (Rom. 8:31). Satan and a godless world will ever be lined up against the saints, but in spite of all assaults they are invincible, emerging from the conflict more than conquerors. From the Psalms Paul gathered inspiration to encourage believers to stand firm. "The Lord is for me, I will not fear; What can man do unto me?" (Ps. 118:6).

If there is no suggestion of doubt here, we should read the verse, "Since God be for us." Is not his name *Emmanuel*—God with us? Therefore, all the perfections of his nature are arrayed for the defense and safety of those fighting the good fight of faith. God is committed by his covenant, his oath, and his promise to support and sustain us and to bring us through to victory. Our cause is his. Thus he is opposed to all who are against us and has pledged to deliver us in six contests and not to forsake us in the seventh.

Amid all opposition to our faithful witness let us take fresh heart, for our ally is the Lord God omnipotent who is able to clothe us with invincibility. None can prevail over us, for he that is in us is greater than satanic foes in the world. Because God is with and for us, we can overcome the world, conquer death, and eternally inherit glory. God is ours, and we are God's. Why then should anything or anybody alarm or terrify us?

Let Gentleness My Strong Enforcement Be

"Thy gentleness hath made me great." *Psalm 18:35.*

The word *gentleness* is translated in many ways. The Book of Common Prayer has it, "*Thy loving correction* has made me great." Our developing character owes much to divine correction. "Thy *goodness* hath made me great." David often gratefully ascribed all his greatness, not to his own goodness, but to the unfailing goodness of God. Another reading puts it, "Thy *providence*," and divine providence is nothing more than goodness in action. "Goodness is the bud of which Providence is the flower." Some render it, "Thy humility hath made me great" or "Thy condescension hath made me great!" Spurgeon said, "We are so little, that if God should manifest His greatness without condescension, we should be trampled under His feet; but God, who must stoop to view the skies, and bow to see what angels do, turns His eye yet lower, and looks to the lowly and contrite, and makes them great." The Chaldean clay tablet reads, "Thy word hath increased me." But the virtue of gentleness—the Roman emperor Aurelius called it *invincible*—is a prominent feature of deity. Shakespeare wrote in *As You Like It:*

> ... *Your gentleness shall force*
> *More than your force move us to gentleness.*

In childhood days we were taught to sing, "Gentle Jesus, meek and mild," and marvelous has our experience been of his gentleness. How gentle he has been in his corrections, his forbearance, his instruction, and his patience! As we meditate upon such a theme as his gentle treatment of us, may gratitude be awakened, love quickened, and humility deepened. It is only thus that spiritual greatness can become ours. St. Aidian would have us remember that God "gently deals with souls untaught." May we ever be found beseeching others by the gentleness of God.

He Sung of God—the Mighty Source

"Bring them hither to me." *Matthew 14:18.*

Because the Son of God was "the hidden source of every precious thing," he knew he could feed the starving, fainting multitude around him. Christopher Smart, godly poet of the eighteenth century, praised the psalmist in "A Song to David":

> *He sung of God—the mighty source*
> *Of all things—the stupendous force.*
> *On which all strength depends.*

In the command of Jesus, "Bring them to me," there was power to perform miracles with the little we may have to give him. One of our hymns speaks of him as "Thou source of all our store" and as "The source of all our bliss." We can bring the poor and needful and sinful to him because he alone has the resources to relieve them.

Have we learned the secret of bringing everything to him—our homes, our children, our business obligations? *Bring them to me!* Are trials, sorrows, heartaches, disappointments, and losses ours? Jesus, the source of sympathetic tears, is saying, Bring them to me, and my provision will sweeten your bitter cup. Have you a particular, peculiar problem or trouble facing you just now? Then close your eyes for a moment and hear Jesus say, "Bring it hither to me." As you do, yours will be assurance that as all things are possible to him he will give you grace to surmount your trial and joy in God. An unknown author wrote:

> *How sweet to be allow'd to call*
> *The God whom heaven adores my Friend,*
> *To tell my thoughts, to tell Him all;*
> *And then to know my prayers ascend.*

The Crown of Sovereignty

"Thy God reigneth." *Isaiah 52:7.*

With united voice Scripture acclaims the sovereignty of him who is the almighty one. As the Lord God omnipotent he is worthy to wear the crown of sovereignty, for his supremacy in every realm cannot be disputed. He sits upon the throne of the universe he created and can use the forces of nature as he deems best. His will as the sovereign Lord cannot be frustrated. No one and nothing can frustrate the accomplishment of his designs. All events are under his control as the superintendent of all things. In these days of international and national crises and upheavals, those of us who love God should encourage our hearts in his supremacy. Laws may be proposed contrary to his will, but he can dispose of them. He rules and overrules. None can stay his hand or say to him, What doest thou?

He reigns, not as a tyrant lord, but as our heavenly Father, seeking to secure our well-being and his glory. He reigns to crush his foes and convert them into his friends. Is this not the sublime truth that should calm and compose our minds at all times—my God reigneth? Amid crumbling empires, look up and see him on his throne as King forever and rejoice. His sovereignty ensures your safety, happiness, and deliverance.

Are the reins of the government of your life in his hands? Does he reign without a rival in your heart? If so, then you will have no doubt as to his universal dominion and supremacy both now and in the future. Sir Robert Grant could write:

> *O worship the King, all glorious above,*
> *And gratefully sing His wonderful love.*

Knit Together in One Fellowship

"Whether we be afflicted, it is for your consolation."
2 Corinthians 1:6.

A portion of the collect for All Saints' Day in the Book of Common Prayer reads, "Who hast knit together thine elect in one communion and fellowship, in the mystical body of Thy Son." One aspect of this fellowship of kindred minds concerns pain and comfort, as the chapter from which our text is taken clearly proves. This is preeminently the Comfort Chapter of the New Testament. Paul had had some dark experiences, including an affliction when he would have died had it not been for God's intervention. But through all his suffering the apostle experienced the comfort of God and was brought to see that his severe trials and the unfailing consolation of God through them all were but a preparation for his ministry of comforting others.

Often God afflicts us first and then heals and consoles us because he wishes to fashion us into missionaries of comfort among those in any trouble. Our own sorrows and trials are not squandered or lost when they mold us into sons and daughters of consolation. Alexander Smellie reminded us that "there are many around me on whom griefs like my own are laid; and who upholds and strengthens them so well as one who has been in the wilderness of desolation and the gloomy Valley of Death's Shade before them?"

If we have never known heartbreak, we are not qualified to assure the brokenhearted of reality of divine comfort. A world of pain and grief is a grim reality, and there are secrets we could never learn unless we become personally acquainted with the trials and afflictions of those around. One of these secrets is the presence of the divine comforter in our trouble, resulting in the ability to comfort others as we ourselves were comforted of God.

I Tremble for My Country

"His heart trembled for the ark of God." 1 Samuel 4:13.

Thomas Jefferson, the American president who died in 1826, said, "Indeed I tremble for my country when I reflect that God is just." Aging Eli knew that God was just and trembled for his country as the ark was being taken by godless hands. The prophet shuddered to think what it would mean for Israel if the ark were lost to the nation. Israel's glory would depart, for the ark had been at once the symbol and pledge of the presence of Jehovah in the midst of his people—a presence to which they owed everything. Behind Eli's trembling of heart was a smitten conscience, for he had permitted flagrant abuses in its holy precincts and had allowed the ark to go from its holy and peaceable habitation out to the clamor and carnage of the battlefield. Yet Eli dearly loved the ark, which acted as a magnet drawing the warmth and emotion of his soul.

Christ is the Ark of the Covenant, and if all he represents as the mercy seat departs, we have a creed with life and a temple without the presence of the Lord. Eli felt he could not live if the ark were disgraced or banished. In fact, at its removal he died. Is this our estimate of Christ in spite of the wounds we have inflicted upon him?

When Principal Fulloch, conservative theologian, was dying in Torquay, his wife, Jeanie, was at their home in St. Andrews. As he died, he kept uttering a plaintive cry, unconscious of what he was saying but conscious of the one earthly thing he wanted—*Jeanie! Jeanie!* As he went down into the valley, his whole being called for her who had been his constant companion. Can we say that this is our longing when Christ our ark seems removed? *Jesus, Jesus, leave me not.* Bless him, we have no need to tremble, for nothing can separate us from him!

A Victorious Name

"The breaker is come up before them." *Micah 2:13.*

Of the many names and titles of the Lord, *breaker* is one of the most forceful. Micah, stirred by the injustice and oppression associated with the house of Jacob, envisaged a decisive deliverance for the people. As Charles John Ellicott, late eighteenth-century bishop of Gloucester, commented, "The Breaker shall go before them as their Saviour and Deliverer, yea, even Jehovah at their head. . . . This Breaker is, by confession of the Jews, the title of the Messiah. A saying of one of their famous Rabbis reads—'the explanation from above as Messiah, as it is written, *The Breaker is come up from before them.*'"

He is a mighty breaker, able to break down all opposition and clear a road out of all captivity. By his death and resurrection Jesus broke down and destroyed the forces of darkness and was victorious over every foe. As those delivered from the penalty and thralldom of sin, we do not march on *to* victory but *from* it, for the great enemy was overcome at Calvary. By faith we appropriate his triumph as ours. With Samuel Medley we

> Sing the dear Saviour's glorious fame,
> Who bears The Breaker's wondrous name;
> Sweet name, and it becomes Him well,
> Who breaks down sin, guilt, death, and hell.

The Lord is able to break in pieces all oppressors and go before his own as their victorious protector. May we take fresh heart from the fact that all our enemies were conquered beforehand and the prey taken from the mighty. Through the conquest of the cross, satanic foes, bent on hurting us, have had their weapons severely blunted. The old serpent would still try to destroy us, but his fangs have been extracted. As the roaring lion, his teeth have been broken. So let us praise our blessed *breaker.*

A Happy Issue out of All Their Afflictions

"In their affliction they seek me early." *Hosea 5:15.*

In the Book of Common Prayer is a petition for those in "any ways afflicted, or distressed, in mind, body, or estate." It pleads that for them there may be "a happy issue out of all their afflictions." Hosea described how the people could find a happy issue out of their national affliction, namely, by seeking the Lord, not only *early* or at once, but earnestly. "In their affliction they will earnestly seek me." Hosea said that God's withdrawal from his people was not absolute and final but was a method intended to produce a result which could make his return possible. And when his people sought him earnestly, God returned to them.

Often God uses our adversities and afflictions as the means to bring us nearer himself—always a happy issue! Charles H. Spurgeon said that afflictions are frequently "like fierce dogs to worry wanderers back to the fold." If we are rich and increased with goods and boasting like David, "In my prosperity . . . I shall never be moved" (Ps. 30:6), God often applies the rod, and what we have treasured disappears. Our carnal security vanishes, and, stripped of our pride, we earnestly seek the Lord. Then our emptiness is sanctified to the enrichment of our soul. In abject poverty the prodigal son said, "I will arise, and go unto my father." If we are heirs of affliction, as he rebukes us, let us recognize that it is a loving hand that chastens us and a loving heart that forgives us. The happy issue out of all afflictions is embodied for us in the words of the hymn by Elizabeth P. Prentiss:

> Let sorrow do its work, Come grief and pain;
> Sweet are thy messengers, Sweet their refrain,
> When they can sing with me,—More love, O Christ, to thee,
> More love to thee!

That Man's Silence Is Wonderful to Listen To

"But he answered her not a word." Matthew 15:23.

Thomas Hardy in *Under the Greenwood Tree*, described a character thus:

> *Silent? Ah, he is silent! He can keep silence well.*
> *That man's silence is wonderful to listen to.*

Over sixty years ago Percy Ainsworth left the church a precious heritage in his volume *The Silences of Jesus*, in which he makes us feel that it is wonderful to listen to the silences of the Master.

The silence that greeted the heartcry of the woman of Canaan for the healing of her sick daughter is called the "silence of love." This distressed soul had come a long way and had crossed the strong barrier of race when, as a Gentile, she made a request of a Jew. But she thought of Jesus more as a great healer and presented a simple plea, "Have mercy upon me, O Lord, thou Son of David; my daughter is grievously vexed with a devil" (Matt. 15:22). She expected an immediate reply, "but he answered her not a word." His silence was sympathetic and was designed to bring the distressed woman nearer the heart of infinite love and pity. Her second cry and answer to the refusal of Jesus brought forth his commendation, "O woman, great is thy faith: be it unto thee even as thou wilt" (Matt. 15:28).

Are there not times in our experience when, in spite of our pleading, heaven is silent? It is said that that great man of faith, George Muller, prayed for fifty years for the salvation of a friend before God answered his plea. God's silences do not mean denials. His silence is the richest test of our faith, for we have the assurance that if our requests are according to his will he must answer us. Another silence wonderful to listen to was his own when before his crucifiers he was dumb and opened not his mouth. By his silence he conclusively proved himself the true lamb of God. In the silence of our own hearts may we ever hear the voice of his love.

A Pleasant Shade, a Grove of Myrtles Made

"Instead of the brier shall come up the myrtle tree."
Isaiah 55:13.

Isaiah is conspicuous among the sacred writers in his love of, and unique ability to use, natural objects to symbolize spiritual truths. Briers have no beauty, yield no fragrance, and bear no fruit. They only cumber the ground and occupy soil well able to produce something more beneficial. Briers are, therefore, symbolic of all that is worthless and mischievous in the world and must be got rid of so that a wilderness can be turned into a garden. Myrtles, however, provide "a pleasant shade," as the fifteenth-century poet Richard Barnfield reminded us.

Looked upon as emblems of youth and loveliness, myrtles were deemed sacred by the ancients. They were used in all joyous festivals, especially those in honor of Venus. The bark of myrtles was used for tanning. The berries and leaves provided medicine, wine, and oil and thus remain as types of all that is pure, fragrant, and serviceable in the world. Changing briers for myrtles is a change for the better; and our age is in great need of the destruction of briers and the planting of myrtles.

History is laden with stories of courageous men who have uprooted briers and planted myrtles. In the days of William Wilberforce slavery was an ugly, cruel brier that died very hard, but self-denying patriots like Wilberforce and Abraham Lincoln labored unceasingly to expose the horrors of the slave trade. They lived to see the day when the brier of slavery was killed and the myrtle of freedom planted in its place. Godly souls, like John Bunyan, believed that persons should worship God in their own way and according to the dictates of their heart and consequently suffered torture, imprisonment, and even martyrdom for the sake of religious liberty. They succeeded in uprooting the brier of religious persecution and planting the myrtle tree of religious freedom. In the narrower world of our own hearts we must cast out the briers of disobedience, pride, selfishness, and sin and substitute the myrtles of obedience, humility, love, and holiness.

Watch Your Step

"Walk circumspectly, not as fools, but as wise."
Ephesians 5:15.

What an engaging term Paul used in his description of the walk and warfare of the believer! *Circumspect* means wary, taking everything into account, exercising caution. The Revised Version expresses the verse, "Look therefore carefully how ye walk, not as unwise but as the wise." We are to walk accurately, looking around, watchful on every side. As those redeemed by the precious blood of Jesus, we must be strict about our character and check up on our daily living with the deliberate purpose of correcting wrong decisions taken and of being self-controlled in every habit. Strictest consistency in common things is obligatory, for we are taught to avoid every appearance of evil. Only thus can we buy up every opportunity of doing good.

Surrounded as we are by the wiles of the Devil, we have to be careful of every step. In *Julius Caesar* Shakespeare wrote:

> It is the bright day that brings forth the adder,
> And that craves wary walking.

We live in a hostile, godless world surrounded by manifold temptations. Our heart is deceitful above all things and desperately wicked, and unless we keep close to Jesus, we cannot be victorious as we walk in the midst of snares. Honoring him in every phase of life should be our constant aim, and for such a purpose the precious promises covering life and service were given. Isaac Watts suggested:

> So let our lips and lives express
> The holy Gospel we profess;
> So let our works and virtues shine,
> To prove the doctrine all Divine.

Beside a Human Door

"I am the door." John 10:9.

Wordsworth had Lucy Gray in mind when he wrote:

> —*The sweetest thing that ever grew*
> *Beside a human door.*

When Jesus said, *"I am the door,"* he declared himself a "human door" through which all people could enter. What an understandable presentation of our adorable Redeemer this is! He is the ever-open door so that we can go in and out.

An ordinary door has two functions: it admits, yet excludes. We can open the door of our home and allow all welcome friends to enter. The same door, however, can be kept closed against others who have no wish to entertain. The allegory as used by Jesus of himself is consoling. He is the only entrance into the fold in which his sheep find safety, sustenance, and liberty. He is the only door into salvation now and heaven hereafter.

But the time is coming when, as the foolish virgins proved, the door will be closed. In this age of grace he is the ever-open door. His sorrow is that the door of the heart is fast closed against him, and his repeated knocking goes unheeded (Rev. 3:20). How unkind it is to keep him standing outside in the cold! To quote the Scottish Metrical Psalm 24:

> *Ye gates, lift up your heads on high;*
> *ye doors that last for aye.*
> *Be lifted up, that so the King*
> *of glory enter may.*

How assuring is his word, "If any man open the door, I will come in"! The blessed fact is that when he comes in he closes the door behind him.

The Want of a Nail

"I will fasten him as a nail in a sure place." *Isaiah 22:23.*

When Jesus became the recognized Son of a carpenter, then a carpenter himself, he learned all about the value and purpose of nails. Nails were daily *in* his hands, and when he came to die, cruel men drove nails *through* his hands. Among the varied and significant titles and types of Jesus, none is more expressive than that of a nail, for as such, he had been fastened by the Father in a sure or safe place. Does this not imply that he will never come loose, causing what depends upon him to fall? Applied to Jesus, the figure of a nail suggests fixity, the sense of security in his relationship to the throne of God.

We find nails useful in two ways, namely, for hanging things on and for binding things together. Isaiah says, "They shall hang on him all the glory of the Father's throne" (Isa. 22:24). Have you discovered Jesus as the nail on whom you can hang all that concerns you, which is but another way of casting all your care upon him? No weight is too heavy for him to carry. As nails join things together, so Jesus is the only nail able to unify his people and hold them together.

But Isaiah issued this warning: "The nail that is fastened in a sure place shall be removed." When this age of grace ends, a sinning world will no longer hear the joyful news that Jesus saves. Presently, he is its nail of salvation in the holy place (Ezra 9:8). Our hope is that when he does appear we shall see the print of the nails in his wonderful hands and also, as Shakespeare reminded us, in *1 Henry IV:*

> . . . *those blessed feet*
> *which fourteen hundred years ago were nail'd*
> *For our advantage on the bitter cross.*

The Throned Monarch Better Than His Crown

"In that day the Lord of Hosts will become a beautiful
crown and a glorious diadem." *Isaiah 28:5,* ASB.

What a fascinating two-sided cameo of the Lord this is—a crown of
glory and a diadem of beauty. On the one side we have the excellence,
worth, sovereignty, and glory of the Lord. How visible this crown will
be when he returns as the Lord of glory (Ps. 24)! On the other side we
witness in the diadem of beauty the incomparable loveliness, luster, and
radiance of our Lord: Who is like unto him, so glorious in holiness?
Well might we pray with Charles Wesley, "Fill me, Radiancy divine!"

Too few of us have learned that he wishes us to have dominion with
a "quality of mercy . . . [that] blesseth him that gives, and him that
takes [and] becomes the throned monarch better than his crown"
(Shakespeare, *The Merchant of Venice*)—achieving worth, radiance, and
attractiveness of character. We sometimes sing, "Let the beauty of Jesus
be seen in me," but is he, as the diadem of beauty, diademing our lives
with his love and loveliness?

How ugly and despicable are the sins of the flesh when brought alongside him! Would that ours could be the ever-deep longing and determination to become his crown of glory and diadem of beauty! Such a
combination of qualities delighting the sight and mind, however, cannot
be acquired by human effort. They must be accepted from him who is
altogether lovely and the source of all that is beautiful. An unknown
writer gave us these lines:

> As some rare perfume in a vase of clay
>   Pervades it with a fragrance not its own,
> So when Thou dwellest in a mortal soul,
>   All Heaven's own sweetness seems around it thrown.

The Church's One Foundation

"For a foundation a stone, a tried stone, a precious corner stone, a sure foundation." *Isaiah 28:16.*

How different is the prophet's stable foundation to "the refuge of lies" which the ungodly fashion for their safety! Paul agreed with Isaiah when he called the Lord *a foundation*, for did he not say, "Other foundation can no man lay than that is laid, which is Jesus Christ" (I Cor. 3:11)? Thus the foundation of our faith is not a precept, but a Person, not a fact, but a figure, even him, who cannot be moved. This wonderful truth inspired Samuel J. Stone to pen his great hymn:

> *The Church's one foundation*
> *Is Jesus Christ her Lord;*
> *She is His new creation,*
> *By Spirit and the Word.*

The metaphor of foundation suggests the thought of stability or a solid base. Jesus, in his parable of the building of two houses, illustrated how the foundation made all the difference between them. One house was doubtless built all right, but the foundation was all wrong. Being of *sand*, it was not *sure* and fell when a storm arose. But the other house stood the test of the hurricane since it was built on rock. Jesus himself is our foundation on a tried stone, and John Newton wrote:

> *On the Rock of Ages founded,*
> *What can shake thy sure repose?*

Philosophies, precepts, morals, and axioms may be commendable in a way, but they do not offer a safe foundation on which a sinner may build. Life can only be secure and stable if built upon Jesus, the unmovable rock in a weary land. If rejected, he becomes "a rock of offense."

159

Sermons in Stones

"The stone which the builders rejected." *I Peter* 2:7.

Peter, quoting from Isaiah, wrote of Jesus as "a chief cornerstone, elect, precious," "the stone the builders rejected," "a stone of stumbling" to them which "stumble at the word" (I Pet. 2:6–8). How full of spiritual import this symbol of Jesus is! As the *chief cornerstone* he possesses peculiar honor in the most wonderful temple ever built.

As the *living stone* he is not an inert mass of particles as stones out of the ground, but a living and life-imparting stone. As the *elect stone* he came out of the council chamber of heaven as God's chosen one to die as the Savior for the salvation of a world of stony hearts. As the *precious stone* he is a jewel beyond compare. To all who receive and love him he is precious or, as the Scofield Reference Bible margin states, "He is the preciousness" since he sacrificed his precious blood to redeem us.

As a *stone of stumbling* he is the one over whom many will fall into the abyss of eternal despair since they disobeyed his word and warning. As the *stone or rock of offense* he is related to his ancient people, the Jews, the rulers of whom were ever offended because of his life and teaching. As the *stone cut out of the mountain* he warns of his judicial authority and power in crushing godless nations to powder. It is to be hoped that you are not among the builders trying to fashion a successful life by rejecting Jesus as your fountain stone. But if your hope is built on nothing less than Jesus' blood and righteousness, then when you finally see him, he will reward you with a *white stone.*

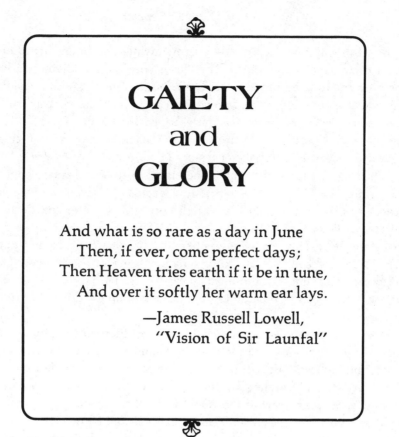

GAIETY
and
GLORY

And what is so rare as a day in June
Then, if ever, come perfect days;
Then Heaven tries earth if it be in tune,
And over it softly her warm ear lays.

—James Russell Lowell,
"Vision of Sir Launfal"

Build, Broad on the Roots of Things

"The Root of David." Revelation 5:5.

Robert Browning advised us to "burrow awhile and build, broad on the roots of things." John told us that Jesus, the root of divine things, is the only one to build broad upon. Is he, as the root of any matter, firmly embedded in the soil of your heart? In his prophetic portrayal of the messianic mission of Jesus, Isaiah described him as coming like "a root out of a dry ground," destitute of any comeliness, and when seen, undesired because of his lack of beauty (Isa. 53:2).

When Jesus entered his public messiahship, Jewish leaders could not see in him the kind of Messiah they expected. To them he was only a dead, dry root. His human life was obscure and humble, and those who rejected him as their Messiah could not find in him any resemblance to a stately tree, only one who was like a tender plant or a root struggling to exist in arid soil. We are to understand Jesus as the Root of David. Scripture often traces the human lineage of Jesus back to King David, whose root he was in relation to the throne and kingdom rights promised to David.

What possibilities are imprisoned in a root! Planted in suitable soil, it springs up into beauty or benefit for mankind. Jesus came as a root, and what fruit he has produced! In his parable of the sower he described how some seeds were scorched by the sun "because they had no root." Is Jesus deep in your heart as the Root? If so, then no sun can scorch you, and barrenness is impossible. Blessed be his name! None can dig him up, but sin can prevent him as the Root producing the fruit of the Spirit in our lives. He ever remains the root whence mercy ever flows.

Sanctuary within the Holier Blue

"Yet will I be to them a little sanctuary." Ezekiel 11:16.

In "The Ring and the Book" Robert Browning wrote these expressive lines:

> *Boldest of hearts that ever braved the sun,*
> *Took sanctuary within the holier blue,*
> *And sang a kindred soul out to his face,*
> *Yet human at the red-ripe of the heart.*

Is it not consoling to know that the Lord himself is our sanctuary within the holier blue of heaven! "He shall be for a sanctuary" (Isa. 8:14). Ezekiel assured those he wrote for that no matter in what country they found themselves they would find the Lord as a small sanctuary to whom they could gather.

Amid the turmoil of the street, busy cares of home, exacting responsibilities of business, or necessary travel, we have a sanctuary closer than breathing, nearer than hearts or feet. No sanctuary has ever surpassed the Temple Solomon built. For magnificence and marvel it was incomparable; yet where is it today? But our sanctuary never decays.

It is fitting and scriptural to gather in a house of worship, whether it be a simple or a cathedrallike structure. The sphere of worship, however, as Jesus taught the woman at the well, makes little difference. Many dear shut-in ones cannot journey to a sanctuary of stone; yet hidden from earth's eyes and from all earth's din and confusion, they take advantage of him who offers himself as a sanctuary. Are we not privileged to have a person as well as a place to draw nigh to? Although he calls himself "a *little* sanctuary," in him there is room enough for all who worship in spirit and in truth.

The Tide of Times

"At that time Jesus answered and said, I thank thee
O Father." *Matthew 11:25.*

The Gospel is replete with illustrations of the timeliness of Jesus who was never before his time or after it. He knew the exact moment to speak or act. To borrow Shakespeare's phrase in *Julius Caesar,* Jesus studied "the tide of times." *At that time!* Matthew never forgot the precise time Jesus uttered his prayer to the Father. The very hour never vanished from his memory. Jesus had been speaking of his rejection, and darkness around him was deepening into tragedy, but at that very time he rose to exultant thanksgiving to God.

From then on the disciples began to watch the times of Jesus as if in those very times there was a message for their hearts. For us, as well as for the disciples, there is much spiritual profit in studying the timeliness of Jesus. At the marriage feast of Cana he said to his mother, "Mine hour is not yet come." Jesus meant that she must not interfere; when the hour struck, he would perform his task.

This reiterated insistence on his *hour,* when others sought to hasten or retard him, illustrates his perfect timeliness. He silenced people by speaking of his hour. Jesus refused to let himself be hurried or, when the hour struck, to be delayed. As he faced Calvary, he said, "Mine hour is come." There was one perfect moment and one only. As one reads the Gospel narrative, one cannot fail to be impressed with the exquisite timeliness the words and works of Jesus were. His words were timely, and yet they have proved timeless. Although they were occasional, they are yet immortal. This is why at the very time of some crisis or sorrow his words to our hearts are so timely, even though centuries have passed since they were first uttered for the comfort of others.

164

Songs of Deliverance

"There shall come out of Sion the Deliverer."
Romans 11:26.

It is amazing to discover that the term *deliver* and its cognates occur over seven hundred times in the Bible. In the majority of references divine deliverance is implicated, proving Scripture to be the Magna Carta of emancipation. Jesus was appointed and anointed to deliver the sin-bound. Authority over all flesh was given to him, as was every attribute of deity which he exercised for the deliverance of his own whenever they had need of his aid.

Happily we are not left to struggle against the pull of the old nature within; nor are we left to the mercy of humankind to deliver us. We look to Jesus who came to deliver us from all evil. To him we repair in every trial, assured that he will preserve us from any danger since it is his office to hear us, set us free, and bless us. As our Deliverer he performs in temporals as well as in spirituals, from internal and external foes.

More than ever in a Devil-driven world we need to cling to his title as the *Deliverer*, making use of him as such in preference to any other. We should apply to him *first* in every difficulty, rely on him with confidence in every need, and believe that he will deliver until his aid is no longer required. The promise is, "He shall deliver the in six troubles: yea, in seven there shall no evil touch thee" (Job 5:19). From an unidentified source we have the words:

> *Lord, Thou canst help when earthly armour faileth,*
> *Lord, Thou canst save when deadly sin assaileth,*
> *Lord, o'er Thy Rock nor death nor hell prevaileth,*
> *Grant us Thy peace, Lord.*

165

Power Which Seems Omnipotent

"Upholding all things by the word of his power."
Hebrews 1:3.

Shelley wrote of those who "defy Power which seems omnipotent," but the power of God *is* omnipotent. Christ's omnipotence extends to every realm, for all power is his in heaven and on earth. He unfolds not some things but *all* things by his authoritative Word. Where the word of such a king is, there is power, and one sovereign Lord holds the reins of creation, redemption, history, prophecy, and personal life in his almighty hand.

Sometimes we hear it said, "Why, the world is going to pieces!" Broken it may be by wickedness and war, vice and violence, but it is still among the "*all* things" upheld by his power, for he never ceases to do according to his will among the inhabitants of earth. He overrules as well as rules and is therefore still able to change wrath to praise of him.

In the narrower world of our own lives do we believe in his power to uphold the daily things concerning us? Do we believe that, as of old, he can still speak and it is done? Does not trouble assail us when we take the control out of his hands and transfer it to our own hands? Did he not warn his own, "Without me ye can do nothing"? What folly it is to try to do and be something apart from him! Paul was very careful to say that it was only through Christ and his omnipotent strength that he could do all things. Job affirmed that the Lord is "excellent in power" and can do "everything" (Job 37:23, 42:2). Problems, difficulties, and needs may face you today and seem almost insurmountable. Do not panic or despair. By faith, rest in his power to prevail on your behalf, and you will prove that he is able to accomplish far more than you could ask or think.

Crowding in Their Heavy Burdens at the Narrow Gate

"Bear ye one another's burdens, and so fulfil the law of Christ." *Galatians 6:2.*

There is a sense in which all saints are among the *porters* that Shakespeare depicted in *Henry V* as unloading their heavy burdens at the gate. Paul urged us to make the burdens of others our own, irrespective of the personal load we carry, if we would be like Jesus whose law or custom it was to shoulder the weighty loads of others. Are we not told that he *bore* the sin of the world? He carried our sorrows and shouldered our infirmities. That heavy cross he was made to carry as he trudged to Calvary was our burden, for he was going out to die as our substitute.

Experimentally, do we know what it is to cast our burden upon this burden-bearing Lord? Said the psalmist, "Cast thy burden upon the Lord, and he shall sustain thee" (Ps. 55:22). The Scofield Reference Bible margin gives *gift* for "burden," or as the New American Standard Bible has it, "What He has given you." Who thinks of a burden as a *gift*? Is it not rather something to be rid of as quickly as possible? Yet any burden is a gift from the Lord if it results in drawing us nearer to himself and opens our eyes to the truth that he not only bears the burden but its bearer.

Whatever burden he may permit is *light*. But the question is, Are we emulating the Master in the art of burden-bearing? Is it our joy to lift the load of others? True, there are some burdens we cannot share; yet there are others we can help to carry. We live twice over when, Christlike, we make it easier for some heavy-laden heart to walk with a lighter step. We may heed the advice of a Sankey hymn:

> Hearts growing a-weary with heavier woe
> Now droop amid the darkness—go, comfort them, go!
> Go bury thy sorrow, let others be blest;
> Go give them the sunshine, tell Jesus the rest.

The Dear Remembrance of His Dying Lord

"Remember Jesus Christ." "In remembrance of me."
2 Timothy 2:8; 1 Corinthians 11:24.

Edmund Spenser, quaint poet of the sixteenth century, wrote of a saint:

> *But on his breast a bloody cross he bore,*
> *The dear remembrance of his dying Lord.*

Knowing how faulty the human memory is and how soon we are likely to forget, Jesus left us blessed tokens of remembrance of his agony in the broken bread and outpoured wine. J. R. Miller told of a mother who lost her longed-for baby and would constantly go to a drawer and take out the baby's shoes and clothes, fondly remembering the little one taken from her.

Jesus constituted the Supper to keep us in unfailing remembrance of his dying love. This is why the Holy Feast means very much to those who love him. As Alexander Smellie expressed it, "In the weekdays with their work and worry, a hundred interlopers hide my dying and undying Friend from me. But when the fair white cloth is spread, I see once more the Lord Who is all my Boast: Him I see, and none beside."

If remembrance is a paradise from which we need not be driven, then our constant remembrance of Jesus himself and of all he has accomplished on our behalf will bring us a daily paradise. His declaration is that he never forgets: "Yet will I not forget thee." How can he fail to remember us when our very names are written upon the palms of his hands? May we never be guilty of forgetting him who has us in everlasting remembrance. Thus we can sing with an unknown writer:

> *Our Master's love remember,*
> *Exceeding great and free;*
> *Lift up thy heart in gladness,*
> *For He remembers thee.*

The Sweetest of All Singers

"When they had sung an hymn." *Mark 14:26.*

How moving is Longfellow's "Hiawatha's Lamentation":

> *He is dead, the sweet musician!*
> *He is the sweetest of all singers!*
> *He has gone from us for ever,*
> *He has moved a little nearer*
> *To the Master of all music,*
> *To the Master of all singing!*
> *O my brother, Chibiabos!*

Without doubt Jesus is the master of all music and of all singing. Was he not one of that singing company of which Mark reminded us? Jesus had just broken bread with his disciples. Having explained the mystic significance of the bread and wine, he turned aside from the chamber and stepped out with his own into the dark night.

Where were their footsteps taking them? "They went to the Mount of Olives." Their faces were set toward the garden and Golgotha, but the marvel is that they faced the sorrowful future with a song. Surely it is not irreverent to suggest that Jesus, "the Master of all singing," led the chorus on that dark night. Possibly some of the Degree Psalms (120–134) he knew so well formed the hymn he prompted the small company to sing. We know he died that he might give us songs in the night, as he gave Paul and Silas when at the midnight hour, suffering in a filthy cell, they "sang praises unto God." Pain could not silence their song. Gladness banished their grief.

Francis Beaumont and John Fletcher, joint poets of the early seventeenth century, wrote:

> *Come sing now, sing; for I know ye sing well,*
> *I see ye have a singing face.*

Whether or not we have a singing face, let us be sure that we have a singing heart.

The Second Chariot

"Pharoah made Joseph to ride in the second chariot."
Genesis 41:43.

Although laden with spiritual import, this detail in the fascinating biography of Joseph, Jacob's favorite son, is generally overlooked. First, it displays Joseph's rise from prison to palace and to a position of second importance in Egypt. Many have gone from a palace to a prison, but very few from prison to palace; yet Joseph went through the experience gracefully.

Many evidences of royalty became his. The *ring* was a token of friendship between Pharoah and Joseph; the *chain of office*, a symbol of authority; the *white robe*, an official recognition of his purity; marriage to a *prince's daughter* and the chariot enabling him to travel through Egyptian provinces, tokens of the authority of a royal personage. No fleshy ambition brought Joseph to his high office. It came as the reward of nobility of character. This godly ruler had no aspiration for the *first* chariot but was content with the *second*. Upright and innocent, he had suffered far too long to gender ambition for national prestige. Although he rode in the second chariot as the savior of Egypt, he exercised more power and influence than the Pharoah riding in the first chariot. Joseph's trust was not in chariots because he could always hear, as Andrew Marvell of the seventeenth century wrote in "To His Coy Mistress":

> *Time's wingéd chariot hurrying near,*
> *And yonder all before us lie*
> *Deserts of vast eternity.*

Are you content with riding in the *second* chariot or occupying the *second* place, believing that character is greater than any chariot and that only those who humble themselves are exalted? It is often so hard for us to learn that the only way *up* is *down*, that only those who abase themselves earn the right to exaltation.

Homeless near a Thousand Homes

"The Son of man hath not where to lay his head."
Matthew 8:20.

How truly descriptive of Jesus are the lines of Wordsworth in "Guilt and Sorrow":

> *And homeless near a thousand homes I stood,*
> *And near a thousand tables pined and wanted food.*

I am moved by Samuel Crossman's remarks on the humiliation and poverty of Jesus in a verse of his hymn "My Song Is Love Unknown":

> *In life, no house, no home*
> *My Lord on earth might have;*
> *In death, no friendly tomb*
> *But what a stranger gave.*
> *What may I say?*
> *Heav'n was his home:*
> *But mine the tomb*
> *Wherein He lay.*

Jesus spoke of the way inferior creatures were well-provided for. *Foxes* have their holes, and *birds* of the air, taking no care of themselves yet taken care of, have their nests. Their Creator, however, did not know the convenience of a certain resting place he could call *home*, or place of repose. Such a settlement was not his, not even a pillow of his own upon which to lay his head.

Christ here calls Himself *the Son of Man*, a Son of Adam, partaker of flesh and blood. Matthew Henry said, "He glories in His condescension towards us, to testify His love towards us, and to teach us a holy contempt of the world, and a continual regard to another world. Christ was thus poor to sanctify and sweeten poverty to His people." Paul knew what it was to share the homelessness of his Master, for he wrote of having no "certain dwelling-place." The main thing is to know that we have given Jesus a home in our hearts.

He Shareth in Our Gladness

"Jesus rejoiced in the Holy Spirit." *Luke 10:21,* RV.

Cecil F. Alexander, unique composer of children's hymns, in his appealing verses, "Once in Royal David's City," described the tears and smiles of Jesus when he was "little, weak, and helpless" and then said:

> *And He feeleth for our sadness,*
> *And He shareth in our gladness.*

The Gospels may not record his laughing with joy; yet his gladsomeness is only too evident. The word Luke used for *rejoiced* is very strong and expresses exaltation and ecstatic delight. What caused this deep thrill of joy to the Savior's heart? Did he not praise the Father for the *method* which he had chosen for the proclamation and establishment of his kingdom? More generally, despite all the sorrows that lay upon his heart, and the heaviness of the Cross he had to bear, there can be little doubt that Jesus impressed people as a very gladsome person.

When he spoke about his joy, nobody had to ask him what he meant, for he was the embodiment of it. He called himself the *bridegroom,* and who ever saw a bridegroom with a long face? What, then, was the secret of the gladness of this Man of Sorrows? How did he maintain, even in the darkest hours, the joyful, undisturbed, radiant heart?

He was supremely faithful in his appointed vocation, never swerving from the fulfillment of God's will. He shone in the tranquil radiance of fidelity. One of the deepest attributes of duty is that the doing of it always leads to gladness. Only thus can we be glad in the Lord. Carlyle said, "Give me the man who sings at his work." Do we have a gladsome mind?

Christ Is Thy Strength

"Gathered together in my Name." *Matthew 18:20.*

Whenever and wherever the saints gather for worship, such is only acceptable when they meet for fellowship in his name. Alas, multitudes assemble for worship on Sunday, not in his name, but in their own denominational name. "Christ is thy strength," wrote John S. B. Monsell in "Fight of Faith." If Jesus is not recognized as Savior and as a King whose name has strength, or if all that belongs to him is denied, such as his virgin birth, his deity, his miracles, his efficacious death and resurrection, even though the apparent worshipers have a form of religion, how can they be said to have gathered in his name?

Matthew Henry's wise comment should be considered by every church member: "When we come together, to worship God in a dependence upon the Spirit and grace of Christ . . . having an actual regard to Him as our Way to the Father, and our Advocate with the Father, then we are met together in His Name . . . [and] are encouraged with an assurance of the presence of Christ, *There am I in the midst of them.*" How seriously we have departed from God's New Testament principles honoring worship! Jennie Garnett wrote:

> *Here in Thy Name we are gather'd,*
> *Come and revive us, O Lord:*
> *"There shall be showers of blessing,"*
> *Thou hast declared in Thy Word.*

As those who bear his name, let us ever honor it by lips and life, doing nothing that would detract from its worth and power.

The Continual Dew of Thy Blessing

"The Lord be with you all." *2 Thessalonians 3:16.*

How unique Paul is in his pronouncement of salutations and benedictions! The apostle loved to greet the saints and then dismiss them with a blessing such as the one before us which portrays Jesus as the ever-present companion of his people. Cervantes, of the sixteenth century, gave us the proverb, "Where there's no more bread, boon companions melt away." This may be true as far as some earthly companions are concerned, but in Jesus we have a companion who never leaves us and who, when there is no more bread, is able to provide it. Repeatedly, we are reminded of his abiding presence. He is always at hand, consoling our hearts with his blessing and bounty. We need nothing more to make us safe and serene, and we could wish nothing better for ourselves and our friends than the promise of his unfailing companionship.

It is the presence of God that makes heaven to be heaven, and this will make this earth to be like heaven. But note who it is that accompanies us. It is the Lord. Paul's benediction then implies that as the Lord he is the master of every situation. His miracles prove that he is able to undertake for us accordingly. Further, his lordship is not exercised on behalf of a few elect souls but for *all* who are his, even for you and me, simple, ordinary, and inconspicuous though we may be. All he is and has can be appropriated by each and all.

May we be spared negligence in taking advantage of the abundant provision of such an ever-present companion on life's pilgrimage. As daily we face "the trivial round, the common task," is ours the privilege and joy of knowing what it is to have Jesus walking with and talking to us? Do others detect the fragrance of our unseen Master?

174

An Incomparable Storyteller

"Without a parable spake he not unto them."
Matthew 13:34.

In *Tales of a Traveler* Washington Irving wrote, "I am always at a loss to know how much to believe of my own stories." Jesus had every faith in the stories he told, for all of them were a picturesque way of declaring the truth people needed to hear. And what a matchless storyteller Jesus was! No wonder the common people gladly listened to his preaching. For naturalness, conciseness, color, and effect his parables, metaphors, and illustrations are without equal. If a parable is an earthly story with a heavenly meaning, then he knew how to draw from a wide range of subjects, stories, or parables so full of spiritual import.

The story of the husbandman smote the consciences of those Pharisees who listened to it with deep interest. They knew that Jesus told the story against them, and had it not been for his popularity among the people, they would have taken him prisoner.

All who are called to preach and teach the Word can learn precious lessons on the art of illustration from the oral ministry of Jesus. Usually his illustrations were taken from human life and were never used simply for the sake of telling them. Alas, some preachers are guilty of padding their sermons with too many stories, containing no connection with their main thought. Illustrations should always function as windows letting the light in on truth being expressed. The function of a good illustration is to make clear, and it is this that makes Jesus the storyteller *par excellence*.

175

To the Tent-royal of Their Emperor

"Prince of the kings of the earth." Revelation 1:5.

An emperor is a supreme monarch or the ruler of an empire in which lesser kings may be yielding him obedience. Among the many titles Christ possesses, none is so expressive as prince, monarch, or controller of all earthly kings. We have Shakespeare'e saying in *2 Henry IV*, that "Uneasy lies the head that wears a crown." But on Christ's head are many crowns speaking of universal sovereignty; yet his head is never uneasy. He never has any fear that he will lose his multiple crown to a usurper. As the King of kings he will yet reign as world emperor with no dread of a rival, and his kingdom will last until moons shall wax and wane no more.

Earthly kings are sometimes deposed, shorn of their power, or assassinated. In Victorian times Britain was an empire, holding sway over vast dominions with their rulers, but no longer. Christ's empire will never shrink, for "of his government there shall be no end" (Isa. 9:6). His reign is to be universal, prosperous, and perpetual, with multitudes crying, "Hail to Thee, Thou princely King!" From a hymn by James Watts we shall sing:

> To Him shall endless prayer be made,
> And princes throng to crown His head,
> His name like sweet perfume shall rise
> With every morning sacrifice.

While our hearts thrill at the thought of the universal coronation he is to receive, the present question of paramount importance is, Have you crowned him king of your life? If he is not Lord of all within your life, he is not Lord at all. Does he reign supreme, without a rival, in your heart? If not, then give him his coronation as king of your life.

I Conquer but to Save

"Our Saviour Jesus Christ who hath abolished death."
2 Timothy 1:10.

What a glorious gospel is proclaimed in this verse as a whole! Here Jesus emerges as a conqueror with garments bloodstained after treading the winepress alone to save a lost world. Existing before the world began, he appeared among men in order to redeem them from sin and bless them with his eternity. Calvary was a grim conflict, but as the Lord of life he abolished death. By dying, death he slew. Through his grief and gospel brought life and immortality to light.

Until Jesus' death and resurrection there was no full revelation of the afterlife. True, "life and immortality" were hidden in Old Testament Scriptures, but Jesus banished their obscurity and made them shine. As the result of the cross and the empty tomb, the shadows have fled away, and we now have clear guidance as to where we are bound.

He abolished death! This is a marvelous truth, but saints and sinners still die, and countless graves gain the victory. How then did Jesus abolish death? First, he proved himself to be its conqueror when he rose from the grave. Second, he abolished death by robbing it of its sting and of its climax in "the second death"—the terrible condition of all who die in their sin! May we be found basking in the full light the Gospel sheds on all that awaits us when our bodies return to their native element. Said Jesus, "He that believeth in me shall never die." D. W. Whittle wrote a hymn with which we may identify:

Dying with Jesus, by death reckoned mine;
Living with Jesus, a new life divine;
Looking to Jesus till glory doth shine
Moment by moment, O Lord, I am Thine.

A Privileged Association

"Why persecutest thou me . . . I am Jesus whom thou persecutest." *Acts 9:4–5.*

This historic, memorable chapter opens with Saul breathing out threatenings and slaughter against the disciples of Jesus; yet when smitten with a heavenly, blinding light, this hater of "the way" heard a voice from heaven calling his name and asking, "Why persecutest me?" When Saul requested the speaker to identify himself, he received the reply, "I am Jesus whom thou persecutest."

Is there not a precious truth in such a revelation? Ignorant Saul thought he was persecuting a small band of poor, deluded religious zealots, little thinking it was one in heaven that he was all the while insulting. "Why persecutest thou *me?*" Jesus was not on earth among those saints to be brought in chains to Jerusalem, but because he and his own are one, Saul, in persecuting the disciples, was persecuting their Lord himself. Graciously, he identifies himself with his suffering disciples and takes what is done against them as done against himself. In effect, Jesus said, "Persecute them, any of the members of my body, and I, as the head, likewise endure the same affliction. Touch them, and you touch the apple of my eye."

The same precious truth of this privileged identification or association is emphasized when Jesus said, "Inasmuch as ye have done it unto one of the least of these . . . ye have done it unto me" (Matt. 25:40). When we suffer for his cause and sake, may consolation be ours that Jesus suffers with us. Because he has all power in heaven and on earth, he can deal effectively with those who persecute us since he is still able to transform blasphemers into believers. The union making Christ and the redeemed as one is the constant theme of the Gospels and the Epistles. Hymn writer James George Deck asked:

> *Lord Jesus, are we one with Thee?*
> *Oh height! Oh depth of love!*
> *With Thee we died upon the tree,*
> *In Thee we live above.*

178

The Eternal Beam

"Now unto the King eternal." *1 Timothy 1:17*.

The description John Milton gave of Lucifer in *Paradise Lost* is truer of our Blessed Lord:

> ... *Th' Eternal co-eternal beam,*
> *May I express Thee unblamed? Since God is light,*
> *But never but is unapproach light*
> *Dwelt from Eternity*

While Paul's great and glorious portrait presents our heavenly sovereign in a fivefold way, it is as the "King Eternal" or of the Ages that we are to consider. To apply Shakespeare's lines in *Macbeth* to Jesus, he is:

> ... *Mine eternal jewel*
> *Given to the common enemy of man.*

We know that Jesus was born a King and will yet be seen as the King of kings, but how is he the *eternal king*? The answer is simple: Jesus was a King *before* his birth and therefore a King *at* his birth. Did he not come as "the Father of eternity" (Isa. 9:6, 7)? Jesus lived before he was born. Majesty, honor, and glory were his in the past eternity. Thus before God gave him to die for the salvation of his common enemies, he could say of his "eternal jewel," "Yet have I set my King upon my holy hill of Zion" (Ps. 2:6). As the blessed and only Potentate his was no acquired or anticipated sovereignty. It goes back before the beginning of time when Jesus dwelt in eternity. Did he not affirm, "Before Abraham was, I am" (John 8:58)?

From everlasting he was established as the daily delight of his Father, rejoicing always before him (Prov. 8:22–31). John went beyond the beginning of creation when he wrote, "In the beginning was the Word, and the Word was with God, and the Word was God" (John 1:1). Jesus came as the eternal Word.

There Grows the Flower of Peace

"The Lord of peace." *2 Thessalonians 3:16.*

Henry Vaughan, religious poet of the seventeenth century, in his verses on peace spoke of one born in a manger as "Sweet Peace is crown'd with smiles." He went on to describe him as "the One, Who never changes, thy life, thy care" and then said:

> *If thou canst get but thither,*
> *There grows the flower of peace,*
> *The rose that cannot wither,*
> *Thy fortress and thy ease.*

In the apostolic benediction of peace several aspects appear. First, Paul named Jesus as the *Lord of peace.* He is the source of all true peace; he is our peace in a person. Second, he is the *giver of peace,* personal and universal. As "the Prince of Peace" he is princely in his bestowal on those willing to receive his gift. Third, this peace can be ours *always.* Whether our experiences are tranquil or turbulent makes no difference, for his blood ever whispers peace within. Did he not say that we may meet with tribulation in the world but that there is ever peace in him for those who are *in* him? Fourth, Paul, in his benediction, reminded us that the Lord's peace can be ours "always *by all means.*"

Peace comes to us directly from its prince through his Word and by his Spirit. Sometimes the most unusual experiences contribute to our peace of heart. Samson is not the only one to discover honey in the carcass of a lion! Is yours an inner peace nothing can disturb or destroy? If we would constantly experience his perfect peace in this dark world of sin, our mind must be stayed upon him in whom we profess to trust. Only as we are stayed upon Jehovah do we find tranquillity and rest.

The Shadow of a Great Rock

"The spiritual Rock that followed them . . . was Christ."
1 Corinthians 10:4.

We usually think of a rock as an immovable object, like the Rock of Gibraltar. Many famous rocks have remained steadfast through millenniums, never moving an inch. But Paul reminded us of a rock on the march, for as the Israelites journeyed through the wilderness, the rock of refreshment followed them. Such a rock was not something but *someone.* "That Rock was Christ." Charles John Ellicott commented, "As Christ was 'God manifest in the flesh,' in the New Dispensation, so God manifested in the Rock—the Source of sustaining life—was the Christ of the Old Dispensation. The Jews had become familiar with the thought of God as a rock, 1 Sam. 2:2 etc. The point the Apostle brings forward is that of the abiding presence of God."

As pilgrims, is it not comforting that thirst will never afflict us in the desert? No matter where we may go, the life-giving rock follows. The margin has it, "The Rock went with them." Thus anywhere and at all times we can stoop down and drink and live. How mobile Jesus is! He ever moves with his own who are built on him as the rock, and the water he gives is sufficient for their need. May we be found constantly appropriating him as the rock whose shelter and sustenance are unfailing. Emily Brontë could write of those:

So surely anchored on
The stedfast rock of immortality.

Are you safely anchored in such a rock in this weary land? Can you sing out of a redeemed heart, along with William O. Cushing, "Thou blest 'Rock of Ages,' I'm hiding in Thee"? He only is our shade by day and our defense by night.

To Give Thanks Is Good, and to Forgive

"The same night in which he was betrayed."
1 Corinthians 11:23.

Extolling nature as being "full of blessings," Wordsworth gave us this expressive sentiment in "Tintern Abbey":

> *Knowing that Nature never did betray*
> *The heart that loved her.*

The tragedy of our Lord's last hours was the way in which one of the disciples he loved betrayed him. While a good deal of mystery shrouds the choice of Judas and his dastardly act of selling his Master for thirty pieces of silver, the truth we should never lose sight of is that Jesus himself carried no animosity in his heart toward his betrayer. What particularly interests us in the phrase *"the same night* in which he was betrayed" is what happened shortly after Jesus was sold with a kiss. "The same night . . . he gave thanks." Think of it! Gratitude followed the committal of Judas' foul crime! Immediate thanks dried up any thought of anger, bitterness, or revenge. This was the same Jesus who taught his own to agree with their adversary *while in the way.*

Wrong feelings are like babies: the longer we nurse them, the larger they grow. The longer we take to forgive those who injure us, the harder it becomes to forgive. Have you been wronged by someone who is close to you, as Judas was to Jesus? Then remember the same-night attitude of your Master and give thanks even for a bitter cup. "To give thanks is good, and to forgive," wrote Swinburne. The way in which we immediately respond to any form of betrayal by others is an indication of our likeness to him who is ever ready to forgive. We repeat with an unknown writer:

> *Knowest thou Him?——Who forgave,*
> *with the Crown of Thorns on His temples?*
> *Earnestly prayed for His foes, for His murderers,——*
> *say dost thou know Him?*
> *Ah! thou confessest His name,*
> *so follow likewise His example!*

An Interpreter of the Cogitations Thereof

"Open the seals thereof; for thou wast slain."
Revelation 5:9.

The above title from Ecclesiasticus is certainly true of Jesus, the redeemer-interpreter. The worshipful host, singing the new song, extols the worthiness of the slain lamb to take the Book and open its seals or reveal its fascinating contents. Such ability and authority of Jesus to unveil the judgments and the joys contained in the last book of the Bible are based upon his redemptive work at Calvary, "For thou wast slain." As the central truth of the entire Bible is the cross, only he who died upon it can unfold its mystery and message. As the crucified, risen Lord he was able to expound in all the Scriptures the things concerning himself. Thus as the redeemer he alone has the right to function as the revealer.

If we would know how to take the Book and open its seals, then, as with the divine interpreter, there must come a death. Sin and self must be slain if we desire to discover the treasures of the Word. Are we worthy to take the Book and break its seals? Does our life correspond to its precepts? An ever-expanding knowledge of the secrets of the Lord depends upon obedience. If I disobey what I discover today, the Spirit will not grant me further and fuller light tomorrow. Disobedience closes the door of revelation; death, identification with the death of the cross, opens it. Is this not what Job meant when he prayed, "That which I see not, teach thou me: if I have done iniquity, I will do no more"? Revelation results in sanctification. The more we gaze upon divine holiness as set forth in Scripture, the deeper our sense of personal unworthiness. Yet, what the vision reveals of sin, the blood can cleanse.

All Combin'd in Beauty's Worthiness

"Worthy is the Lamb that was slain." *Revelation 5:12.*

I have no hesitation in taking Christopher Marlowe's phrase and applying it to Jesus who combined in all his virtues "beauty's worthiness." Although he was the one "of whom the world was not worthy," the vast angelic host, along with the living creatures and the elders of which John wrote, exalt his worthiness because he became the Lamb. This ascription of praise is fitting, for Jesus is worthy all he requires, all we can give, all his people have done for him or suffered in his cause. The Book of Revelation provides us with many striking cameos of Jesus as the *Lamb*. In the verse before us he is the "worthy Lamb."

Think of all he is worthy to receive as the Lamb, "freshly slain" as the original suggests! *Power* is his—all power in heaven and on earth. *Riches* are his whether spiritual or material. The wealth in every mine belongs to him. *Wisdom* is his, for he became wisdom personified, and his teachings contain the highest wisdom. *Strength* is his. Ultimately the strength of the strongest vanishes, as Samson experienced, but Jesus' strength remains undiminished because it is eternal. *Honor* is his. Every knee, Paul said, will yet acknowledge him as Lord. *Glory* is his. With his ascension came the restoration of the glory for which he prayed (John 17:1–4). Before long the whole earth will be filled with his glory. *Blessing* is his. The fullness of every blessing is now his to bestow. Because he became the Lamb, all he is and has can be ours. Sir Isaac Watts recognized:

> *Jesus is worthy to receive Honour and power divine;*
> *And blessings, more than we can give, Be, Lord, for ever Thine.*

It will take all eternity to magnify and praise his intrinsic worth.

A Coiner of Sweet Words

"The words of our Lord Jesus Christ." *1 Timothy 6:3.*

The magic power of words to blast or bless has been dealt with by many writers. Samuel Johnson would have us know that "words are the daughters of earth, and that things are the sons of Heaven." Alexander Pope wrote of one "grac'd as thou art with all the pow'r of words." Robert Louis Stevenson would have us remember that "bright is the ringing of words, when the right man rings them." Tennyson, who was a master of words, reckoned that "words, like Nature, half reveal—And half conceal the soul within." Thomas Gray wrote the line, "Thoughts that breathe, words that burn."

I take, however, the phrase Matthew Arnold used of another writer as "a coiner of sweet words" to describe the wonderful words of life that Jesus, a wizard of short, simple words, uttered. He was not afflicted with a barren superfluity of words and did not conform to those Philip Massinger described as being "All words / And no performance!"

As the prince of preachers Jesus knew how to seek out acceptable words which were as goads and as nails fastened in a sure place. His lips were like lilies, dropping sweet-smelling myrrh, and like a thread of scarlet uttering comely speech (Song of Sol. 4:3, 5:13, 16). How privileged were the multitudes to listen to the gracious words proceeding out of his mouth! Vain and idle words never left the lips into which grace had been poured. Every word was a benediction. He was never verbose or guilty of using unnecessary or long and involved words. Each word was rightly coined and timed and shot as an arrow to a given target.

Life for us would be saved much of its friction if only we would set a watch upon our lips. All our words will be acceptable to God if only we "weigh them in a balance, and make a door and a bar for our mouth" (Ecclus. 28:15). How apt are the lines of George MacDonald: "Thou Comforter! be with me as Thou wert When first I longed for words, to be A radiant garment for my thought, like Thee."

May of Thee Be Plenteously Rewarded

"The Lord, the righteous judge." *2 Timothy 4:8.*

From the Book of Common Prayer we gather the petition that God's faithful people may be found "plenteously bringing forth the fruits of good works, and may of Thee be plenteously rewarded." Through all his arduous service for the Master, Paul kept before him the judgment seat and its rewards. The smile and benediction of the judge at the end of the day was the apostle's constant incentive. One look from this righteous adjudicator, and the sound of his voice saying, "Well done, good and faithful servant," spurred on the apostle, enabling him to be indifferent to his sufferings for Christ's sake. This was the prize of his high calling he strove to attain.

Paul knew that because the Lord is the *righteous* judge he would assist his labors and longings for what they were worth and reward him accordingly. Being the judge he is, the Lord cannot deny any servant of his any earned reward. Ours is the assurance that if we are faithful to him unto death the judge of all the earth will do right. If we have plenteously brought forth the fruits of good works, ours will be a plenteous reward. There is, of course, a great difference between gifts and rewards. A gift is bestowed, gratis. It would cease to be a gift if we had to work for it. But a reward has to be earned. Alas, many at the judgment seat will be saved because of their reception of the gift of God's salvation but will be rewardless because of a lost life.

Do we share Paul's confidence that an unfading crown is laid up for us? By God's grace and power are we pressing toward a full reward? May we be spared the sorrow of standing before the judge with a saved soul but a lost life. May ours be a full reward.

Without an Original There Can Be No Imitation

"Be ye imitators of God, as dear children."
Ephesians 5:1, RV.

The apostle Paul set before the Ephesians, and us, an astonishing yet reasonable demand, namely, to be godlike in all our ways, works, and words. As a child watches his or her father and unconsciously becomes like him in habits and nature, so God sets the standard for his redeemed children to follow. As he is and does, so are we to be and do. The word *followers* in the Authorized Version means "imitators." "Therefore be imitators of God as beloved children."

At the outset let it be said that by ourselves we cannot emulate the divine example. This is no mere human effort to strive in every possible way to be like God who proposes himself to us as our pattern. But he not only presents himself for our imitation. He imparts the grace and power whereby we can exhibit all of his divine virtues. Christ left us an example to follow his step, but he is within us enabling us to walk even as he walked. An unknown essayist of the eighteenth century said that "without an original there can be no imitation." Christ is our original and by his indwelling Spirit helps us to imitate him.

Horace, in his *Epistles*, wrote of those in Roman days, "O imitators, ye slavish herd." But as the imitators of God we are not driven by fear and force to imitate him. Certainly, he commands us to imitate him, but our relation to him requires it; and our peace is involved in it. From the context it would seem as if the one attribute above others, recommended for our imitation, is God's *love*. As his dear children we are to "walk in love." This should be the divine principle to practice. Alas, however, we are bad imitators of the original when we come to loving all that he loves. May grace be ours to exhibit more godlikeness in a godless world.

Escaped Even As a Bird out of the Snare

"God . . . will with the temptation make also the way of escape." *1 Corinthians 10:13*, RV.

While God permits temptation, he does not provide it. He allows the enemy to try us in order that we might be sifted. God suffered his well-beloved Son to be tempted of the Devil, but he emerged from the grim conflict with his sinlessness unimpaired. God's *way of escape* from temptation then consists in preventing the attack of the enemy or in divesting temptation of its force. Whether or not we are conscious of it, God prepares you and me to bear the siege before which, if it were not for his faithfulness, we would fall to the foe.

During the hour of temptation, God is at hand and, with the trial under his control, adjusts it to our capacity. We can trust God for victory over Satan because God makes the temptation flee through his omnipotence. We emerge from the contest richer in humility since we have discovered our own feebleness. We are also richer in faith, for the struggle with our adversary draws us near the captain of our salvation. We are richer too in sympathy because of our manifold temptations, for experience enables us to guide and help fellow believers who are being assailed by the enemy.

Without fail, God makes the way of escape for us, but we must seek it by abounding in prayer, by guarding against any shameful surrender, and above all by depending upon the indwelling Spirit who is able to make us more than conquerors. Paul would have us remember that our sheet anchor in seasons of testing is the faithfulness of God. The apostle gave us one of those blessed *buts* of Scripture: "But God is faithful who will not suffer you to be tempted above that ye are able" (I Cor. 10:13). We are encouraged by an unknown author to:

> *Trust on! the danger presses, Temptation strong is near*
> *Over life's dangerous rapids, He shall thy passage steer.*

More Than Enough, for Nature's Ends

"God has dealt graciously with me, and because I have plenty." *Genesis 33:9, 11,* ASB.

Like the hired servants in our Lord's parable of the prodigal son, both Esau and Jacob had bread enough and to spare. The Authorized Version reads, "Jacob said, I have enough, or I have all things." I prefer, however, the translation given above from the American Standard Bible. David Mallet, a lesser known Scottish poet who died in 1765, left us this verse:

> O grant me, Heaven, a middle state,
> Neither too humble nor too great;
> More than enough, for nature's ends,
> With something left to treat my friends.

The contrast between Jacob leaving home and returning to it years later is most striking. He was forced to leave his father's house and took nothing with him but a staff. But the Lord greatly prospered him, as Esau could see in the large family and abundant possessions of his brother. Yet the kindness of Esau's approach after the long estrangement and the grace and goodness of God led Jacob to say, "I have plenty."

Spiritually, is our cup full and running over? As objects of Jehovah's everlasting love we are entitled to all the riches he offers. In him there is more than enough to make us holy, to fill us with gratitude, to fill angels with wonder, and to fill the Devil with envy. Why then do we live as spiritual paupers when there is bread enough and to spare in our Father's house? If God is an all-sufficient store, why not buy of him all we need without money and without price? Plenteous in mercy and grace, God invites us to partake of his bounty and live as those who are rich in faith. David could say, "My cup floweth over" (Ps. 23:5). Is yours the overflowing cup?

His Life Is a Watch

"I say unto all, Watch." *Mark 13:37.*

This clarion call of Jesus must be interpreted in light of the parable of the men taking a journey into a far country but who may return at any time. It apparently applies to our being watchful in view of the return of Jesus himself. Oliver Goldsmith depicted "the broken soldier" who was prompt at every call and who "watch'd and wept, he pray'd and felt for all."

Is this our attitude as we anticipate his glorious appearing? As we watch and wait, are we weeping over, and praying for, the multitudes of erring ones around us? John Keats wrote of the bright steadfast star hanging aloft, "Watching, with eternal lids apart." May this be the character of our watching for the dawning of "the Bright and Morning Star."

The coming of the Savior is the grand object of our hope and should be our daily desire and prayer. In wisdom and mercy God has purposely concealed the time of his Son's return. He commands us to be *awake* and, as watchmen, to keep awake as night approaches. By the Spirit's aid we should discern the signs of Christ's return and at the same time watch over our daily conduct, thus being ready to hail his arrival. We should watch and walk as we wish death or Jesus to find us. We should transact all our affairs as though the Master were at the door, as he may well be. Surely you would not like Jesus to come and find you idle, contentious, at enmity with a fellow believer, murmuring over God's providence, indulging in any sin. May your life, as Swinburne put it, be a watch. The Master calls you to watch and pray. Wrote an unknown author:

> *Passing along the street—Among those thronging footsteps,*
> *May come the sound of My feet.*
> *Therefore I tell you Watch!*

190

God's Anonymous Army

"Yet have I left me seven thousand in Israel." 1 Kings 19:18.

We do well to remind our hearts that there are vastly more unknown than known saints to human fame, both in the Bible and in the history of the church. Elijah had imagined that he was the only remaining champion of the Lord and that the cause might perish if he were killed. But he had to learn that though God had called him to a special task he was not the only loyal servant of Jehovah. Scattered up and down the land were seven thousand obscure individuals whose knees had not bowed to Baal and who were manifesting in less prominent ways their fidelity to God. Elijah has always remained in the limelight, but these others of his time have ever lived in the shadows of obscurity. Because we do not know them, we are in danger of ignoring them.

Is this not also true of the seventy elders appointed to assist Moses and of the seventy disciples Jesus sent forth? If your name has never appeared in print, take courage. The known and famous are in the minority, and the unknown majority are the privileged soldiers in God's host of warriors since they outnumber the generals and captains we know. Never forget that much of the Bible itself was written by God's anonymous scribes. How much poorer the Bible would be without those books whose human authors are unknown.

What would the church do without the majority who render anonymous service? God does not forget the army of quiet helpers upon whom any pastor relies and who manifest fidelity and integrity in their daily lives and are ever ready to serve him. They may be unknown to the world, yet well known to God they have the assurance that his approval is their highest reward. Alexander Pope wrote of one who was "content to breathe his native air" and "live, unseen, unknown." If prayer is the native air we breathe, recognition and fame will not trouble us.

PART III

Fulfillment and Splendor

Continuing our journey around the circle of the year, we find ourselves in the last half when summer reaches its fulfillment and brings us to the season *par excellence*. For lovers of flowers and fruit, July is a paradise. What a perfect month it is with all its glory and splendor! The seventh month suggests perfection, a virtue it displays. In summertime Jesus drew attention to a nearby field profuse with lilies and preached a powerful sermon on God's concern for us in all things.

Entering the lovelist time of the year, we discover so much pleasing to the eye. What better month is there for holidays when the problems of the rest of the year seem to fade? Farmers too hail this month of fulfillment with its rich harvest of golden grain and ripe fruit. Reaping what we have sown also reminds us that whatever we sow in conduct and character we will surely harvest, if not in time, then in eternity.

The golden year climaxes in the month of golden sun, golden leaves, and the golden harvest moon. What can compare to the glorious rainbow hues and satisfying sense of fullness and beauty September brings? How eloquent it is of the serenity of an accomplished destiny! Yet it is the month of shortening days and lengthening nights, reminding us of our gradual decay and likewise of God who is the length of our days.

FULFILLMENT and SPLENDOR

I sing of brooks, of blossoms and
  of bowers
. . . and July flowers.

  —Robert Herrick,
    "Argument of His Book"

194

A Portion of the Eternal

"The Lord is my portion, saith my soul, therefore will I hope in him." *Lamentations 3:24.*

In the Old Testament God is frequently referred to as the *portion* of his people. Since the word *portion* means "share," how privileged the saints are to have a share of, and in, God, or to adopt Shelley's phrase, "A portion of the eternal." The surprising thing is that God condescends to call his people *his portion*. "The Lord's portion is his people" (Deut. 32:9; Zech. 2:12). But he does not have a share in them; *he owns them.* They are his redemption right, and all who own him as their portion must recognize his claim to the sovereignty of their lives.

Courageous Chrysostom, church father of the fourth century, was not ashamed to tell the Roman emperor that there was nothing he could do to harm him since God was his portion. The pagan monarch replied, "I will take your riches."

"My treasure is in Heaven," the fearless saint answered.

"I will banish you from your friends," the ruler threatened.

"My best Friend will never leave me," Chrysostom replied.

"I will exile you from your country," the emperor said.

"Heaven is my Fatherland: Heaven is my home," was the church leader's ready answer.

Last of all, the godless emperor said, "I will take away your life."

The dauntless warrior met the threat boldly: "My life is hid with Christ in God. There is nothing you can do to hurt me."

If we believe that God is our portion, then let us by faith appropriate all we have in him. A. H. Waring wrote:

> My heart is resting on my God,
> I will give thanks and sing.
> My heart is at the secret source
> Of every precious thing.

Light a Candle, and Sweep the House

"I will search Jerusalem with candles." *Zephaniah 1:12.*

The unexamined life is not only fruitless but fatal. This is why the Bible presents the divine and human side of the examination of the human heart. Paul stressed self-*examination*. "Let a man examine himself." "Examine yourselves whether ye be *in* the faith" (1 Cor. 11:28). It is sadly possible for a person to work for the faith and yet not be *in* the faith. Therefore, such a search is imperative for the soul's eternal welfare.

Psalmists, however, stress the divine side of the search. "Lord, thou hast searched me out—or through and through" (Ps. 139:1). "Examine me, O Lord" (Ps. 26:2). Searching with candles intimates the minuteness of the heavenly searcher of hearts. Nothing must be left in the corners of one's life. A proverb has it, "Take heed you find not that you do not seek." When we work with God in the thorough examination of our hearts, we often discover those forbidden things we did not seek.

Are we prepared to examine ourselves carefully, deliberately, and prayerfully, taking God's Word for our rule and guide? Do we pause and look within to discover whether we are growing in grace or declining spiritually, whether we are being daily quickened by the Spirit, whether the love of God is being shed abroad in our hearts, whether we possess the evidence to prove the reality of our profession of faith in Christ? The psalmist prayed to be searched to see if there were any wicked way in him. Is this our daily prayer? We have no need to fear what the search may reveal, for what the candles bring to light of a forbidden nature the Holy Spirit can remove. Joseph Morris in "Poems of Inspiration" wrote:

> *Searcher of hearts! oh, search me still:*
> *The secrets of my soul reveal:*
> *My fears remove: let me appear*
> *To God and my own conscience clear.*

I Have Learned to Be Content

"Be content with such things as ye have." *Hebrews 13:5.*

How apt and appealing are the lines on the virtue of sweet contentment in John Bunyan's *Pilgrim's Progress*:

> *I am content with what I have,*
> *Little be it, or much:*
> *And, Lord, contentment still I crave,*
> *Because Thou savest such.*

Bunyan went on to describe how it is best for those on pilgrimage to have

> *Here little, and hereafter bliss,*
> *Is best from age to age.*

Baron Houghton, poet of the nineteenth century, could write of "the land of lost content." Do we not live in such a land? Is not discontent the most conspicuous feature of the multitudes around who are bent on seeking out some new thing? In our industrial world we forget the biblical declaration, "Be content with your wages." We may not have what we wish, but if we are the Lord's, we certainly have what he thinks best for us, and such godliness ever breeds contentment. We find it hard to learn Paul's lesson, "I have learned, in whatsoever state I am, therewith to be content" (Phil. 4:11). Several poets have followed Thomas Dekker of the early seventeenth century in writing of "Sweet Content":

> *Art thou poor, yet hast thou golden slumbers?*
> *Oh sweet content!*
> *Art thou rich, yet is thy mind perplexed?*
> *Oh punishment!*

With Christ as their abiding companion all believers should manifest such content, for he has promised to meet their needs. Grass grows content through the heat and the cold. Does not the old Book tell us that godliness with contentment is great gain?

The Secret Sympathy

"In all points . . . like as we are." *Hebrews 4:15.*

The word *sympathy* is not in the Bible, but all that it represents is. Are you not told that Jesus is "touched with the feeling of our infirmities" (Heb. 4:15)? The gospel hymn speaks of him as "the sympathizing Jesus." Walter Scott in "The Lay of the Last Minstrel" embodied such fellow feeling:

> *The secret sympathy,*
> *The silver link, the silken tie,*
> *Which heart to heart, and mind,*
> *In body and in soul can bind.*

When Jesus became man, he forged a "silver link" with humanity and came to know for himself its sorrows, temptations, and needs. Often we confuse *sympathy* with *sorrow.* But you can have genuine sorrow for a person afflicted in some way or another without experiencing personally the anguish he or she may be bearing. You cannot have sympathy for the person, however, if you have never known in your own heart what he or she is enduring.

The word *sympathy* implies an affinity or relationship, a correlation, the capacity of entering into and sharing the feelings, interests, and trials of others. The prophet Ezekiel said, "I sat where they sat" (3:15), implying that he shared the captivity of those around him. This fellow feeling makes us wondrous kind and is what Shakespeare had in mind when he wrote in *Troilus and Cressida,* "One touch of nature makes the whole world kin." Because Jesus became acquainted with our grief, he is able to help us in *our* grief. He enables us to learn life's secrets in the school of experience and then uses us in the world of tears to weep with those who weep and help them dry their tears. There would be fewer broken hearts around if only more of the virtue of sympathy were shown.

The Fountain of All Goodness

"How great is thy goodness, which thou hast laid up."
Psalm 31:19.

The psalmist told us that God treasures up his great goodness. It is *laid* up, or kept in reserve, for those who fear him until they need it; then he graciously disburses it. Is this not what the farmer does when his harvests are golden—store them up for when they are required? So it is with the goodness of God which is not emptied out in heaps all at once for our appropriation.

One of the most blessed features of him who gives us so many rich things to enjoy is that he never gives us in bulk all he has to bestow. It is impossible for him never to have more to give. "Have you received? Still there's more to follow," wrote P. B. Bliss in a hymn. Is it not encouraging to know that we never reach the limit in divine blessings? As J. R. Miller expressed it, "Every door that opens into a treasury of love shows another door into another treasury beyond. We need not fear that we shall ever come to the end of God's goodness, or any experience for which He will have no blessing ready." God's storehouses are always opened to us when we need the provision they contain. This is as true of nature as it is of grace, for when God created the world, he *laid up* in it supplies for every human need. Alas, how slow we are to learn that God's goodness is always found as need arises, as his many promises declare, "When thou passest through the waters, I *will be* with thee" (Isa. 43:2).

Once we find ourselves in the circle of need, we discover he is there to supply us with all that is necessary—a supply we often find in the valley of shadows. Bless God, the best of his goodness is *laid up* in heaven. This is why death for the Christian is far better, for then he is in the treasurehouse itself.

199

Boundless His Wealth As Wish Can Claim

"But thou art rich." Revelation 2:9.

The wealth of the believer that Jesus described is so different from the wretch depicted by Sir Walter Scott. The wretch, although "boundless his wealth," was "concentred all in self" and died "unwept, unhonour'd, and unsung"! The saints at Smyrna were materially poor yet rich. "I know thy . . . poverty," Jesus said, "but thou art rich" (Rev. 2:9). Broadly speaking, the majority of his followers are really poor in respect to what the world counts wealth, but he chooses the poor of this world, rich in faith, makes them heirs of his kingdom, and bestows upon them as much spiritual wealth as they wish to claim. An unidentified hymn writer said:

> *Call'd by grace, the sinner see,*
> *Rich though sunk in poverty;*
> *Rich in faith that God has given,*
> *He's a legal heir of Heaven.*

As poor sinners enriched by grace, we have *donated* wealth since Jesus has bequeathed us unsearchable riches. We likewise have the wealth of all the good things he has promised us. We are rich in relationships, having God as our Father, Jesus as our Savior and advocate, and the Holy Spirit as our invisible companion.

Because all who believe inherit all things, we should be rich in good works and rich in expectation, having before us the eternal city God is preparing for us. Our wealth is beyond compare, for his righteousness justifies us, his blood cleanses us, his Spirit sanctifies us, his angels minister unto us, and his heaven is to be our everlasting habitation. May grace be ours to claim our boundless wealth, here and now, and live as the heirs of God.

He's a Good Fellow, and 'Twill All Be Well

"It shall be well." 2 Kings 4:23.

Edward FitzGerald's portrait of one whose visage was daubed "with the smoke of Hell" but was yet encouraged to believe that all would be well with him since he was a "good fellow" illustrates the assertion of the Shunammite woman. Although she was a good person, as she set out on her journey to Elisha, she carried bitterness in her heart because of the death of her son. She came to experience that all is *well* to those who fear God, even when trials and sorrows are present.

It is always *well* with the righteous. When brought up against the fact of inherent corruption, all is well for you since you are not under the law but under grace. Sin cannot have victory over you. When you face the wiles of the Devil and are alarmed at his evil suggestions and subtle temptations, all is well. The God of peace is ever near to bruise Satan under your feet and to make you more than a conqueror. When your heart is cast down within you because of the trials, tears, and testings besetting your pathway, remember that *it shall be well.* Your Lord is at hand to cause all things, even the untoward experiences, to work together for your good. An unknown writer advised us to remember that:

Not a shaft can hit,
Till the God of love sees fit.

No matter what sorrows or separation overtake you, your lot is not singular but similar, for no testing can be yours that is not common to all. Further, because of his love and faithfulness God will not permit you to be tested and tried above that "ye are able." At all times let your exclamation be, "It shall be well," providing, of course, that it is well with your soul as far as God is concerned.

Then Heaven Make Me Poor

"The poor committeth himself unto thee." *Psalm 10:14.*

Ben Jonson of the sixteenth century coined the phrase, "When I mock poorness, then Heaven make me poor." When the psalmist referred to the perils of the poor (Ps. 10:9, 10), he doubtless had in mind impoverishment of means and ability to stand up to "the strong men," seeking their captivity. The *poorness* from which Ben Jonson sought to be free was a material poverty. Many of those who are denied earthly riches and appear friendless know what it is to have Jesus as their nearest friend to care for them. Jesus himself was poor, eating often at the table of others; yet he could rejoice in the friendship of those who ministered unto him of their substance.

Whether we are poor in substance or in spirit, may we be found ever committing ourselves unto him who is able to meet our very need. We must commit all to him, as debtors to him as our surety, as clients to him as our advocate, as those who are destitute to him as our rich and generous benefactor, as sinners to him as the Savior, as those who form the bride to him as the bridegroom. But why and how should we commit ourselves daily, deliberately, and unreservedly unto him? We commit ourselves

> To His grace, to be saved by it—
> To His power, to be kept by it—
> To His providence, to be fed by it—
> To His Word, to be ruled by it—
> To His care, to be preserved by it—
> To His arms at death, to be safely carried to Glory!

Committal to the Lord means that he will bring to pass all that concerns us for our present, spiritual good and for his glory.

A Double Blessing Is a Double Grace

"Thou shall be a blessing." *Genesis 12:2.*

We are not sure what Shakespeare actually meant when in *Hamlet* he wrote:

> *A double blessing is a double grace;*
> *Occasion smiles upon a second leave.*

What we do know, however, is that Abraham, as he answered the call of God to journey out into the unknown, received a "double blessing" which was indeed a "double grace." *I will be with thee . . . thou shalt be a blessing.* Being a blessing was contingent upon being blessed.

Unless ours is the continual dew of heaven's blessing, we cannot be a blessing to earth's needy. God cannot bless and use us above the level of our own spiritual experience. God's grace saves us, forms our characters, and fits us for service. By his wisdom he charts our course, imparts strength to accomplish his will, supplies all that is necessary to complete his design, and ultimately crown our efforts. He said, "*I* will bless *thee,*" and how richly he does!

Blessed of him, we are a blessing to others by a meek and gentle spirit, by the imitation of the example of our Savior, by our intercession and service for the lost, and by our efforts to spread about by lip and literature the knowledge of the power of the Lord to save. Ours is a double grace, for both our salvation and service are of divine grace. Is your desire to be made a blessing since God has abundantly blessed you? If so, eternity alone will reveal all who have been blessed as the result of your fragrant life and consecrated service. Harper G. Smyth wrote:

> *Is your life a channel of blessing,*
> *Is the love of God flowing thro' you?*

A Graceless Zealot

"Come with me, and see my zeal for the Lord."
2 Kings 10:16.

Alexander Pope depicted those who fight for "modes of faith" as "graceless zealots," and Jehu was certainly *a graceless zealot.* He drove furiously, smote and did not spare, was consumed by ardent passion, and acted with speed and thoroughness as an instrument of divine judgment upon Ahab and upon Baalim. Although Jehu was carrying out the judgments of God, his own life was corrupt. We read that "he departed not from the sins of Jeroboam" and that "he took no heed to walk in the law of Jehovah" (2 Kings 10:31). Thus his zeal was not according to the knowledge of God's will, and his invitation to Jehonadab to accompany him on his ruthless mission revealed in a flash the central pride of his spirit.

How perilous is self-glorification in carrying out a divine mission! Jehu had zeal, but he was destitute of grace and of the passion to act only for the glory of God. Jehu was proud of his zeal, and such pride is always perilous, wherever it exists, since it leads to other personal evils. We manifest a perverted zeal when we strive to promote the cause of God by lack of tenderness toward others. Such graceless zeal is strange fire upon the altar, as Saul of Tarsus came to realize in his passion to destroy the church. There is a message for our hearts in Shakespeare's impressive lines in *King Henry VIII:*

> *Had I but serv'd my God with half the zeal*
> *I serv'd my king, he would not in mine age*
> *Have left me naked to mine enemies.*

God will never forsake us if we are consumed with a pure zeal for his house and glory and are always zealous of good works and of manifesting spiritual gifts.

O World Invisible, We View Thee

"Open his eyes, that he may see." *2 Kings 6:17.*

Francis Thompson, who gave us "The Hound of Heaven," also left us his appealing poem "The Kingdom of God." In it he affirmed the Christian's ability to see the invisible:

> O world invisible, we view thee,
> O world intangible, we touch thee,
> O world unknowable, we know thee,
> In apprehensible, we clutch thee!

Elisha's prayer for his young servant, when he was troubled about the visible hosts compassing the city of Dothan, was "Fear not: for they that be with us are more than they that be with them. . . . open his eyes, that he may see" (2 Kings 6:16, 17). The Lord opened the eyes of the young man, and he saw the "world invisible"—a mountain full of horses and chariots of fire round about Elisha. These enveloping hosts which ordinary eyes could not see filled the young man with fear, and his faith in "the king . . . invisible" was intensified.

Moses was able to endure manifold trials, for he saw him who is invisible. Is ours not the constant need to pray, "O Jehovah, open our eyes that we may see"? Invisible satanic foes surround us, and their antagonism and strength are great, often causing us to feel there is no way of escape from principalities and powers. The consciousness, however, that God's chariots of horses and fire are round about us delivers us from panic and despair and maintains our hearts in courage and in quietness, which is our strength. Such a faith is not the imagining of unreal sources of deliverance but the assurance that "invisible things are clearly seen" by those who constantly pray, "Lord, open thou my eyes, that I may see!"

205

Leave Nothing of Myself in Me

"Though I be nothing." *2 Corinthians 12:11.*

Richard Crashaw, who died in 1649, remains a star among godly poets. He penned this expression of his faith:

> *I sing the Name which none can say*
> *But touch'd with an interior ray.*

In his poem "The Flaming Heart" Crashaw confessed that his all was in Christ. He wrote:

> *Leave nothing of myself in me.*
> *Let me so read Thy life, that I*
> *Unto all life of mine may die!*

Paul's estimate of himself was that apart from Christ he was nothing but the chief of sinners and least of all the saints. Shakespeare's *Macbeth* says:

> *. . . nothing is*
> *But what is not.*

The apostle experienced such nothingness; yet destitute of "what is not," he abundantly possessed "what is," for he could say, "Having nothing and yet possessing all things" (2 Cor. 6:10). It may be humbling to our innate pride to sing, "Nothing in my hands I bring"; yet the only way up is down. We want to be *something*, but if we want God's best, we must realize that in his sight we are nothing and that all we need is in Christ. Nothing can come out of nothing, nothing can go back to nothing.

All we are is *by* Christ; all we have is *from* Christ; all we shall be is *through* Christ. Of ourselves we have nothing to boast. Are we willing to be nothing, even *scum* as Paul put it, that Christ may be all in all? The vision of his all-sufficiency destroys all pride of the flesh and brings us to the place where God can reveal his power.

Various Are the Tastes of Men

"Is there any taste in the white of an egg?" Job 6:6.

To gather together all the natural facts related in the Bible would make a most profitable volume. Here Job is asking about the white of an egg having any taste. What is the white of an egg? Well, an egg has two inner parts. The *yolk*, or yellow part, is the first section to be formed by the bird. The *white* surrounds the yolk and is a tasteless, odorless sort of jelly, made up mostly of water and known as *albumen*. The white is the chick's ration. As soon as the chick gets its beak, it pecks away at the white. By the time this is consumed, the chick is ready to leave its confined shell world for the larger world outside. Without this white of the egg the chick would die of starvation. Thus, although it has very little taste, the white is of great strength to the chick.

Reduced to abject poverty Job was forced to eat unsavory meats. He became so poor that he did not have a grain of salt to give a little taste to the white of an egg, now the choice dish on his table. Some of the most tasteless articles of food are the most profitable; yet they are despised because they do not appeal to the palate. This is also true in respect to spiritual food; those who lust after the flesh deem soul nutrition most distasteful.

The psalmist advised, "Taste and see that the Lord is good" (Ps. 34:8), and once the Lord is thoroughly tasted and appropriated, he becomes living food for our souls. Taste is something that can be cultivated. In spiritual things this is certainly so. If you have little taste for the Word, for prayer, for holiness, like the chick without the white of an egg, you will die of starvation. So do not be fastidious; eat and live!

The Mystery of Migration

"The stork in the heaven knoweth her appointed times."
Jeremiah 8:7.

The stork knows the time of her migration, and the dove, the crane, and the swallow observe the time of their return. The miracle of bird migration is a mystery and a striking evidence of the unsearchable greatness of the Lord. The ability of birds to fly to parts thousands of miles away and return home—often to nest in the very same house where they nested the year before—is one of the most marvelous yet strangest features in nature. Despite all the efforts of naturalists to explain how birds fly to warmer climes to obtain food and reproduce under the right conditions, we still do not know how they leave and return as they do or what signals and guideposts they note to direct them.

We believe that on the fifth day of creation, when God fashioned "fowl that may fly above the earth in the open firmament of heaven" (Gen. 1:20), he created the birds with a built-in instinct. He is thus responsible for their flight of thousands of uncharted miles over land and water.

At creation humankind was made with a built-in instinct for God. St. Augustine wrote, "Thou hast made us for Thyself, O Lord, and our hearts are restless until they rest in Thee." By his indwelling spirit, the same creative God guides and directs us through the days and years of our earthly sojourn to the land of pure delight which he is preparing for us. Our spiritual instinct tells us that our flight from this godless, blood-soaked earth is not far distant. The question is, Are we ready for our heavenly migration which is nearer than we may realize?

208

Men's Eyes Were Made to Look

"Any man, when he looked unto the serpent of brass,
he lived." *Numbers 21:9,* RV.

We are indebted to Shakespeare for the phrase in *Romeo and Juliet,*
"Men's eyes were made to look, and let them gaze." The serpent-bitten
Israelites of old put their eyes to good use when they looked and gazed
upon the brazen serpent lifted up on a pole. There was, of course, no
healing virtue in the metal serpent which Moses was commanded to
make. Relief came through the look which indicated obedience to the
divine edict, *Look and live!*

All who refused to look perished from the poisonous sting of the
serpents which God sent upon the people as a punishment for their sin.
But the remedy he provided was in the form of what he permitted for
the disobedience of the people. Bitten by death-dealing serpents, they
had to look at the brazen serpent if they wanted to live. As any man
looked, he lived because in looking he bowed to the divine will and thus
made it possible for God to restore and heal him. The *look* required was
not to be a mere glance or "the only loveless look, the look with which
you pass'd" that Coventry Patmos wrote about. The look of the dying
Israelite indicated repentance for sin, longing to be free from the fire
of poison, and faith in the remedy God had provided.

Jesus used the serpent lifted up on a pole as an illustration of himself.
Made in the likeness of sinful man but without his sin, Jesus was
lifted up on a tree for the sinner's restoration. And the divine command
is, "Look unto me, and be saved." Bless God, there is life for a look
at the crucified one! It is to be hoped, my friend, that you looked to him
for salvation and that your gaze has never wandered from his face. We
repeat with C. H. Spurgeon:

> *I looked at Him—He looked at me,*
> *And we were one forever.*

Memory, the Warder of the Brain

"Lest thou forget." Deuteronomy 4:9.

Shakespeare in *Macbeth* not only gave us the striking function of memory in the title of this meditation, but also phrases like "the table of my memory" and "the memory be green" (*Hamlet*). Evidently God desired his people to keep their memories green in respect to all he had accomplished for them. In *Kidnapped* Robert Louis Stevenson wrote, "I've a grand memory for forgetting, David."

With the Israelites of old we too have a "good forgettery" and need the constant plea of Scripture to remember the Lord and all his mercies. On more than one occasion Moses warned the people not to forget their spiritual ideal, for he knew that forgetfulness of the solemn and majestic manifestations they had witnessed would be a sin against God and evidence that their exalted privileges were not of great value.

How apt we are to forget the commands, the deliverances, the disciplines, and at times the very love of God! "Memory is a non-moral function of the soul," said Dr. G. Campbell Morgan, an English Bible teacher and preacher who died in 1945. "If it is either to help or hinder it must be trained and used. When it is employed to key certain facts in the mind, so that they may influence the will, it is one of the greatest forces for good. Memory serves us as an inspiration to true conduct." In his first inaugural address as president, Abraham Lincoln spoke of "the mystic chords of memory," influencing "the better angels of our nature." In *Recessional* Rudyard Kipling delineated the beneficial ministry of memory:

> *Lord God of Host, be with us yet.*
> *Lest we forget—lest we forget!*

210

I'll Put On My Considering Cap

"Consider how great things the Lord hath done for you."
1 Samuel 12:24.

With old John Fletcher, who died in 1625, we too have need to put on our "considering cap"—and keep it on! Scripture employs the word *consider*, which means "to look at attentively," almost one hundred times. A glance at these references reminds us who and what we are to consider and how consideration influences conduct. Samuel emphasized this latter aspect of consideration when, rehearsing the deliverances of Jehovah, he told the people that their constant consideration of the great things accomplished for them would incite them to "fear the Lord, and serve him in truth with all your heart" (1 Sam. 12:24).

Too often we consider our miseries and fail to count our mercies. Taking to our own hearts the constraining plea of Samuel to "consider how great things the Lord hath done," what else can we do but magnify him for the love that prompted him to surrender his beloved Son for our salvation. Consider how Christ himself never fails and never forsakes us and will remain with us until he perfects that which concerns us. Consider how he supplies us with all we need from day to day, corrects our mistakes, conquers our foes, withholds no good thing from us, and gives us his promises to plead. Consider the innumerable proofs of his faithfulness and, above all, the unmeasured marvel of his best treasure—*himself*!

When we consider all these things and many more, what else can we do but praise him for the past and pledge ourselves to trust him in the future, confident that, having blessed us, he will do still greater things for us. Is your considering cap well fixed upon your head? May God not have to say of us, "My people doth not consider" (Isa. 1:3).

But We, Like Sentries, Are Obliged to Stand

"As the Lord God of Israel liveth, before whom I stand."
1 Kings 17:1.

The standing sentries which John Dryden described in "Don Sebastian" stood "in starless nights, and wait the 'pointed hour." But when the appointed hour arrived for Elijah the Tishbite, he came, not only standing before the Lord, but daring to stand *up* for him in a most dramatic way as a courageous sentry until his chariot ride to heaven. In a startling way the prophet broke in on the national life of Israel. Like a bolt from the blue upon the prevailing spiritual darkness, he initiated a new method of divine rule, namely, prophetic ministry. From this point on the prophet was superior to the king in the kingdom of Israel. Elijah's very first message declared his God-given authority. He affirmed that Jehovah, Israel's God, lived and that the message he was about to deliver was direct from Jehobah's throne before which he stood.

Elijah challenged all earthly authority and swept aside human protection. He stood before the Lord, and he believed the Lord would stand up for him, which he did, protecting and providing for him in wonderful ways.

Paul exhibited the same fearless spirit as Elijah when he confessed, "God whose I am, and whom I serve" (Acts 27:23). God ever breaks in upon human history, as he did in Elijah and Paul, and in Martin Luther who also said, "Here I stand, I can do no other," and asserts his authority and displays his power. Men may refuse the message, and persecute the messenger: but the word he speaks is the word of Jehovah, and it is the word by which men live or die, according to their response to it. Are you standing before the Lord and the world as God's messenger, unafraid of your adversary the Devil?

The Secret Things Belong to God

"The Lord shall be thy confidence." Proverbs 3:26.

Scripture has much to say about our confidence in God and that in such confidence is strength; but in the verse before us Solomon spoke of God as our confidence, or *confidant*. He is a confidential friend or one to whom secrets are confided. As the friend sticking closer than a brother, his ears are ever open to hear the secrets of our hearts. The secret things about his children belong to him, are never repeated to others, and are forever locked up in his heart. What we tell him about ourselves in the secret place never travels beyond him because, being who he is, he cannot betray the trust of any child of his.

The margin of the New American Standard Bible reads, "The Lord will be *at your side*," and this translation is apt, since the rest of the verse reads, "and will keep your feet from being caught." Thus our heavenly confidant is also our protector.

The word *confide* is from a Latin root meaning "to trust," and we confide in the Lord because we trust him. Our assurance is that he always listens sympathetically to all we have to tell him. God presents himself as being honorable, as the one to whom we can communicate all that concerns us, and as the one from whom we can receive wisdom, guidance, and peace. The promise is that if we trust him as our confidential friend we shall be as Mt. Zion which cannot be removed. Such is the marvel of divine grace that our heavenly confidant reciprocates by confiding in us. Has he not said that he will share his secret with us and reveal his covenant to us? "The secret of the Lord is with them that fear him" (Ps. 25:14).

213

To Sing of Time or Eternity

"The angel sware . . . that there should be time no longer."
Revelation 10:5, 6.

Tennyson described his fellow poet John Milton as "God-gifted organ-voice of England" and as one who was "Skilled to sing of Time or Eternity." Revelation, the final book of the Bible of which it has been said that without tears it was not written and without tears it cannot be understood, sings of both time and eternity, with emphasis upon the eternal blessedness of the redeemed. John wrote of the welcome oath and cheering promise of the angel concerning the ending of time and the commencement of eternity for the redeemed. Wordsworth would have us know the

> *Characters of the Great Apocalypse*
> *The types and symbols of Eternity*
> *Of first, and last, and midst, and without end.*

Joseph Addison, English essayist and poet of the early seventeenth century, remarked, "Eternity! thou pleasing, dreadful thought!"

But whether we are to find eternity pleasing or dreadful depends upon our relationship to him who inhabited eternity. William Blake reminded us that

> *. . . He who kisses the joy as it flies*
> *Lives in eternity's sunrise.*

Is our joy of the Lord enabling us as pilgrims to eternity to live in its sunrise? The moment Christ calls us home, "there shall be delay no longer" for those redeemed by his precious blood. There will be nothing to dread as we forsake time and pass into eternity for union with the glorified and immortal saints of all ages already there. May we be found living as those ready for the end when time shall be no more.

214

The Continual Dew of Thy Blessing

"I will be as the dew unto Israel." *Hosea 14:5.*

Poets of all ages have extoled the virtues of "bespangling herb and tree." Tennyson, however, referred to a day when "there rained a ghastly dew." A fiat of divine judgment was, "Let there be no dew" (2 Sam. 1:21). For those living in the East, heavy dew was absolutely necessary since the earth depended upon it; hence, its significance in Scripture.

What dew is to fields and fruits, God offers to be to his redeemed people. As the dew cools and refreshes the dry, barren earth, so God waits to refresh our hearts with the assurance of his love and tokens of his favor. As the dew softens and breaks up the clods of the valley, so God softens and dissolves hard and impenitent hearts. As the dew prepares the ground for the seed and causes it to vegetate and grow, so God prepares hearts to receive his Word and causes it to bring forth fruit in our lives. As the dew falls insensibly and when it is most needed, namely, in the evening, so God comes to us when we need his quickening and fructifying operations.

By nature our hearts are dead and but for the grace of God cannot manifest life, beauty, or fruit. Regeneration by the Holy Spirit requires God's continual dew and the need to sing always, along with an unknown writer:

> Come, Holy Ghost, as heavenly dew,
>   My parchéd soul revive;
> The former mercies now renew,
>   Quicken and bid me live:
> Thy fertilizing power impart
> And sanctify my barren heart.

215

That Kiss, Which Is My Heaven to Have

"Let him kiss me, with the kisses of his mouth."
Song of Solomon 1:2.

Fundamentally, a kiss is an evident token of love or affection between two persons; symbolically it is intended to express the manifestation of love the Lord God has for his children. Said the Roman poet Catullus, who lived before Christ, "Kiss me a thousand times o'er." The spiritual mind can see in "the kisses of his mouth" the varied evidences of his boundless love for his beloved ones. Shakespeare had Cleopatra say of Antony's embrace, "That kiss, which is my heaven to have."

God's *kiss of reconciliation* was received in the moment of our surrender to his claims and meant heaven to us in a very real sense, just as the kiss of the father for his prodigal son meant installment in the father's home. God's *kiss of acceptance* is ever warm on our brow as our hearts are assured that we are his through grace alone. The *kiss of communion* is our daily enjoyment of his unfailing love; the lips of his blessing meet the lips of our asking.

Judas prostituted such a token of affection when he hailed his master with a kiss, not of love but of treachery, that resulted in his death. Previous kisses of his mouth, however, will be lost in his *kiss of consummation* when we finally meet him whom our hearts have loved. Richard Greene of the fifteenth century wrote of one, "My kisses are his daily feast." May the kisses of the mouth of our heavenly lover be our daily feast! The lines from "St. Paul" by the English poet F. W. H. Myers are impressive:

Moses on the mountain
Died by the kisses of the lips of God.

The Lord grant that each of us who have kissed the Son die thus. Surely there is no better way to die.

A Door to Which I Found No Key

"The Lord shut him in." *Genesis 7:16.*

Omar Khayyám said in the *Rubáiyát*:

> *There was the Door to which I found no Key;*
> *Here was a Veil through which I might not see:*

The door that shut Noah and his family in the ark had no key, for God shut them in. It is important to observe that when the hour came for those who were to be saved from the deluge, God did not say, "Go in," but "Come in." Such a request implies that he was already inside the ark and that he would remain with his servant and his family all through the flood. Once the ark rested on dry ground, he would open the door for them to enter a renewed world.

Doubtless many doors had been shut in Noah's face because of his unflinching faith in God and his Word, but such refusals mattered little now that God had opened a door of escape from death and then closed the door upon the world that had despised the testimony of his servant. The hand of divine love shut Noah and his family in the ark away from a wicked and condemned world.

How grateful we are that we responded to the divine call, "Come thou and all thy house into the ark" (Gen. 7:1), and that the door of electing purpose interposed between us and an evil world! It is blessed to know that we are shut in *with him* and enclosed in the same circle as the Holy Trinity. Outside the ark all was ruin, but the disastrous floods only lifted Noah nearer heaven, and all within the ark was rest and peace. Out of Christ, our ark, we perish. In him we are saved and safe, for as the door, he has no key, and once shut in with him, no man can open such a door. Are you on the right side of that door?

217

While Memory Holds a Seat

"We will remember thy love." *Song of Solomon 1:4.*

Lifting the following lines from Shakespeare's *Hamlet*, I link them to Solomon's affirmation:

> ... *Remember thee?*
> *Ay, ... while memory holds a seat*
> *In this distracted globe.*

Only our constant remembrance of the undying love of God for us can save us from being engulfed in our distracted globe. Wordsworth could write "that nature yet remembers" as a "perpetual benediction." Surely there is no theme so sweet and precious to God's children as that of the love of his heart fixed on them immutably and eternally. The Son of his love will not let us forget his love. Did he not institute his Supper that we might remember the matchless history of his love? Samuel Rutherford, seventeenth-century Scottish theologian, teacher, and writer, would often sigh, "Oh, for as much love as would go round about the earth, and over heaven—yea, the heaven of heavens, and ten thousand worlds—that I might let all out upon fair, fair, only fair Christ!"

If only we could give all the love in all pure hearts in one great mass, a gathering together of all loves to him who is love and altogether lovely, what a perpetual benediction would be ours. May grace be ours to remember his eternal love, to comfort our hearts amid changing friendships, to encourage our minds amid the gathering darkness in the world, to inspire us with fortitude in times of testing, to begat patience when we find ourselves burdened and oppressed, to reconcile our troubled minds under bereaving dispensations, and to produce and maintain zeal and devotedness in the Master's service. If we forget all else beside, let us remember his love and daily rest in it.

There's a Divinity That Shapes Our Ends

"Ye meant evil against me; but God meant it for good."
Genesis 50:20, RV.

Scripture and also personal experience confirm Shakespeare's dictum in *Hamlet* that

> *There's a divinity that shapes our ends,*
> *Rough-hew them how we will.*

With kind and tender words Joseph consoled his brothers who were fearful that he would punish them for their past treatment of him now that their father was dead. How assured they must have been of his love and favor! They heard him say that God had made use of their wicked action, when they sold him as a slave, in order to preserve the life of many people and to fulfill his plans concerning both Hebrews and Egyptians!

It is comforting to know that there are never any mistakes in the divine government. The blunders and failures of men are overruled and resolved into the perfect wisdom, might, and purpose of God. Religious leaders were bent on evil against the Lord Jesus and succeeded in crucifying him. A divinity was shaping the end of his agonies and death, and a vast, unnumbered multitude rejoices in the shed blood of the Redeemer. God is superb in making crooked things come out straight, and he can cause even the most unwelcome events of life to work together for our good. "*All* things come of thee" (1 Chron. 29:14). The words by Frederick W. Faber apply to that which Joseph came to experience, as saints in every age do:

> *Ill that He blesses is our good,*
> *And unblest good is ill:*
> *And all is right that seems most wrong,*
> *If it be His sweet will.*

The Greater Man, the Greater Courtesy

"Rabbi, where abidest Thou? He said, Come and ye shall see." John 1:38–39, RV.

Mother Julian of Norwich, a saint of long ago, loved to call Jesus "our courteous Lord." Speaking of prodigals returning to him, she said of his welcome to such wanderers, "Then showeth our courteous Lord Himself to the soul, with friendly, welcoming, saying sweetly thus: My darling, I am glad thou art come to Me; in all thy love I have been ever with thee; and now seest thou My loving." What a joy is ours when, at his courteous bidding, we come in faith to him!

We cannot read the above Scripture without seeing how courteously Jesus dealt with the two men who followed him after hearing John describe him. What sympathy and understanding Jesus revealed! Strangely drawn to him, the two travelers hardly dared to take the initiative of speaking, but Jesus turned to them in friendly inquiry, "What seek ye?" Enraptured by his kindness, all that they could say was, "Master, where dwellest thou?" (John 1:38). He did not rebuke them by answering, "That's no business of yours," but answered their unspoken desire with a sweet invitation, "Come, and ye shall see." And he took them home with him. We can imagine how those two men came to listen with growing wonder and deepening joy to his precious conversation.

This is always the manner of Jesus. What must be borne in mind is the fact that part of the same courtesy is seen in that he never thrusts himself upon us. So delicate is this courteous one, he will not enter where his company is not really desired. But how good and kind he is to those who seek him. Old Thomas Dekker wrote of him:

> *The best of men*
> *That e'er wore earth about Him, was a sufferer,*
> *A soft, meek, patient, humble tranquil spirit,*
> *The first true Gentleman that ever breath'd.*

220

The Footstool of the Virtues

"Be strong, and of a good courage," *Joshua 1:6.*

Writers and poets all down the ages have praised the excellencies of courage, whether physical, moral, or spiritual. Robert Louis Stevenson called it "the footstool of the virtues, on which they stand." In his rectoral address on courage given at St. Andrew's University, Scotland, in 1922, James Barrie said, "Courage is the thing. All goes if courage goes."

The Bible has a good deal to say about saints living courageously. In his last counsels to the people he had guided for forty years, Moses instructed them to "be strong, and of a good courage." His successor, Joshua, several times repeated the same exhortation as he commenced to lead the Hebrew nation. Joshua received the solemn charge from God to "be strong and of a good courage; be not afraid, neither be thou dismayed: for the Lord thy God is with thee" (Josh. 1:9). The courage he was to manifest was a mixture of the physical and spiritual.

Plato declared that the guardians of his ideal city should be men whose courage to defend the citadel was grounded in sound training in the true nature of the human spirit. The courage the Bible commands and commends is of the sort God himself inspires, and such courage "mounts with the occasion." Moral courage often transcends physical courage, and this is the brand we need to stand up for the cause of God and his righteousness in the face of a godless, hostile world. George Farquhar, the seventeenth-century dramatist, wrote:

> *Courage the highest gift, that scorns to bend*
> *To mean desires for a sordid end.*

John Milton asked for "courage never to submit or yield." We too may sing the words of an unknown writer: "Since I must fight if I would reign, increase my courage, Lord!"

A Joyous Exchange

"Thy statutes have been my songs in the house of my pilgrimage." *Psalm 119:54.*

David, the sweet singer of Israel who has a good deal to say about singing, tells us where the substance of his songs came from: they were all borrowed from the Word of God. It is amazing how many of our hymns—ancient and modern—are founded upon different phrases of Scripture. Commenting on David's exchange of statutes into songs, Alexander Smellie said, "It seems strange that one should break into melody and music over *statutes*, the enactments of the law and restraints of authority; for are not the imperatives *Thou shalt* and *Thou shalt not* a curtailment of delight, a crippling of ambition, a checking of impulse? Must I not be free, if my mouth is to be filled 'with laughter and my tongue with singing?' But no! the commandments of God do not really fetter; they introduce my soul to joy and peace."

Have we not abundant reason for making God's statutes our songs? Scripture ends turmoil within and changes confusion into order. It delivers one from the burden of guilt, from fear of the world, and from the sting of death. Scripture sets eternity in the heart and guides into a knowledge of a Savior outside ourselves and into a life of likeness to him who died for our redemption on the cross.

David knew that the terms of the Law were not only melodious but strictly prosaic and harsh; yet salvation and stability were secured to the psalmist by that Law, and so he put it to music and sang of him who had become his strength and deliverer. Not only did those statutes become David's delight, affecting him like music, they were likewise great treasure he discovered—honey, pleasant to his taste, and of more value than silver and gold. May the Word of God excite the same wonder in you as it did in David and give you a singing heart.

A Little Cloister within the Heart

"Thou wilt keep him in perfect peace, whose mind is
stayed on thee." *Isaiah 26:3.*

When Catherine of Siena was only a girl, she chafed against the family
claims and duties and longed for the solitude of a convent cell. A wise
teacher, however, bade her remember that she could always keep a little
cell within her own heart to which, in the midst of outward occupations,
she could inwardly retire and find a deeper peace for which she longed.
St. Theresa of Avila called it an "interior castle of the soul" that no
cares or fears could storm. As we know from Paul's teaching, at the
door of this innermost fortress God's peace stands as sentinel, challenging every thought that seems to enter and chasing away every harassing
form of anxiety. How blessed we are if we have discovered this secret
place of peace to which we can retreat in the most crowded hours of life.

In *The Spiritual Guide* the Spanish mystic Molinos said: "This Divine
Lord desires only that He may rest in thy soul, and may form therein
a rich throne of peace, that within thine own heart, by means of internal
recollection, and with His heavenly grace, thou mayest find silence in
tumult, solitude in company, light in darkness, forgetfulness in injuries,
vigor in despondency, courage in alarms, resistance in temptations, peace
in war, and quiet in tribulation."

Can we say that we walk with God amid the crowded duties of life
in such a way that we can sink deep into the quietness which is within
and not without, and then emerge, as it were, from that stillness at a
word, at a touch, and yet remain within it? Charles Wesley would have
us sing:

> *Here I find a house of prayer,*
> *To which I inwardly retire,*
> *Walking unconcerned in care,*
> *And unconsumed in fire.*

In the Heavens Write Your Glorious Name

"Upon the stone a new name written, which no one
knoweth but he that received it." *Revelation 2:17*, RV.

Edmund Spenser was a spiritual poet of the sixteenth century. In his poem "Amoretti" he described how a name was traced in the sand, only to be washed away by the waves, but that there was a name that would never die in dust:

And in the heavens write your glorious name,
Where when as death shall all the world subdue,
Our love shall live, and later life renew.

John assured us that God writes such an imperishable name upon a white stone and gives it to every victorious child of his. What can this promise mean but that the experience of God within each believer's heart is individual, secret, and uncommunicable? Does this new and undisclosed name by which God himself is made known to the soul suggest that God discloses himself in some unique and personal way to each faithful heart? Can it be that we find in God the completion of our own distinctive lives, the answer to our own solitary needs, and a name that stands for all that he is to *each of us*? Can it be that this new and secret name is a particular name God chooses for, and bestows upon, the child of God?

If this is the explanation, then we have the gracious suggestion of the tenderness and intimacy of God's ways with his redeemed ones. For each of us he has his own name that expresses what he alone sees. It is comforting to know that we are to carry in our hearts like an amulet the white stone with its new name written thereon, a token of all that is between the glorified one and his God, a name no other knows, for no one can tell to another all he or she has found in God.

HOLIDAYS
and
HARVESTS

Dry August and warm
Doth harvest no harm.

—Thomas Tusser,
"August's Husbandry"

A Commodity We Can All Buy

> "Redeeming the time, because the days are evil."
> *Ephesians 5:16.*

Modern translations of Paul's exhortation on "redeeming the time" are varied and profitable: "Making the most of your time" (rsv); "Making the most of every opportunity" (C. B. Williams); "Buying up every opportunity" (Amplified Bible). The latter interpretation is significant, for time is a commodity we can all buy and use to the best advantage. Said Benjamin Franklin, "Dost thou love life? Then do not squander *time*, for that is the stuff life is made of." Our employment of time shapes our character and determines our eternity. How rich in significance are the lines of Tennyson in "Lockley Hall":

> *Love took up the glass of Time, and turn'd it in his glowing hands;*
> *Every moment, lightly shaken, ran itself in golden sands.*

What wisdom we can gain from "the great Instructor, *Time.*" A plaque in my home bears this motto:

> *TIME IS*
> > *Too slow for those who wait,*
> > *Too swift for those who fear,*
> > *Too long for those who grieve,*
> > *Too short for those who rejoice,*
> > *But for those who love*
> > *TIME IS ETERNITY*

People speak of "killing time." Let us not be guilty of such murder but realize that time comes each new day, hand in hand with its companion, opportunity. All who have time have opportunity—the privilege of serving God and humanity. If we lose time, opportunity slips away from us too. If we deliberately kill time, then opportunity lies dead at our feet. Because our days are so evil, may we be found buying up every opportunity to glorify God in our personal advance in holiness and in warning the lost to get right with God while they have time to seek him in penitence and faith. Only thus can we leave behind footprints on the sands of time for others to follow.

Who Like Thyself My Guide and Stay Shall Be?

"Thou shalt guide me with thy counsel." Psalm 73:24.

John Bunyan would have us remember that:

> *He that is ever humble,*
> *Has God to be his Guide.*

A guide, Webster informed us, is one who directs, regulates, orders, superintends the training of, instructs. He who has promised to be our guide, even unto death, functions in all these ways. And in the Book of Common Prayer we read, "Where Thou art Guide no ill can come."

Not only does God guide us unto death, but beyond it, for the psalmist affirmed that when guidance by divine counsel ends, "and afterward receive me to glory" (Ps. 73:24). But if we are to experience how the Lord can guide us continually, we must surrender entirely to him to be guided how and where he pleases. We must trust him implicitly to know all the future holds, and being infinitely gracious, perfectly wise, and immutably faithful, he is able to direct our steps aright. We must be careful about taking one step without his orders and aid.

It is blessed to know that all whom God guides he protects from foes, preserves amid trials, and provides in any time of need. Having redeemed us by the blood of his dear Son, God has made us his charge and care, and he will superintend all that concerns us until we reach the throne of his glory. His reputation as a perfect guide has never been tarnished. He never loses his way and has never lost a follower. Well might we sing with all faith and confidence these words by William Williams:

> *Guide me, O Thou great Jehovah,*
> *Pilgrim through this barren land.*

227

Like Children with Violets Playing

"Except ye turn, and become as little children, ye shall in
no wise enter the kingdom of heaven." *Matthew 18:3*, RV.

A saint of a few centuries ago prayed that "each day and every day
I surrender myself utterly and in all things to Divine Providence . . . like
a little child in the bosom of its good and tenderhearted mother, to
want everything and yet to want nothing—everything that God wills,
nothing that He does not will." Mother Julian of Norwich spoke of
God as "our courteous Mother." Like children who have fallen in the
mud, we pray, "My kind Mother, I have made myself foul and unlike
to Thee, and I neither may, nor can, amend it but with Thine help and
grace." Jesus said we must exhibit this trustful life of a little child if we
would enter heaven. St. Theresa of Lisieux called it the "Little Way,"
or the way of the little child. Jesus told Nicodemus that he must be born
anew if he would see the kingdom of God.

Until we become as little children, weak and frail and having no
strength of our own, we are not able to receive all "our courteous
Mother" waits to give us. Many are too proud, self-willed, and self-
sufficient to be saved. They scorn the helplessness of a little child. St.
Augustine lamented, "Behold my childhood is dead!" But the childhood
Jesus spoke of as being essential for the assurance of eternal life can be
acquired anew into undying life.

In the face of a child there are no hard and haughty lines of self-pride,
no blatant self-assertion. There is only the look of helplessness and
dependence upon others. When the Spirit of God convicts a sinner of
his or her need, the sinner in self-abhorrence and as a weak child, rests
a feeble hand in the mighty hand of God and is at peace.

Fear Not, but Trust in Providence

"All things work together for good." Romans 8:28.

Before we consider all the glorious truths wrapped up in these six simple words, it must be emphasized that the providential goodness of God does not extend to all. No one can have the assurance that God is over-ruling in one's life, protecting, preserving, and providing for the person, *unless* one loves God and has been called according to one's purpose. Only the Christian can view *everything* as having a place in God's plan for his or her life.

All things. This means all circumstances, events, and experiences, whether pleasing or painful, are directed by God to fulfill his purpose and end. Omnipotence has servants everywhere, and whether they come dressed in gay colors or garments of distress and sorrow, the child of God is assured that God is able to bring good even out of evil.

Work. This word suggests planning and activity. Day by day God labors at his task of seeing that we never lose anything worth keeping of his dispensations.

Together. Harmony and unison are associated with his adverb. Because of God's perfect wisdom, there is never any conflict in his ordering of our lives. In his marvelous way he is able to fit all the pieces into a complete pattern. Those who love him know that nothing can occur which ought not to arise and that with him nothing is out of joint. Because of all he is in himself, God can make no mistakes. Thus the true believer in the spirit of true resignation can pray, "What Thou sendest is best."

Good. The harmonious overruling of our gains and losses, joys and sorrows, successes and failures, results in our present and eternal benefit. J. J. Lynch wrote:

> *Say not my soul, "From whence can God relieve my care?"*
> *Remember that Omnipotence has servants everywhere.*
> *His method is sublime, His heart profoundly kind,*
> *God never is before His time, and never is behind.*

Enslave Me with Thy Matchless Love

"Present your bodies a living sacrifice." Romans 12:1.

Paul, with his expert knowledge of the Jewish ritual of sacrifice, knew that when a beast was set apart for sacrifice it was considered sacred and was carefully preserved from all disease or injury. The apostle, spiritualizing the offering up of a lamb without blemish, said that the Christian is intended for the altar, not as a *dead* offering, but as a *living* sacrifice, holy and acceptable to God. Not only his body but all he represents must be kept from defilement, being daily cleansed by obedience to God's Word. Such a holy sacrifice is not only well-pleasing to God but is our "spiritual service of worship."

This presentation of ourselves is not the sullen submission of those who have been beaten but a joyful surrender or yielding up of ourselves to him who gave his all for us and therefore reserves our best. Certainly, we are to become his captives, but *willing* ones, ever ready to follow him in his triumph. Only when we are enslaved with his matchless love can we move freely.

The full surrender to God of all we are and have does not mean the loss of individuality. In the sacrifice of ourselves each of us finds a deeper, fuller life. Giving back the life each of us owes, we find that in God's deep love, life's flower becomes richer. Yielding ourselves as clay to the potter, we discover how he can mold us into a beauty we could not develop. As James Montgomery has taught us to sing:

> *Then with the gift of holiness within us;*
> *We not less human, but made more divine;*
> *Our lives replete with Heaven's supernal beauty,*
> *Ever declare that beauty, Lord, is Thine.*

Oh, To Be Content

"I have learned . . . to be content." Philippians 4:11.

Evidently Paul had reached the contented state, but when he used the word *content*, he did not mean what has been described as the torpor of a foul tranquility. What he implied was the acceptance of inevitable conditions as the sphere in which we are to do the will of God. "I know how to be abased, and I know how to abound," he reminded the Philippians (4:12). By divine grace Paul could handle both poverty and prosperity as they alternated in his experience because at all times he sought the kingdom of God and his righteousness.

Only as we seek the will of God in all circumstances can we possess an inward peace that enables us to find the most profitable way of dealing with every kind of situation. *Discontent* is written large over present-day society and causes so much of our industrial strife. Not content with such things as they have, people want more and still more. Solomon could write of one who would not "rest content, though thou givest many gifts" (Prov. 6:35). Our Lord told the soldiers of his day, "Be content with your wages" (Luke 3:14). Today the word is *contest*, not *content*. Unfortunately, some seem to have no regard whatever for the hardship they inflict upon others as they strike for what they want. But *godliness with contentment* is ever great gain, no matter what our material position may be.

Travel Stains of the Day

"He who has bathed needs only to wash his feet . . . you
are clean, but not all of you." *John 13:1–15,* RV.

Washing the disciples' feet in the Upper Room at the Last Supper was
more than a sign of Jesus' love for his friends. It was even more than a
lesson for them, and us, in the dignity of lowly service. In light of the
conversation between Jesus and Peter, the feet-washing was an acted
parable having a twofold application. First, Jesus was facing his betrayal,
and he knew that Judas, whose heart had resisted him, would sell him
to his enemies. But the rest of the disciples loved him. They were all
clean, but Judas was not, and he died tragically in his uncleanness. "The
Lord knoweth them that are his" (2 Tim. 2:19) and whose hearts have
been "sprinkled from an evil conscience," whose bodies have been
"washed with pure water" (Heb. 10:22). He made them clean, and
they are his.

Second, every saint needs a daily cleansing from the travel stains of
the road. Coming home from the dusty lanes, the traveler does not need
to wash all over again; he needs only to wash his feet. The soul made
clean by the blood cannot be reborn a second time; yet he does need
a daily renewal of cleansing by which the travel stains are washed from
his feet.

Ye are clean. What comfort there is in this truth! We learn from an
unknown source:

> Once, definitely and irrevocably, we have been bathed in
> the crimson tide that flows from Calvary; but we need a
> daily cleansing. Our feet become soiled with the dust of
> life's highways; our hands grimy, as our linen beneath
> the rain of filth in a great city; our lips—as the white
> doorstep of the house—are fouled by the incessant throng
> of idle, unseemly, and fretful words; our hearts cannot
> keep unsoiled the stainless robes with which we pass
> from the closet at morning prime.

Before we retire at night, we need cleansing from the contagion of the
world's slow stain.

The Morning Watch

"In the morning . . . Jesus rose up . . . and prayed."
Mark 1:35.

Many who love the Lord are able to give more extended hours than others to set seasons for prayer. But for the majority of saints who have to work, the day demands mental or physical exercise, with very little time for relaxation or spiritual worship. Hence it is necessary to begin each day with God in order to prepare for arduous tasks ahead and to receive poise and balance to live and labor through the working hours of the day as those who have a friend at hand. We read that this friend, whose days were crowded with preaching, teaching, and miracle works, rose "a great while before day . . . and departed into a desert place, and there prayed" (Mark 1:35, RV).

We may have no desert place to retire to in order to prepare ourselves prayerfully for the day ahead; yet we must each have a quiet spot within our homes where we can begin the day with God. If we are not able to provide spaces of silence and solitude in our daily life, times consecrated to the business of prayer, it is essential to maintain the morning watch with as much time as possible. If we start the day prayerless, we cannot expect to be kept in perfect peace as we meet problems, responsibilities, and decisions.

Mechthild of Magdeburg, a thirteenth-century German woman mystic, would have us remember:

> Prayer makes a sour heart sweet, a sad heart merry, a
> poor heart rich, a foolish heart wise, a timid heart
> courageous, a sick heart well, a blind heart full of vision,
> a cold heart ardent. For it draws down the great God
> into the little heart; it drives the hungry soul up to the
> plentitude of God; it brings together those two lovers,
> God and the soul.

Therefore, after we rise in the morning, let us meet the lover of our souls and with him journey through the rest of the day. "Early will I seek thee" (Ps. 63:1).

233

Far Beyond My Depth

"Hast thou entered into the springs of the sea? Or hast thou walked in the recesses of the deep?" *Job 38:16*, RV.

St. Teresa of Avila used to say that "it is only in this life that we have the chance of walking by faith and not by sight." When with our glorified beings we are with God, we will have the privilege of walking in the recesses of the deep truths of his being and character as we cannot presently do with our finite minds. Now he is past finding out, but in heaven what wonderful revelations of the mystery of his ways will be granted us.

As nature has her secrets, so has God, and until he reveals them unto us, we can but trust his wisdom and his love. We are indeed wise when we confess that human knowledge, no matter how extensive it may be, has its bounds beyond which it cannot pass. With all our searching, we cannot find God out. We are no more able to fathom deep and dark truths, or to discover the reason of his providences, the motive of his actions, the design of his visitation, that we can comprehend the depth from which the ancient ocean draws her watery stores. Charles H. Spurgeon, nineteenth-century English preacher, wrote:

> Let me not strive to understand the infinite, but spend
> my strength in love. What I cannot gain by intellect I can
> possess by affection, and let that suffice me. I cannot
> penetrate the heart of the sea, but I can enjoy the healthful
> breezes which sweep over its bosom, and I can sail over
> its blue waves with propitious winds.

Love to God and obedience to his will are more profitable than trying to walk in the recesses of the deep. Thus we pray, My Lord, I leave the infinite to Thee, and pray Thee to put far from me such a love for the tree of knowledge as might keep me from the tree of life!

The Crown of Love and Friendship

"Abraham my friend." Isaiah 41:8.

How rich in suggestion is John Keats's tribute to divine friendship in his poem "Endymion":

> *Wherein lies happiness? In that which beckons*
> *Our ready minds to fellowship divine,*
> *A fellowship with essence.*
> > *The crown of these*
> *Is made of love and friendship, and sits high*
> *Upon the forehead of humanity.*

Abraham, more than any other person, seems to have had such "fellowship with essence" in abundance, for God called him *my friend.* Jehoshaphat spoke to God of "Abraham thy friend for ever" (2 Chron. 20:7); while James says of the patriarch, "He was called the Friend of God" (Jas. 2:23). Although so highly privileged, Abraham was not alone in wearing upon his forehead the crown of divine friendship. Cowper wrote:

> *Throned above the heights He condescends,*
> *To call the few that trust in Him, His friends.*

Jesus said to his disciples, "No longer do I call you servants . . . but friends" (John 15:15, RV). Through grace we too are brought into a fellowship of heart and mind, a sharing of the thoughts and purposes of Jesus. How arrestive are Shakespeare's lines in *Hamlet*:

> *Those friends thou hast, and their adoption tried,*
> *Grapple them unto thy soul with hoops of steel.*

As Jesus is the friend who sticks closer to us than a brother, may we be found grappling him to our hearts with hoops of steel. He laid down his life for his friends—and enemies.

Every Creature . . . Depends on His Creator

"Apart from Me you can do nothing." John 15:5, ASB.

Nature is a parable of God, and in each of her forms we have a revelation of God. In using the emblem of the vine and its branches, Jesus illustrated and enforced the truth of our utter dependence upon him. Both the vine and its branches constitute one plant, and Jesus and his own are one. The vine root is not sufficient in itself; it must have branches to bear the fruit. It is the same with him who called himself the true vine; he has fruit-bearing branches, or "long lines of saved souls extending down the centuries—through which to communicate Himself to a barren world." So wrote Alexander Smellie, renowned early twentieth-century Scottish minister.

The fruit comes from the sap in the main stem. Thus, Smellie said, "the vine is in the branch; no self-sustained life is throbbing through twigs and tendrils; they are dependent for all that they are and all that they can produce on the quickening currents, that flow to them from the root and stem of the tree."

From me is thy fruit found. As all the life of the vine lives in each fragile tendril and as all the fruitfulness of the vine finds its fulfillment in each branch containing all the sweetness of the vine in each cluster, so all the life and grace and beauty of Jesus dwells in you and me as branches. Since branches can only live and bear fruit as they abide in the vine, apart from him we are but fruitless, withering branches.

Andrew Murray, South African leader of the Dutch Reformed Church who died in 1917, exhorted us:

> Think not so much of thyself as a Branch, nor of the
> abiding as thy duty, until thou hast first had thy soul
> filled with the faith of what Christ as the Vine is. He
> will really be to thee all that a vine can be, holding thee
> fast, nourishing thee, and making Himself every moment
> responsible for thy growth and fruit.

He is indeed the true life-giving vine.

Patient Endurance Is Godlike

"After he had patiently endured he obtained the promise." *Hebrews 6:15*.

Longfellow gave us this impressive phrase from "Evangeline": "Sorrow and silence are strong, and patient endurance is godlike." Abraham had plenty of "sorrow and silence," and they helped to make him the strong character he became. By his godlike patient endurance he inherited and obtained the promises of God (Heb. 6:12, 15).

The word used here for *patience* means more than endurance. It is the word elsewhere rendered *long-suffering*. It is active rather than passive. There was "faith in patience," and the safe cure for sluggishness is ever the activity which persists in conforming the life and its habits to the faith which is professed, even as Abraham did.

Long and sorely tried, this friend of God never questioned God's delay in fulfilling his promise. There is no evidence of his doubting God's veracity, limiting his power, questioning his faithfulness, or grieving his love. Ultimately, Abraham received the promise of a son because he bowed to divine sovereignty, submitted to divine wisdom, and was silent under delays, waiting God's time. As a patient waiter Abraham has left us an example to imitate. His manner of life wrote an unknown author, "condemns a hasty spirit, reproves a murmuring one, commends a patient one, and encourages quiet submission to God's will and way." We sing with Thomas Olivers:

> The God of Abraham praise,
>   Whose all-sufficient grace
> Shall guide me all my happy days
>   In all my ways.
> He calls a worm His friend: He calls Himself my God:
> And He shall save me to the end, Through Jesus' blood.

Freedom Has a Thousand Charms to Show

"The truth shall make you free." *John 8:32.*

In "Table Talk" Cowper informs us that:

> *Freedom has a thousand charms to show,*
> *That slaves, howe'er contented, never know.*

The emancipating truth Jesus taught has indeed a "thousand charms" and proclaims a glorious liberty of which contented slaves of sin are grossly ignorant. There is the *double curse*, for sin both *blinds* and *binds.* That it blinds is evident from the assertion of the Jews who listened to what Jesus had to say about freedom and said, "We were never in bondage to any man." Somehow they had forgotten the long and bitter slavery of Egypt. Prejudice had blinded them. "The eyes of their understanding are darkened" (Eph. 4:18, paraphrase).

Sin binds and enslaves those who began by thinking they could take up sin and lay it down at their will. They became slaves of sin. But, through grace, there is *the double cure*, for, as the hymnist John Addington Symonds, put it, there is a "loftier race":

> *With flame of freedom in the souls,*
> *And light of knowledge in their eyes.*

Our Lord's two phrases the "Son shall make you free" and "The truth shall make you free" are not contradictory but complementary, for he said, "I am . . . the truth" (John 14:6). Freedom from the tyranny of sin must come from without, and it has through him who by his mastery over Satan and sin provided a glorious liberty for all who receive him.

But spiritual freedom does not mean that we may do as we like. Deliverance from sin does not imply license. In the Lord's service there is perfect freedom to do only what pleases our blessed emancipator.

It Becometh Well the Just to be Thankful

"In everything give thanks." *1 Thessalonians 5:18.*

Each of us should pray daily the following petition which is found in the Anglican Order of Service: "We beseech Thee to make us truly sensible of Thy mercy, and give us hearts always ready to express our thankfulness, not only by words, but also by our lives, in being more obedient to Thy holy commandments."

In Paul's quartet of words there are precious truths to ponder. *In.* The apostle did not say *"for* everything give thanks," and we are glad. Certain calamities overtake us for which . . . we cannot kneel down and express gratitude. But we can give thanks *in* them because we know that our all-wise God never makes a mistake and that what he permits must be for his glory and our good.

Everything. Paul did not say *some* things but *everything.* We find it easy to be grateful for the good things of life but not for the bitter cup. Yet the dark threads are as needful as the threads of gold and silver in God's pattern for your life and mine. Apart from his supporting grace it is hard to pray as did an unknown writer:

> *Through dark and dearth, through fire and frost,*
> *With emptied arms and treasures lost,*
> *I thank Thee while my days go on.*

Give. This is a sacrificial word and implies, as Whittier suggested, "each loving life a psalm of gratitude." Are we not enjoined to "offer the *sacrifice of praise* continually" (Heb. 13:15)? We must take time to meditate upon all the benefits so freely and fully bestowed and praise him from whom all blessings flow.

Thanks. Thanksgiving for all things is never out of season, for we have always so much to be thankful for, and gratitude pleases the bountiful giver. With another unknown writer we sing:

> *A thousand blessings, Lord, to us Thou dost impart,*
> *We ask one blessing more, O Lord,—a thankful heart!*

A Double Bounty

"The Lord will give grace and glory." *Psalm 84:11.*

The gifts of God are as freely given to man as the light of the sun, and two of these gifts are grace and glory. Spurgeon wrote that "the little conjunction *and* in this verse is a diamond rivet binding the present with the future: grace and glory always go together. God has married them, and none can divorce them. The Lord will never deny a soul *glory* to whom He has freely given to live upon His grace." *Grace.* If you drop the *G*, you have *race*, and Grace has been abundantly given for all within the human race, for God so loved the world. All who repent and believe can receive the free gift of grace. Then when we are saved by grace, he gives us more grace. No matter how good a person may try to be, no merit can entitle a sinner to grace, which God gives liberally to the repentant, believing sinner. To all who are redeemed, grace in all its forms he freely renders. Grace is to fit us for service, support us in trial, and sanctify our hearts. All we are and have is of his matchless grace.

Glory. What is glory but grace in perfection? If by his grace we have been saved, then we shall be glorified with him. He cannot deny glory to those to whom he has given grace. To quote Spurgeon again, "Glory is nothing more than grace in its Sabbath dress, grace is full bloom, grace like autumn fruit, mellow and perfected. Glory, the glory of Heaven, to glory of Eternity, the glory of Jesus, the glory of the Father, the Lord will surely give to His chosen". So let us cling to this rare promise of our faithful God. Two lines by an unknown writer are inspiring:

> *Two golden links of one celestial chain:*
> *Who owneth grace shall surely glory gain.*

A Sabbath of the Heart

"A rest for the people of God . . . . Give diligence to enter that rest." *Hebrews 4:9, 11.*

That the Bible is a manual on the necessity and methods of rest is proven by the fact that the word *rest*, as applied to spiritual relaxation, occurs over two hundred times. Rest is a gift of heaven, yet something we must find. Peace, concord, silence, quietness, to be at ease, and to lean or rely upon are some of the various meanings of our English word *rest*. In several passages it means Sabbath. Thus Dryden wrote about breaking "the eternal Sabbath of his rest." Wordsworth used the same thought:

> . . . *Every day should leave some part*
> *Free for a Sabbath of the heart;*
> *So shall the Seventh be truly blest,*
> *From morn to eve with hallowed rest.*

The rest that remains is not in heaven alone; it is for all the people of God on earth to enter into deeply and possess as they linger amid the shadows. Such a rest does not imply cessation from work or freedom from conflict and suffering. God's ideal for us is "in our labour rest most sweet." Cowper expresses it:

> *Absence of occupation is not rest,*
> *A mind quite vacant is a mind distress'd.*

The true rest we are to seek diligently comes when we cease from self and find our all in Jesus. In his rest he gathers round our restlessness, as Robert Browning puts it. This rest is not so much a possession as a person. *"Thou* art my Rest." The Lord is the true peace of the heart; out of him there is nothing but disquiet and restlessness. What a Sabbath for the heart it is to rest *in* him with unshaken, confiding, and ardent love.

They Came at a Delicate Plain Called Ease

". . . His soul shall dwell at ease." Psalm 25:13.

While the noun *ease* is understood as meaning freedom from pain, annoyance, constraint, effort, or anything that disquiets or oppresses, in the verse before us the term does not imply laziness or indolence. A "woe" was pronounced upon those who were at ease in Zion. God never intended any child of his to live idly. "Son, go work today in my vineyard" (Matt. 21:28). Shakespeare could have the ghost find Hamlet "duller . . . than the fat weed that rots itself in ease." In the original Hebrew text, *ease* has several meanings. In the verse above it means "good," and so the phrase has been translated, "His soul shall lodge in goodness" or "His soul will abide in prosperity." In the darkest, saddest, loneliest hour, the soul can find a home in the goodness of God. Our hearts can be free from slavish fears and from soul-distressing anxieties and dwell in a state of contentment and solid peace only when we place our faith in God's Word. Our cares are replaced with a realization of his omniscience and omnipresence, a longing to please him in all things, a fear to offend him in anything, and an unceasing desire for his return.

Beloved, has your soul found a resting place in which your heart is at ease because you are at peace with God? Are you lodging in the goodness of God who is the storehouse of every blessing, the supply of every need, and the one who alone can silence all our fears? Undue and unbelieving anxiety about anything vanishes as we cast all our cares upon God and live on "the delicate plain, called *Ease*," as John Bunyan expressed it. With God as our portion, his precious promises are as security, his glorious atonement as our plea, Jesus as our constant advocate, and heaven as our final home, why should we charge our soul with any care? May grace be ours to be at home in ease.

God's Nonconformists

"Be not conformed to this world." Romans 12:2.

Emerson said that "whoso would be a man must be a non-conformist."
In modern parlance, a nonconformist does not adhere to the order of the
established Church of England; a conformist acts in harmony with all
the edicts of the church. All who are members of the church, which is
the body of Christ, are nonconformists since they do not agree with the
ways of a godless world. Every believer should have a nonconformist
conscience when it comes to separation from the world. Are we not
urged to come out from among unbelievers and touch not the unclean
thing? If we confess to be Christians, let us be marked and distinct
Christians.

The miracle of Pentecost was the placing of the church in the world.
The masterpiece of Satan is placing of the world in the church, which
results in spiritual barrenness. The church's Pentecostal power has been
lost through its conformity to the world. Spurgeon said:

> Would you attain the full assurance of faith? you cannot
> gain it while you commune with sinners. Would you
> flame with vehement love? your love will be damped by
> the drenchings of godless society. You cannot become a
> great Christian—you may be a babe in grace, but you
> never can be a perfect man in Christ Jesus while you yield
> yourself to worldly maxims and modes of business of men
> of the world. It is ill for an heir of Heaven to be a great
> friend with heirs of Hell.

That Jesus was an unflinching, unashamed nonconformist can be
gathered from his explicit declaration, "I am not of the world." And he
spoke of his own as being in harmony with his nonconformity, "Ye are
not of this world" (John 17:16).

243

The First-rate for the Having

"But seek ye first the kingdom of God and his righteousness." *Matthew 6:33.*

One of the most colorful and controversial figures in English life and literature is Malcolm Muggeridge. In the second volume of his entertaining autobiography *The Infernal Grove* he is by turn elegant, amusing, and sour, but always honest about himself, as the following quotation proves: "The saddest . . . thing to me . . . is the preference I have so often shown for what is inferior, tenth-rate, when the first-rate was there for the having."

Is this not the folly of many who seek the fleshpots of Egypt rather than the kingdom of God and his righteousness? They prefer the tenth-rate of the Devil rather than the first-rate Jesus urges us to seek. But why hanker after the inferior when the superior is for the having? A place in God's kingdom and being robed in his righteousness are ever first-rate even though all else of inferior value be ours.

The caesars of Rome had all they could wish for in wealth, palaces, slaves, and soldiers. Were they happy and content with such inferior possessions? No. From an unknown source we learn that "Augustus became morose and suspicious in his old age; Tiberius fled from Rome to the loneliness and sin of the little island of Capri; Nero had to hide at last from his enemies in a miserable hut outside the city." Because God made us for himself, we must seek him first and always. Georgiana M. Taylor wrote:

> Seek ye first, not earthly pleasure,
> Fading joy and failing treasure,
> But the Love that knows no measure
> Seek ye first.

May None Those Marks Efface!

"The print of the nails." John 20:25.

Byron in his "Sonnet on Chillon" wrote the following lines:

> *. . . May none those marks efface!*
> *For they appeal from tyranny to God.*

The marks Jesus eternally bears appeal from the tyranny of those who caused God in the dateless past to surrender his beloved son to be a sacrifice for the sins of the world. None will ever be able to efface the marks of the nails in his hands and feet, for they represent our eternal salvation. They are marks of indelible grace, and eternity cannot erase them. We shall know our Redeemer by the print of the nails in his hands, when redeemed by his side we stand. Cruel men pierced his hands and feet, but the only cry the pain wrung from his lips was a prayer for his enemies. The blood from his gaping wounds became the blood of redemption. Charles Wesley sang:

> *Five bleeding wounds He bears, received on Calvary;*
> *They pour effectual prayers, they strong plead for me.*
> *"Forgive him, oh, forgive," they cry,*
> *"Let not that ransomed sinner die."*

Staupitz cried to Martin Luther, "Look at the wounds of Jesus!" and there is no other way by which a sinner can be saved. Thomas said he would not believe what others said about Jesus unless he saw the print of the nails, and when Jesus showed him his hands and his side, Thomas cried, "My Lord and my God!" (John 20:28). Any religion or plan of salvation destitute of the print of the nails is to be rejected. Paul prayed that he might bear in his body the Calvary marks of the Lord Jesus. Crucified hands are careful what they handle; crucified feet are careful where they go; crucified hearts are careful who and what they love.

He Views His Children with Delight

"The Lord takes pleasure in them that fear him, in those that hope in his mercy." *Psalm 147:11.*

Mother Julian of Norwich loved to write of the saints as "the bliss of the Lord." In *Revelation of Divine Love* she said:

> Our good Lord said blissfully, Lo, *I have loved thee,* as if
> He had said, . . . See what satisfying and bliss I have in
> thy salvation, and rejoice with Me. . . . Now in all My
> bitter pain and all My hard travail turned to endless
> joy and bliss to Me and to thee.

Thomas Traherne in the seventeenth century expressed the same thought of divine delight in his poem:

> . . . *O my soul, ours is far most bliss*
> *Than His is ours; at least it so doth seem*
> *Both in His own and our esteem.*

Jesus finds a deep and satisfying joy in those who have been redeemed by his blood and are lovingly obedient to his will. God could say of him, "This is my beloved Son, in whom I am well pleased" (Matt. 3:17). As the sons of God through grace, ours is the privilege of giving God pleasure. It is on record that Job was well-pleasing unto God. Then it seems as if God almost boasted about Job when he asked, "Hast thou considered my servant Job? For there is none like him in the earth" (Job 1:8).

Does he find the same pleasure or bliss in you and me? Is he delighted in us since we love him, share his thoughts, and serve the cause so dear to his own heart? Is he not saddened when he cannot find in us the fellowship he desires? May we so live in unison with his will that he will rejoice over us with singing. Truly, we are his bliss, as we know from the following lines by an unknown author:

> But saints are lovely in His sight,
> He views His children with delight;
> He sees their hope, He knows their fear,
> And looks, and loves His image there.

My Life Is by His Counsel Planned

"My times are in thy hand." *Psalm 31:15.*

What a consoling affirmation this is! When we remember that the ordering of our lives rests in God's hand, what peace of mind should be ours. His omnipotent hand also controls the universe and the destinies of nations. Job reminded us that "times are not hidden from the Almighty" (Job 24:1). This truth prevents us from looking at God through circumstances; instead we should look at circumstances through the environing presence of him whose powerful hand none can stay. God measures out our days, and our hours should obey his loving will.

It is not by chance that we are living in these times, for his will chose this day in which we live, and we must not drift unseeing through such a time of divine opportunity. These are indeed hard and difficult times, but all events are under divine control, nothing being left to chance. Does it not comfort your heart to know that the hand of God is in all that occurs, directing and overruling and sanctifying for our present and eternal good? Whether our times are glad or sad, God knows best about the daily ordering of the course of our lives. William F. Floyd wrote:

> My times are in Thy hand, Whatever they may be;
> Pleasing or painful, dark or bright, As best may seem to Thee.

The psalmist told us that by being in God's hand he is able to deliver us from the hand of our enemies and persecutors. May grace be ours to rest in the assurance that, hour by hour, the varied experiences of life are shaped by God into his program for our lives. Floyd also wrote:

> My times are in Thy hand; Why should I doubt or fear?
> My Father's hand will never cause His child a needless tear.

247

See All, nor Be Afraid

"He shall not be afraid of evil tidings." *Psalm 112:7.*

The only thing a Christian has to fear is *fear* itself, and if our hearts are fixed by trust in the Lord, then of whom or what should we be afraid? Certainly there is much to be afraid of in the evil tidings our daily papers record of violence, hooliganism, crime, brutal murders, lack of integrity among men in high places, immorality, and war. No wonder people are scared as they think of the future; their hearts fail them for fear. But deliverance from all fear possesses the hearts of those who believe that there is no cold fate, no blind, unpredictable chance controlling the world, but a heavenly, loving Father. Clouds may gather, but they will pass away or break in showers of mercy.

A cynic said to a Christian friend, "If I could see all God sees of evil and tragedy in the world, it would break my heart!"

The friend quietly replied, "But God's heart did break at Calvary for the sin of the world."

The godless have every reason to be afraid of evil tidings because they have no God to fly to, no *hid security*, as Rupert Brooke expressed it. If those of us who are the Lord's are distracted and distraught by the state of the world, then where is the value of that grace we profess to have received from him who would have us live without fear? If we gave way to alarm in the day of evil tidings, unable to meet trouble with that calm composure, nerving us for service and sustaining us under adversity, how can we expect to honor him who said, "Let not your heart be troubled, neither let it be afraid" (John 14:27)? Because the days are evil, we must be holy and thereby act as the salt of the earth, arresting its corruption. Let us be found combatting evil tidings by proclaiming the good tidings of the Gospel.

The Fear That Sends Me to His Breast

"Fear him . . . yea, I say unto you, fear him." Luke 12:4–5.

Although as Christians we meet evil tidings with the absence of fear, but there is a fear we must earnestly cultivate, and it is the fear of the Lord. Scripture has a great deal to say about this kind of fear. Jesus told his friends not to be afraid even of those who would seek to kill them, but he warned them to fear God who has power to cast evil men into hell. When this nobler fear dwells in the heart, there is no room for lesser fears. We cease to be afraid of what others can do against us, or of any stroke of trouble that may fall upon us, for such cannot touch one's real life—the hidden life of fellowship with God.

Fear, in respect to the Lord, is not the cringing fear of slaves for the cruel and callous master. Throughout the Old Testament the phrase "the fear of the Lord" represents piety and reverential trust coupled with hatred of evil. As David expressed it, "The fear of the Lord is clean, enduring for ever" (Ps. 19:9). This is the meaning Charles Wesley enshrined in his hymn:

> *Give me, Lord, a holy fear,*
> *And fix it in my heart,*
> *That I may from evil near*
> *With timely care depart;*
> *Sin be more than hell abhorred;*
> *Till Thou destroy the tyrant foe,*
> *Keep me, keep me, gracious Lord,*
> *And never let me go!*

May the Lord teach us to fear nothing but the sin that robs us of our holy fear of his name.

Man Is Immortal till His Work Is Done

> "I must go on my way today and tomorrow and the day following." *Luke 13:33* (RSV).

The title of this meditation is of early origin, but in the seventeenth century Thomas Fuller in his *Church History of Britain* quoted an extended version of the saying: "God's children are immortal while their Father has anything for them to do on earth." Our Lord's specific pronouncement formed part of his answer to the Pharisees and to Herod, all of whom sought to kill him before his God-appointed time. He was immune from death, however, until the work he was sent to do was accomplished. Anticipating Calvary, he prayed to his Father, "I have finished the work thou gavest me to do" (John 17:4). The time periods *today* and *tomorrow* were the days when he would continue unhindered the exercise of his gracious ministry. The *day following* or the "third day" was to be the day he would be perfected, the day of his death, not by those of this earth, but by the prearranged counsel of God.

Whether our days are long or short makes little difference, for in the purpose of God it is not the length of life that counts but the quality of it. Jesus was some thirty-three years old when his task was finished, but what marvelous things he accomplished in those brief years. As we live in true fellowship with him, we have the assurance that until our life's work is ended no hostile power is strong enough to prevent us from finishing our course.

Matthew Henry commented, "It is a comfort to us, in reference to the power and malice of our enemies, that they can have no power to take us off as long as God has any work for us to do." We may lament when a child of God is suddenly cut off because unfinished tasks are left behind. But from the divine side, that person's task was completed— *it is finished.*

250

A Friend in Need Is a Friend Indeed

"Call upon me! . . . I will deliver." Psalm 50:15.

There is no uncertainty whatever about this divine promise. The Lord knows all about our troubles; so there is no need to give him information about them. But if we need his help, he demands that we should call. Days of troubles are often permitted to make us call, and when we are in need, the Lord is a friend indeed. Robert Browning said, "What if this friend happens to be—God?" The friend inviting us to let him know when we require his aid *is* God. The Apocrypha says that "A faithful friend is the medicine of life." How true this is of him who condescends to offer himself as our friend, who is always within call and has boundless resources to help us! He assures us that his ear is not so heavy that he cannot hear us, nor his arm shortened that it cannot help us.

When sore trials overtake us, we must not look to others to undertake for us until God has proved that he cannot or will not lift our burden—*and that will never be*! Because of all he is in himself and all that he has promised, he must respond as we arise and call upon him. God's heart is too kind and his word too faithful for him to turn a deaf ear to our entreaty.

Are you facing a *special* trouble? Without hesitation, pay God a visit, lay your whole case before him, and expect his sympathy, aid, and blessing. He will deliver you, and you shall glorify him. As you trust him as your friend, you honor him. As you expect him to undertake for you in the hour of your need, you have the assurance that you will not be ashamed, for he is ever to be found by those who seek him in all sincerity. *Ask, and ye shall receive.*

The King's Name Is a Tower of Strength

"The name of the Lord is a strong tower: the righteous runneth into it, and is safe." *Proverbs 18:10.*

Shakespeare's praise of King Richard III is true of our heavenly King, whose varied names and titles reveal him to be *the* tower of strength to his people. In his "Ode on the Death of the Duke of Wellington" Tennyson wrote of the famous soldier:

O fall'n at length that tower of strength
Which stood four-square to all the winds that blew.

Since the fall of Lucifer, God has stood foursquare against all satanic blasts and assaults. He has not fallen and cannot since he is the eternal, impregnable tower of strength. What truth this promise holds for our hearts.

The name of the Lord. By his dear name, which is the rock on which I build, my shield and hiding place, we understand all that he is in himself. "As His name, so is He" (1 Sam. 25:25). His name, "sweet in a believer's ear," as a hymn states, represents his nature, character, and being.

Is a strong tower. The idea of the Lord as our refuge, hiding place, fortress, tower, and stronghold permeates Scripture. The strongest towers of men have fallen to enemies, but although the world around us is rocking to its foundations, God is a refuge that cannot be moved. When tumult rages, we have in him a strong citadel of calm.

The righteousness runneth into it. The provision of God as a tower is only for those who are clothed with his righteousness. For the godless there is no hiding place from wrath.

And is safe. Shelter and security are experienced by all those who find in his name a love that never fails, a sympathy always perfect, a sweet omnipotence of grace, and provision equal to every need.

Faint Not nor Fear, His Arms Are Near

"Underneath are the everlasting arms."
Deuteronomy 33:27.

Many figures of speech, like the one before us, have a touch of tender intimacy about them. It is no mere vague goodwill to which we commit ourselves, a kind of friendly tendency in the universe; we commit ourselves to one who personally cares and loves his children. As it is natural for children to run to the arms of their parents when little troubles overtake them, so it is natural for those who believe in the fatherhood of God to cast themselves into the arms of their heavenly Father when the trials of life beset them. J. Drummond Burns taught us to sing:

> As helpless as a child who clings
> Fast to its father's arm,
> And casts his weakness on the strength
> That keeps him safe from harm:
> So I, my Father, cling to Thee,
> And thus I every hour
> Would link my earthly feebleness
> To Thine almighty power.

The arms around and underneath us are the everlasting arms of the eternal God and are, therefore, well able to support and protect us at all times. Think of the double consolation there is for our hearts in the glorious promise, "The eternal God is thy dwelling-place." Our native environment is not earth or time but heaven and eternity. We are assured that the everlasting arms of our eternal God are underneath us, ever there to save us from falling. No matter how deep our distress and affliction may be, underneath are the arms that never flag or lose their strength, embracing and consoling us. Thus sustained, all Satan's efforts to harm us avail nothing. Fanny J. Crosby wrote:

> Safe in the arms of Jesus,
> Safe on His gentle breast,
> There by His love o'ershaded,
> Sweetly my soul shall rest.

The Garment of Praise for the Spirit of Heaviness

"My soul melteth for heaviness: strengthen thou me
according to thy word." *Psalm 119:28.*

Although the word *depression* is not in the Bible, all that it depicts is
scattered throughout the sacred pages and emerges in phrases like "Out
of the depths I cried unto Thee" (Ps. 130:1), "Why are thou cast down,
O my soul?" (Ps. 42:5), "When my spirit was overwhelmed within
me" (Ps. 142:3). David was often despondent. John Trapp, a seventeenth-century English Bible commentator, said of the psalmist's sigh,
"Why art thou cast down, O my soul," that "David chideth David out
of the dumps." His redeemed spirit rebukes the flesh and battles with
its despondency in the name of the most high.

All of us have days when a weight seems to lie on the spirit and the
soul melts for heaviness. A mist hangs over our world, work becomes
a weariness, and depression seizes us. Physical weakness or mental over-
strain produces moments of spiritual darkness and the drying up of
spiritual joy. When such heaviness of spirit overtakes us, a cure for our
depressed state of mind is to don the garment of praise—*Hope thou in
God*!

Brighter days dawn as we leave our brooding over troubles and go
out to help others who are downcast. John Keble's wise word is apt:
"When you find yourself overpowered as it were by melancholy, the
best way is to go out and do something kind to somebody or other."
New hope and strength are ours when we seek to carry cheerfully
another's load. The consoling thought is that even in the gloom Jesus
is with us. He promised to undertake for us "all the days"—days of
despondency and cheerless gloom as well as days of joyous sunshine.
"When my spirit was overwhelmed within me, thou knewest my path."
Only such a faith can save us from despair and bring to us treasures,
even out of our darkness.

The Superfluous Is Necessary

"How much more shall your Father which is in heaven
give good things?" *Matthew 7:11.*

The dictionary informs us that *superfluous* means "overflowing," "more
than is necessary," "an excess of which is sufficient." As a professed
atheist Voltaire did not have the superfluity of God in mind when he
coined the phrase, "The superfluous is necessary." The *much more* that
Jesus spoke reveals that our heavenly Father is not prescribed in his
provision but superabundant. When Jesus fed the hungry crowds, there
was not just enough to go around, but after all had eaten well, there
was the superfluity of twelve baskets full of fragments. Such superfluity
was necessary to prove that he is able to do exceeding abundantly, above
all we ask for or need.

In his teaching Jesus interprets the bountiful heart of God. If an
earthly father gives his child what he asks for—a loaf, stone, fish, or
serpent—our heavenly Father waits to give his children greater and
more numerous good things. So let us cling to these three words, *How
much more!* Human love is a symbol of the divine, but the symbol often
fails. "If ye then know how to give good gifts" (Matt. 7:11)—but
fathers do not always know and in ignorance bestow gifts that prove
detrimental. Our heavenly Father always knows what is best for every
child of his and in his wise love gives only *good gifts*—his beloved Son,
the Holy Spirit, the Holy Scriptures, his grace and glory. In God's giving
we have a sea without a shore. Overflowing blessings are ours here and
now, but the hand that bled to make them ours holds *much more* for us
in heaven. Then we shall turn, as an unidentified author wrote,

> *From the gift looking to the Giver,*
> *And from the cistern to the River,*
> *And from the finite to Infinity,*
> *And from man's dust to God's divinity.*

More Space in My Narrow Heart

"Abraham called the name of that place Jehovah-jireh
[meaning the Lord will provide]." *Genesis 22:14.*

Frederick W. Faber told us in his hymn "Thou Broadenest Out with
Every Year" that God makes more space for himself when he gives us a
clearer vision of his face. After Abraham had witnessed what God did
on the mount, he received, not only a further revelation of the Almighty,
but more space in his heart for his friend.

Divine names and titles are a fascinating theme, as I have sought to
show in my book on this subject. *Jehovah-jireh,* for instance, was not
only a new name for a place, it was also a new name for God—a name
registering a fuller discovery of God and an addition to Abraham's
thought and experience of God. From now on the patriarch was to know
him as *the Lord will provide,* the God intervening at the moment of
need.

As we follow the list of names given to God, we find that each fresh
one further revealed his love and power through some great experience.
Jehovah-nissi, meaning the "Lord my banner," was another name born
of a new sense of God's leadership and protection. Richard Baxter,
seventeenth-century Puritan divine, could write, "Every state and change
of my life, notwithstanding my sin, hath opened to me Treasures and
Mysteries of Love, and after such a life of Love shall I doubt whether
the same God do love me?"

Have we not had experiences, enriching our spiritual store with new
thoughts of God and, like Abraham, found ourselves going forward with
great assurance that he would provide? Coming to a mount of trial, we
found it turned into a mount of mercy. "On the mount of the Lord he
will be seen" (Gen. 22:14, R.V. margin). Only on the mounts of sorrows
and testings do we come to know him as the one ready to supply our
need and display his power on our behalf.

BEAUTY
and
BOUNTY

Up from the meadows rich with
    corn
Clear is the cool September morn.

—John Greenleaf Whittier,
"Barbara Frietchie"

Thou Dost Preserve the Stars from Wrong

"O thou preserver of men." Job 7:20.

God not only preserves the stars from wrong and makes the ancient heavens fresh and strong, as Wordsworth expressed it, he also preserves the saints. Job had deep experiences of God's preserving grace and mercy, for he could say, "I have seen God face to face, and my life is preserved" (Gen. 32:30). We also have the assurance that God will preserve our going out and our coming in until traveling days are done. A modern translation (RSV) gives us, "O watcher of men," and the eye that is on the sparrow watches over us to preserve us from falling. Because of our inherent sinful nature we are liable to fall; we have neither the wisdom nor the strength to preserve ourselves from the hand of the enemy. Corruption within and without is strong, and our hearts are deceitful. Satan is ever vigilant to beguile us.

Therefore, we need a *preserver* every hour to call upon as we are assailed by the enemy, and God is such a one who can and does preserve his own. But divine preservation is ours only as we walk in the way of obedience. How can we expect his security if we are not watchful, prayerful, and walking humbly before him? Without his strong hand to keep us, we fall into the grossest sins. May we be delivered from the folly of thinking we are safe, except as we are found constantly leaning on him and daily cultivating communion with him who is able to keep us safe and secure. The world, the flesh, and the Devil are leagued against us, and nothing but omnipotent grace can preserve us from falling and ultimately present us faultless before the presence of his glory with exceeding joy. "I have heard thee . . . I will preserve thee" (Isa. 49:8).

The Liberality of Our Glorious Boaz

"And Ruth did eat, and was sufficed, and left." *Ruth 2:14.*

Within the world's literature, sacred and secular, no love story is so absorbing as that of Ruth the Moabitess who became the ancestress of the Lord Jesus Christ. Finding herself in Bethlehem, Ruth faced the practical problem of poverty. Looking for work, "her hap was to light on the portion of the field belonging unto Boaz" (2:3). The word *hap* does not mean that the meeting with Boaz was accidental but implies *that which she met with*—an issue revealing divine overruling. There are no accidents in the life of faith. In its music, the accidentals perfect the harmony.

During a break in the hard toil, Boaz was attracted by the charming maiden who had come to glean and offered Ruth some of his own parched corn. We read that "she did eat, and was sufficed and left" (2:14). Thomas Gray, poet of the seventeenth century, wrote of one, "Large was his bounty and his soul sincere." Such was certainly true of Boaz and truer of our heavenly Boaz whose liberality we magnify.

As Ruth was satisfied with the meal Boaz provided, what can we say about the bountiful repast our Lord provides? Where he is host, no guest goes empty from the table but is sufficed. All desires are satiated when we know him and are found in him. Sufficed, Ruth left. Is this not so with us? We have had deep drafts; we thought that we could take in all of Christ, but when we have done our best, we have had to leave a vast remainder. After leaving the satisfying meal, Ruth discovered that a richer bounty was to follow. Likewise we learn that after having our hunger relieved at the feast of sacred love there is an abundance of spiritual meat remaining. There is always more to follow. Samuel Rutherford could say of the Lord he dearly loved, "He was the ever-running-over Lord Jesus."

A Striking Symbol of Neglect

"Ephraim is a cake not turned." *Hosea 7:8.*

The prophet Hosea was rich in his use of arrestive symbols to illustrate spiritual truths, and none was so pointed as that of the cake a housewife failed to make thoroughly. The word *thorough* means "through and through." Ephraim was not wholly the Lord's but was like a cake not turned—uncooked on one side and overbaked on the side nearest the fire. Ephraim was not obedient through and through. The people of Ephraim experienced grace, but such grace had not gone to the very center of their being so as to be felt in all thoughts, words, and actions. It is sadly possible to appear holy in one place yet reign in sin in another.

A cake not turned is soon burned on the side nearest the fire, a symbol of one who is "saint in public but a devil in practice. The assumed appearance of superior sanctity frequently accompanies a total absence of all vital godliness," said Spurgeon.

Can we say that we are like a well-baked cake, brown all around, or in other parts thoroughly consistent and sanctified in every part of our being? Spurgeon gave us the following prayer:

> If I am cake burned on one side, and dough on the other,
> O Lord, turn me! Turn my unsanctified nature to the fire
> of Thy love and let it feel the sacred glow, and let my
> burnt side cool a little while I learn my own weakness and
> want of heat when I am removed from Thy heavenly
> flame. Let me not be found a double-minded man, but one
> entirely under the powerful influence of reigning grace;
> for well I know if I am left like a cake unturned, and am
> not on both sides the subject of Thy grace, I must be
> consumed for ever amid everlasting burnings.

Have we not need to pray a similar prayer as followers of him who was holy all through?

The Purest of Human Pleasures

"The Lord God planted a garden." *Genesis 2:8.*

The eminent essayist Francis Bacon was an ardent lover of gardens. He wrote, "God Almighty first planted a Garden; and it is the Purest of Human pleasures." As soon as God created man, he fashioned him a garden for the promotion of his enjoyment of the creator. A garden rests the soul and cheers the heart, and we should pray that in our hearts and lives God Almighty may find a garden of his own planting where he can talk with us in the cool of the day. The Bible lover will find much inspiration in what the scripture says about gardens and their flowers and fruits. The first home of the first man was a garden, but there are sad reminiscences in this history of Bible gardens. On a tombstone in a Welsh churchyard this epitaph is found:

> In a garden the first of our race was deceived:
> In a garden the promise of grace was received:
> In a garden was Jesus betrayed to His doom;
> In a garden His body was laid in a tomb.

Shakespeare in *Othello* said, "Our bodies are our gardens, to the which our wills are gardeners." If we deem our bodies the temples of the Holy Spirit, then, like watered gardens, they will be full of fragrance rare. Rudyard Kipling's poem "The Glory of the Garden" is superb even though his garden was England. "The Glory of the Garden lies in more than meets the eye," he wrote. He continued:

> Oh, Adam was a gardener, and God who made him sees
> That half a proper gardener's work is done upon his knees,
> So when your work is finished, you can wash your hand and pray
> For the Glory of the Garden, that it may not pass away!

The garden of paradise with its twelve kinds of fruit shall never pass away but ever remain for the health of nations.

261

Enlarge My Life with Multitude of Days

"Be ye also enlarged." *2 Corinthians 6:13.*

Samuel Johnson was somewhat cynical when he wrote the words in the above title, for he went on to say that "life protracted is protracted woe." We who love the Lord who is able to enlarge our steps only want as many days as the Lord can allow us so that our service for him can be lengthened. The Bible has much to say about spiritual enlargement. The carnal Corinthians were static in their spiritual experience, and so Paul exhorted them, "Be ye also enlarged." The apostle assured them, "Our heart is enlarged" or, as the Amplified Bible has it, "O Corinthians, our heart is opened wide, and so pleads, 'Open wide to us also.' "

We need to be enlarged in our knowledge, love, hope, liberality, faith —in every place. God who ever seeks to enlarge our hearts disapproves of contraction in the lives of those who are his. All of his promises warrant enlarged expectations, and he would have us open our hearts as wide as possible to receive all that he is willing to bestow. Because God waits to gratify enlarged, spiritual desires, may our lives exhibit enlargement in prayer, benevolence, pity, and compassion in all our efforts for his glory.

It is essential to guard ourselves against narrow views or feelings, for the heart of God is large; the love of Christ is large; the Gospel commission is large: the provision of mercy is large; and the mansions of Glory are large. I offer this prayer, that we have our narrow hearts enlarged: O Lord, expand my contracted heart, that I may abound in hope, by the power of the Holy Spirit! Thou hast made provision to gratify desires for spiritual enlargement; enable me to open my heart wide to receive all Thou hast for me!

Draw Nearer Me, Sweetly Questioning

"What would ye that I should do for you?" *Mark 10:36.*

Quaint and saintly George Herbert of the early seventeenth century must have had Jesus in mind when he wrote of "quick-ey'd Love" who:

> Drew nearer to me, sweet questioning
> If I lack'd any thing.

An unidentified writer of the past century left us a most profitable book called *The Master's Questions and His Answers.* Sweetly Jesus questioned the sons of Zebedee, "What would ye that I should do for you?" He could not accede to the request, however, since position in heaven was his Father's decision. To the blind man Jesus met near Jericho, he asked the same question, "What wilt thou that I should do unto thee?" Without hesitation, the beggar said, "That I may receive my sight." Then, sweetly as he questioned, Jesus sweetly answered, "Receive thy sight!" (Luke 18:42).

As we commence each new day, may we hear him ask us what he can do for us as we face the unknown hours ahead, and may we have our petition ready, for if we ask according to his will, he will hear and undertake. "Ask, what shall I give thee?" (1 Kings 3:5). How else can we reply but say, O Lord, grant me victory over inward corruption—purify my heart—make me a vessel of honour, fit for Thy service—impart Thy holiness—write Thy Word on my heart, and enable me to be as a living epistle with Thy precepts written large over my life—fashion me into Thy likeness, and enable me to live for the honour and glory of Thy free and sovereign grace!

Let us ever remember that Jesus is always at his pardon office, sitting on a throne of grace, and always in a gracious and loving temper to give us what we ask of him in reply to his question, "What would you like me to do for you?"

When There's Trouble Brewing

"Trouble is near." *Psalm 22:11.*

When troubles were brewing, Charles Knight, an eighteenth-century English publisher, asked:

Are we downhearted?
No! let 'em all come.

Trouble and the believer, and the unbeliever also, are never long apart. The difference is that the believer, who is never apart from Jesus, is never downhearted when trouble is near. Jesus is always a very *present* help in trouble. Trouble may be used by Satan to make us wander from Jesus, but Jesus will not abandon us.

We certainly live in a troubled world, and hearts fail for fear. But we have the assurance that although troubles may be near, whether personal, national, or international, the throne of grace is near and his promises are at hand to calm and counsel us. God invites us to call upon him in the day of trouble, and he promises to deliver us. In turn we are to honor him. Any kind of trouble, then, is meant to make God more precious to our hearts. He does not permit trouble to come our way in order to fill us with confusion, weaken our faith, and drive us from his loving heart. We have his promise, "I will be with him in trouble" (Ps. 91:15). He is ever near to sanctify our trials, to glorify his grace, to deepen his work within us, to brighten our evidences, and to fill us with joy and peace in believing. Our attitude toward God then determines whether our trouble is a bane or a blessing. As Edmund V. Cooke, who died in 1932, put it:

Oh, a trouble's a ton, or a trouble's an ounce,
Or a trouble is what you make it.
And it isn't the fact that you're hurt that counts,
But only, how did you take it?

264

Repairer of Broken Earthenware

"A heart broken and crushed, O God Thou wilt not despise." Psalm 51:17, ASB.

Several years ago Harold Begbie, a gifted writer and an ardent admirer of the work of the Salvation Army, wrote a moving book he called *Broken Earthenware.* In it he described the stories of men and women whose hearts and lives had been broken and crushed by sin but who had been transformed by God through the ministry of the army. Our world today is full of broken earthenware, those brokenhearted people who through one cause or another will end their days crushed and destroyed. In "A Jacobite's Epitaph" Thomas Macaulay referred to them: "O'er English dust. A broken heart lies here."

The Bible, a faithful mirror of human life, has much to say about broken hearts and about the causes of such crushing grief. Jeremiah, the weeping prophet, reflected this sorrow of God when he cried, "Mine heart within me is broken because of the prophets . . . and because the land is full of adulterers" (Jer. 23:9).

Do the apostasy and adultery of our time move our hearts as deeply? Do rivers of tears run down our faces because of a powerless religion and a corrupt society? It is said that reproach broke Jesus' heart and that because he literally died of a broken heart, as evidenced by the blood and water from his pierced side, he is able to heal the brokenhearted. How poignant is the lament of Paul over the effort of friends to deter him from his task: "What mean ye to weep and to break mine heart?" Solomon said that through "sorrow of the heart the spirit is broken" (Prov. 15:13). Is yours a broken spirit? Are you, either through your own mistakes or the action of others, broken and crushed? Then claim the promise, The Lord is near to the brokenhearted, and saves those who are crushed in spirit. He alone can mend broken hearts and lives. As Oscar Wilde expressed it in "The Ballad of Reading Gaol":

> *How else but through a broken-heart,*
> *May the Lord Christ enter in?*

A Bundle of Contradictions

"As having nothing, and yet possessing all things."
2 Corinthians 6:10.

C. Caleb Cotton, essayist of the early eighteenth century, wrote that "man is an embodied paradox, a bundle of contradictions." But the Bible possesses many embodied paradoxes and is a bundle of seeming contradictions. The above assertion of Paul is one of them. How can we be poor if rich? These blessed contradictions are worthy of our study.

The majority of the Lord's family are not materially rich but generally poor, and the world around may look at them as having nothing valuable or calculated to make them content and happy. But how wrong they are. The poorest saints are heirs of God, having him as their portion and inheritance. While they do not have much of the world's wealth, theirs is the gold tried in the fire, making them spiritually rich. Would that we could be found possessing all the things we have in the Lord. He is our never-failing treasury, and James Smith, a British writer, reminded us in *Daily Remembranceer*, of what we have in him:

> His eternity as the date of our happiness; His
> unchangeableness, the rock of our rest; His omnipotence,
> our constant guard; His faithfulness, our daily security;
> His mercies, our overflowing store; His omniscience, our
> careful overseer; His wisdom, our judicious Counsellor;
> His justice, our stern avenger; His omnipresence, our
> sweet company; His holiness, the fountain from which we
> receive sanctifying grace; His all-sufficiency, the lot
> of our inheritance; His infinity, the extent of our
> glorious portion.

Beloved, if we have little of this world's goods, we have a marvelous fortune at our disposal in God who waits to give us all he has, richly to enjoy. Ours is the privilege of living as heirs of heaven, poor yet rich; unknown by the world as heirs of eternal wealth, ye are yet fully known to him who is owner of all. Though poor, we can make many rich, said Paul who owned little more than the clothes he wore.

To Business That We Love We Rise Betime

"I must be about my Father's business." *Luke 2:49.*

How appropriate are the lines of Shakespeare in *Antony and Cleopatra* in respect to Christ's constant endeavor to finish the work his Father had given him to do:

> *To business that we love we rise betime*
> *And go to't with delight.*

The Son delighted to do the will of his Father and would often rise betime to converse with his Father about the business he had entrusted to him. Literally, the word Christ used for business means "affairs" or "the things of my Father." The Revised Version reads, "Knew ye not that I must be in My Father's House?" (Luke 2:49). These are his first recorded words and, although uttered when he was but a twelve-year-old lad, indicate that he knew at that very early age his purpose in the world.

This first saying of his is significant also because it gives us the key to the whole of his life and mission. Bible teacher and writer G. Campbell Morgan, who died in 1945, commented, "The compelling force, the *must* behind all His doing and teaching, was ever the same: the things of His Father. He lived and wrought only to do the will of God."

We are happy parents if our children relate their lives to God by the *must* of complete surrender to his will. Are we found doing the King's business, not only with haste, but with delight? Are we being borne along by the Master's compelling force to finish the task the Father has allotted us? The majority around us have no idea why they are in the world, and having never discovered the divine plan for their lives, they drift with the tide. But if we are the Lord's, then no matter what legitimate business is ours whereby we can work to live, the Father's business must always have our sincere attention. His affairs should be our chief concern.

267

To Know That You Know Not

"I know not how." . . . "The Lord knoweth how."
1 Kings 3:7; 2 Peter 2:9.

Francis Bacon in one of his great essays said, "If you dissemble some-times your knowledge of that you are thought to know, you shall be thought, another time, to know what you know not." With all our acquired and assumed knowledge there are many things we know not. "We know not what a day may bring forth" (Jas. 4:14, free trans.). When Solomon succeeded his father David as king, he was clothed with all humility and confessed, "I am but a little child! I know not how to go out or come in" (1 Kings 3:7). God had said to him, "Ask what I shall give thee" (1 Kings 3:5), and Solomon asked for an under-standing heart and discernment of character.

We know not the way we should take in many decisions that have to be made, but God knows the way we must take; and when he has tried us, we come forth as gold. Job's great triumph of faith can be ours if we have learned to sing with an unidentified writer, "In every hour, in perfect peace, I'll sing, He knows! He knows!"

We do not know how to face the burdens of tomorrow, but do we need to know? Is not today's burden enough, and has not God said, "As thy day, so shall thy strength be" (Deut. 33:25)? Why then add tomorrow's load to today's? If you feel tomorrow's burden will crush, let it happen tomorrow and not today. The Lord knows how to deliver the godly out of the trials awaiting them. We know not how we are to meet this problem, situation, choice, or sorrow, but the Lord knows how; and as we rest in him, he makes our way plain. Perhaps you have recently been bereaved and are saying to your heart, "I know not how I am to face the coming days without the loved one who was so much a part of my life." But God knows how you will fare, for he has made every provision for the vacant place in your heart and home. So why not leave tomorrow in the hands of him who said, "Let the morrow take thought for itself" (Matt. 6:34).

Death Is Entrance into Light

"Seek him that . . . turneth the shadow of death into the morning." *Amos 5:8.*

Our descriptions of death are as somber as the event itself. We speak of "death's dark night," "the terrors of death," "the icy hand of death," "death, the least of all evils." But the declaration of Amos is that God turns the shadow into substance, night into morning. Samuel Johnson in his satiric verse *The Vanity of Human Wishes* said:

> *Faith, that, panting for a happier seat,*
> *Counts death kind Nature's signal of retreat.*

Faith in God enables us to count death as the signal of retreat from the dark shadows of this world into the glorious abode above. Death is the passage way from the mortal into the immortal. During World War II a sincere Christian soldier whose name is unknown was instantly killed in battle, but some time before his death he had set forth his conception of leaving earth for glory in the following poem:

> *Best loved of all I leave behind. I see*
> *O Heaven, pity those who cannot see!*
> *Glory on glory—glory on that face*
> *So near, so dear; gold glory on the wave,*
> *Purple and gold and darting tongues of flame;*
> *Calm glory on the cloud-piled dome of heaven;*
> *Glory of fire on the earth's great face.*
> *So slips my soul, scarce heeding of the change,*
> *From glory unto glory! Heaven breaks*
> *Eternal glory, on the face of God!*

Christ's death and resurrection have given us the assurance that in him only the shadow of death will be transformed for us into glory unspeakable.

Transmuted in the Furnace of Affliction

"When he hath tried me, I shall come forth as gold."
Job 23:10.

The experiences and utterances of Job, which the New Testament presents as a model of patience, are a mixture of confidence and complaint. In the chapter before us, in the midst of Job's bitter complaining and sighing after God, there flames forth a most remarkable evidence of the tenacity of his faith. He was confident that God was behind his trials and through all the processes of testing was seeking the vindication of the true gold in his servant. In the furnace of affliction the divine goldsmith was transmuting Job's life into a most precious vessel. Malachi assured us that God sits as the refiner and purifier of silver.

Dr. Robert G. Lee, master of words whose eloquent preaching often thrilled me, commented on Job's assertion:

> The fire of the furnace and the smoke of the flames—
> these show how God brings deep things out of the dark—
> rich treasures out of darkness. Authorities tell us that the
> potter never sees his clay take on rich shades of silver,
> or red, or cream, or brown, until after the darkness and the
> burning of the furnace. These colors come—after the
> burning and darkness. The clay is beautiful—the vase is
> made possible—after the burning and darkness. How
> wide-lying and universal is this law of life! When did the
> bravest man and purest woman you know get their
> whitened characters? Did they not get them as the clay
> gets its beauty and glory—after the darkness and burning
> of the furnace?

It may be that you are presently being sorely tried and are mystified by what God is permitting to overtake you. Remember that he dwells in "thick darkness" as well as in light and is with you in the darkness of your furnace, trying you, sifting out the dross, and transmuting your life into a golden vessel more fit for his use.

He That Is Down Need Fear No Fall

"God resisted the proud, but giveth grace unto the humble." *James 4:6.*

In his Sermon on the Mount Jesus called those who were humble "poor in spirit." He did not mean, however, that they were poor-spirited. He meant that they were conscious that their own righteousness was but filthy rags in the presence of a thrice-holy God and that their own fleshy wisdom was but folly to Him. Only those who do not shun the valley of humiliation prove it to be a place of hope. Only as we learn of our own poverty and ignorance are we ready to learn of God and to trust him.

Contrary to worldly policy, humility is the root of all progress in knowledge and of all dependence on God from which his bounty springs. Some of the greatest persons in knowledge or personality are generally the most humble. Sir James Simpson of Edinburgh, discoverer of chloroform, was once asked what he deemed his greatest discovery. This was his quick reply: "That I was a sinner, and that Christ died for me!" Knowledge with such persons enables them to realize how little they know.

All who are the Lord's should seek to adorn the garment of true humility, for such a virtue is the basis of further virtues such as a quiet mind, gratitude, contentment, and, above all, robust faith in God's ability to undertake for us in any circumstances of life. The consistent teaching of him who was "meek and lowly in heart" was that the gates of the kingdom of God are ever open to the lowly hearted and to those who knew that there is nothing between them and great darkness, now and beyond, but the pity of God. Thomas à Kempis has taught us to pray, "Surely my heart cannot rest, nor be entirely contented, unless it rest in Thee, and rise above all gifts and all creatures whatsoever." Only as we realize that we are nothing, have nothing, and can do nothing apart from God can we be graced with the humility which James declared to be God's gift.

271

There Was No Leaf upon the Forest Bare

"He hath stripped me." *Job 19:9.*

In a most poignant way Job told us how God had denuded him of his glory, his crown, his honor, his children, his familiar friends, his possessions and position, leaving him as a barren tree. As I write this meditation, I glance out of my study window and gaze for a moment at several trees near my garden. During the summer their foliage was abundant and beautiful, but there they stand gaunt, bare, leafless. Stripped of all their glory, they are not a pleasant sight to behold. This was how Job felt in his wretched and lonely condition. In his own epitaph Benjamin Franklin spoke of his corpse as "the cover of an old book with contents worn out and *stript of its letting and gilding—food for worms.*" Death is indeed the final stripper.

Does your life seem desolate and bare, a leafless tree? Perhaps you have been stripped of all that made life worth living. A dear one, so precious to your heart and upon who you were so dependent, was taken from you, and in that one's death your own heart seems to have died. Now you stand on the bleak summit of your deep grief, no longer sheltered by the one long loved but lost awhile, stripped like a tree of all its summer dress and beauty.

Well, you must not yield to despair but live in hope that, as a tree planted by the Lord in his garden, you will blossom again and no longer stand as a naked tree. Job lost all in his trials but lived to see the day when God gave him back twice as much as he had lost, with his latter end being more richly blessed than his beginning. Above all, think of Jesus who was stripped of all and died naked on a leafless tree but who is now clothed and crowned with honor and glory.

Under His Wings I Am Safely Abiding

"Cover thee with his feathers . . . his wings." Psalm 91:4.

The dominant feature of this great psalm, ascribed to Moses, the man of God, is that of the security of one whose whole trust is in the Lord. The Book of Common Prayer puts the verse as, "He shall defend thee under his wings, and thou shalt be safe under His feathers." How precious is the illustration Jesus used of himself as a hen yearning to shelter her chicks under her warm feathers! The psalm before us, rich in its singular personal pronouns, is fragrant with the satisfaction of the heart that has God as its dwelling place. The psalmist referred to this habitation as "the secret place," and described its complete security by employing the figure of the mother-bird to illustrate "The shadow of the Almighty" (91:1).

As we read this psalm, we must not forget that the safety offered is of a spiritual nature rather than a material experience. As those redeemed by the precious blood of Christ, we are not always immune from physical plagues and pains. "Many are the afflictions of the righteous" (Ps. 34:19). The truth conveyed by promises of security is that the saints are ever guarded from destructive spiritual forces as they dwell in the secret place of the Most High; only through Christ are they admitted to the most intimate fellowship with God. Our life is hid with Christ in God. In Jesus who came as the shadow of the Almighty we are privileged to dwell, now and forever, in the secret place with its eternal safety. William O. Cushing's chorus rings out to each of us:

> *Under His wings, under His wings,*
> *Who from His love can sever?*
> *Under His wings my soul shall abide,*
> *Safely abide for ever.*

The Handkerchief of the Lord

"He maketh the grass to grow." Psalm 147:8.

The splendor of grass is beautifully set forth in the lines from "Songs of Myself" from *Leaves of Grass* by Walt Whitman, who died in 1892:

A child said What is the grass? *fetching it to me with full hands, . . .*
. . . I guess it is the handkerchief of the Lord,
A scented gift and remembrance designedly dropt,
Bearing the owner's name someway in the corners,
      that we may see and remark, and say Whose?

As we clothe our children with attractive and beneficial garments, so, said Jesus, God clothes the fields with lovely grass of various kinds. The psalmist told us that "God causeth the grass to grow for the cattle" (104:14). How could they, or we, although human, exist without it? Where would our milk, butter, cheese, and wool come from if it were not for the grass? Grass is not only for our provision but for our pleasure, for there is nothing more pleasing to the eye than the beautiful green covering the earth like a carpet.

If God so clothes the earth with grass, surely he will not fail to take care of us, as Jesus clearly taught in his illustration of the grass of the field. The psalmist has a further reference to grass: "God maketh the grass to grow upon mountains" (147:8), meaning in the least likely and the most difficult places. The word *maketh* reminds us that the power of God is under the root of the grass, causing it to grow even in shallow soil that is never nurtured. If life for us is not in some sheltered valley but exposed in a most difficult sphere, is it not encouraging to know that God can enable us to grow in grace and in the knowledge of him in the least likely place? Having charmed us with the color of grass, he is able to make us pleasing in his sight—and in the sight of others.

A Most Profitable Exercise

"It is a good thing to give thanks unto the Lord."
Psalm 92:1.

The phrase arresting our attention is this advice from the Hebrew saint, "It is a good thing." Profit in praise was a high expression of approval and took the psalmist back to the first divine approval recorded in the Bible—"God saw the light, that it was good." At creation each divine feat found adequate expression in the repeated word *good*. This highest word of approval God had for his own works is used here by the psalmist. Praise to God is "a good thing" because it is in harmony with the original design of creation. Although sin brought discord into the world, God made all things harmonious, and the response of an unfallen world was in song—"The morning stars sang together, and all the sons of God shouted for joy" (Job 38:7). Is it not a good thing to emulate the divine ideal of things and add to the world's harmonies and not to its discords?

Good to give. Life is enriched in its noblest aspects by giving rather than by constant receiving. It is a good thing when we learn to give.

Good to give thanks. What grander or better virtue is there than appreciating the source of goodness, its value, and the acknowledgment of our own indebtedness. Those who never give thanks miss one of the essential attributes of human nature, namely, gratitude.

Good to give thanks unto the Lord. He is a constant and bountiful giver, and in our thanks to him we give something back, particularly if we offer the sacrifice of praise. Giving thanks is therefore a good thing because it imparts joy to the heart of the Lord himself. No song in God's world that is pure and unselfish fails to reach his ear. As he yearns for our *Thank you!* it must ever be a good thing to rejoice the heart of him from whom all blessings flow. We are urged "to sing praise unto Thy name" (Ps. 92:1). It is a good thing when gratitude melts into song and we find ourselves singing unto the Lord who ever hears "the robins sing on earth."

Thy Kind but Searching Glance

"Examine me . . . prove me . . . try me." *Psalm 26:2.*

Examinations as a rule are not pleasant experiences. Young people dread them at school. Searchings of our persons and possessions for security reasons at airports are inconvenient but not to be feared if we have nothing to hide. David asked God, a very keen and thorough examiner, to search his life for any hidden sin or weakness. He wanted everything known to God to be made known to himself. David sought heaven's vindication of his character. Desiring no wicked way to remain within his heart, the psalmist used three words: *examine, prove, try.* The Amplified Bible presents the passage, "Examine me, O Lord, and try me; Test my heart and my mind."

These are forcible words. *Examine* implies a fiery process, a burning up of all dross, leaving behind only that which can pass through the fire. *Try, prove,* and *test* are likewise expressive; the Hebrew words mean a melting by fire. Thus David prayed for a searching by fire—a symbol of the Holy Spirit—that should burn up all that was contrary to the will of God.

Failure in school examinations often creates a determination never to fail again and is therefore profitable. David felt that if God examined him thoroughly, sin and ignorance would be revealed, and when they were removed, his life would be more fit for God to use. It is encouraging to know that the divine searcher is our loving heavenly Father whose kind but searching glance scans the very wounds that shame would hide in order to heal them. Paul urged the Corinthians to *examine* themselves as to whether they were *in* the faith. It is sadly possible to work *for* the faith yet not be *in* it. Self-introspection can result in despair. It is far better to pray with David, "Search me, O Lord!" He knows how to throw light into the darkened cells until conscience feels the loathsomeness of sin. And, blessed be his name, what his search reveals, his blood can cleanse.

Taking True for False, or False for True

"Old shoes and clouted upon their feet." *Joshua 9:5.*

Tennyson, in *Idylls of the King*, described a "race of miserable men" who:

> *Do forge a lifelong trouble for ourselves,*
> *By taking true for false, or false for true.*

Joshua had to face a good deal of trouble as the result of taking the false for true in his encounter with the deceiving Gibeonites who came with the intent of misleading the wise leader of Israel and cleverly succeeded. The Book of Common Prayer has a supplication for deliverance from "blasphemous fables, and dangerous deceits." Evidently Joshua did not offer such a petition. He was beguiled by the wily Gibeonites with their tattered clothes, worn-out shoes, and moldy bread because he "did not ask counsel at the mouth of the Lord" (Josh. 9:14). Famous for his stratagem as leader of Israel's forces, yet because he acted on his own as he listened to the fabricated story of the Gibeonites, he was found wanting in keen discernment.

Hypocrites fall into two classes. Some profess to be better than they are, and these form a large group. Others profess to be worse than they are or poorer than they are. The Gibeonites were of this latter class. They acted as if they were very poor, not only to gain sympathy, but to save their necks from death. These deceivers likely had large wardrobes, wealthy homes, and plenty of good food.

One lesson we can learn from them is never to act what we are not. May we be saved from all deceitfulness in righteousness. A sign of the last times is the way multitudes will believe a lie, even as, alas, Joshua did. Satan is the archdeceiver who beguiled Eve through his subtlety and who, although the fiend of darkness, can transform himself into an angel of light. Our protection against satanic wiles is the constant effort to seek counsel of the Lord, praying that spiritual intuition may be ours to detect immediately that which is not of the Lord.

To Measure Life Learn Thou Betimes

"He that spake with me had for a measure a golden reed to measure the city." *Revelation 21:15*, RV.

Measures meet us at every turn of the avenue. One wonders if we could exist without measure for many phases of life. The house you live in represents precise measuring. The clothes you wear were made by measure. The food you eat comes in measured form. The light and gas you use come to you through the *meter*, a word meaning "that which measures." The roads you walk on required a good deal of measuring. The laws of the land charges as unlawful the tampering with recognized measurements. All standards of measurement must be maintained accurately and beyond all suspicion.

The Lord is the one with the measuring rod who tests your life and mine to see if it conforms to his standard measurement. The Bible is God's law from heaven for our life on earth and presents Jesus as one infallible standard. Paul prayed for grace to measure up to the stature of the perfect man in Jesus, who had a good deal to say about measures and measuring.

As cities and towns are subjected to endless measurements in their creation, so the Holy City, the heavenly Jerusalem, indicates perfect planning. Precise measuring is found in the details: "The city lieth foursquare" and was measured out by one with his "golden reed" (Rev. 21:15, 16). (A reed from the hedge was the first measure people used.)

One apparent lesson we learn from all this is that God wills us to order our lives systematically, conforming to his standards. Long ago people measured with their thumbs—an inch being the distance between the knuckle and the first joint. This became known as the "rule of thumb" but was not very exact. God, who measures our days, would not have us plan life in any such haphazard way but by his certain and infallible standard. To bring us up to the divine measurement, we have the power of the Holy Spirit who is given to us without measure.

Good Order Is the Foundation of All Good Things

"Make the men sit down by fifties in a company."
Luke 9:14.

Edmund Burke's principle of "good order" is certainly illustrated in the action of Jesus when he commanded the five thousand to sit down by fifties in a company. Had they rushed upon him, crowding around him in a confused, feverish fashion, he would not have been able to dispense the good things he had to satisfy their hunger. So we read, "And they do so." What a sight! A multitude sitting down in groups of fifty, looking up into the face of the one who was the object of all their hope, who alone knew how to command a well-nigh unmanageable crowd.

Phillips Brooks once preached a powerful sermon on the phrase, "Make the men sit down." He indicated that at that moment all the excitement subsided; instead of the people pushing toward and surging around Jesus, they were made to sit down in readiness to receive from him what he was prepared to give. Brooks went on to show that this action is illustrative of two stages in Christian experience: First, when people rush hurriedly after good things, their religious life is full of excitement and even worry. Second, when they sit down, their restlessness and confusion give way to calm patience and watchful waiting—an essential and important part of spiritual experience.

Christ was ever the master of assemblies and knew how to act in an emergency. He never lost command to make people sit down, and as his followers we should never lose our equanimity in the presence of tumultuous trials and cares. Like Mary, we should always be found sitting at his feet, ready to be fed by him. When we fulfill the Master's commands, we discover that there is always more than enough to satisfy our hunger for the bread he alone can give.

He Sat Him Down in a Lonely Place

"Ye shall . . . leave me alone." *John 16:32.*

In "The Poet's Song" Tennyson depicts the poet sitting down in a lonely place and chanting a melody loud and sweet:

That made the wild-swan pause in her cloud,
And the lark drop down at his feet.

Jesus, who inspired some of the greatest lines in poetry, knew what it was to sit down often in a lonely place, but although alone, there was ever a sweet melody in his heart, for he could say, "The Father hath not left me alone" (John 8:29).

There is a twofold aspect of the loneliness Jesus predicted we would suffer. First, he was alone as far as his disciples were concerned. In spite of their ecstatic utterances that they would never be offended by what he said or did and would never forsake him no matter who else did, the great purposes of his life and mission were largely hidden from them because they were not able to comprehend them. Certainly, Jesus was not alone in the sense of being without the love, sympathy, and confidence of his disciples. They believed in him, trusted him, and tried to enter into a living sympathy with his sorrows. What they failed to share with Jesus was the divine purpose of his marvelous self-denial even unto death and the offering up of himself as the sole atonement of the world's sins.

Second, Jesus was alone as far as the world was concerned, for it would not have him to reign over it. The world was ever hostile to his claims and rejected his love and grace. Because of our allegiance to him, we may find ourselves sharing his loneliness, but although lonely, we are not alone. Ours is the assurance that Jesus had throughout his sojourn in a lonely place. His Father was his abiding companion and is likewise our confidence. Hug the promise to your heart, lonely witness, "The Father hath not left me alone."

The Sermon a Penny Preached

"Bring me a penny, that I may see it." *Mark 12:15.*

When we want to emphasize the influence money wields, or "answereth to all things" as Solomon put it, we say, *Money talks*. The small penny in the hand of Jesus certainly did talk although its witness was silent until Jesus gave it a voice in his question. Pointing to Caesar's profile on the Roman coin, Jesus asked, "Whose is this image and superscription?" (Matt. 22:20). Greater in value than our modern penny, the *denarius* Jesus asked for was the principal Roman coin, just as the *drachma*, or "piece of silver" the woman lost, was the principal Greek coin of the day. The miniature piece of silver Jesus asked for bore the name and likeness of the emperor, indicating that he had made it his own and that bearing his superscription he had claim upon it. Distributed among his subjects, such money represented his power and his right to rule.

In a most effective way Jesus told the message of the penny. In reply to his question about the image on it, the people said, "Caesar's." He said, "Render to Caesar the things that are Caesar's; and to God the things that are God's" (Mark 12:17). No wonder the people marveled at the sermon on obligations, heavenward and earthward, that he made the penny preach. The emperor's image was stamped upon silver that had been purified and made ready for use. The question each heart must ask is, Am I as purified silver, fit for the Master's service, and therefore qualified to bear his stamp upon my heart and life?

All who are redeemed by the blood of Jesus are his coinage, and he seeks to use them as his current coin in the world wherever they go. Bearing his image, they are recognized as his property. By their spirit and conduct and by the words they speak and deeds they do, they glorify God as their owner and fulfill in the world all that is legally expected of them, no matter who their governing caesar may be.

If You Were Suddenly to See Me, Could You Recognize Me?

"There standeth one among you, whom ye know not."
John 1:26.

Ovid, the Latin philosopher, affirmed of himself, "Nor, if you were suddenly to see me, could you recognize me." Jesus appeared suddenly to many in the days of his flesh, but they failed to recognize him as the Messiah. When the priests and Levites asked, *"Who* art thou?" he readily confessed, "I am the Christ." But those of his own nationality received him not. That man of vision who heralded Jesus' coming, John the Baptist, had no hesitation in proclaiming that Jesus was the Son of God. Joseph and Mary did not understand why he was in the world, and he rebuked them by affirming, "Wist ye not that I must be about my Father's business?"

One of the mysteries of the ages is the stupidity of human beings, who, although surrounded by natural objects, took thousands of years to discover what God had put close by their side for use. Sorrowfully the Savior of the world lamented, "There standeth one among you"—the supreme fact of life—"whom ye know not"—the supreme folly of life, for to know him is eternal life.

How privileged we are to have God's beloved Son standing among us! His presence is an inspiration, and his grace is sufficient for every need. The tragedy, however, is that so many around us do not know that he is standing at the door waiting for recognition and admission to their hearts as their Savior. It has been said that "the scales of neglect cover the eyes and darken the soul." This statement is true of those who, neglecting the great salvation, fail to see in the Savior the effulgence of the Father's glory and the express image of his person. How blessed you are if with Paul you can say, "I know whom [not what] I have believed (2 Tim. 1:12), and have the assurance that life everlasting is yours through knowing him!

282

As Straight As a Die

"The Lord said unto me, Amos, what seest thou? And
I said, A plumbline." *Amos 7:8.*

In one of his books Arnold Bennett described Half Bursley as having
a grudge against Ralph "because he's as straight as a die, and always
knows what he wants, and is always clever enough to get . . . . People
don't like it—naturally." Those who strive to see the crooked made
straight are not popular in a crooked world. The purpose of the plumbline the Lord showed Amos was to see that a wall went up perfectly
straight. While the modern spirit level is now widely used, bricklayers
still place the plumbline against the wall as it is being built to test
whether it is perfectly perpendicular.

In a way, Israel had been built up as a nation with a plumbline, and
everything being right, God approved of his people. But they fell into
the crooked ways of idolatry, and Amos was raised up to warn King
Jeroboam, the high priest, and the nation of their departure from the
straight road. Tested by the divine plumbline, the people were upright
no longer. God's wall, so gloriously built, was no longer perpendicular,
and grieved with the departure from his ways, he declared that he
would take it down to the foundation.

As with nations of antiquity, so with ourselves. God is ever using
his perfect plumbline, namely, the grand old Book by which lives are
tried, to see if the building of life and character is according to his plan.
The Bible is our law from heaven for life on this earth, and we are wise
if we always test our motives and desires by this infallible plumbline
which God is ever placing alongside our conduct to see whether it is
according to his rule. If there are bulging defects, then we are not to be
discouraged, for the one with the plumbline in his hand is able to make
crooked things straight.

Give Me the Splendid Silent Sun

"For the Lord God is a sun." *Psalm 84:11.*

"Give me the splendid silent sun with all his beams full-dazzling." This phrase of Walt Whitman's can be used of our Lord. Among the many types or symbols the Lord uses of himself, this one—a sun—is the most compelling. This earth cannot exist without the sun, bright and shining in the heavens, and what the sun is to the world, the Lord is to its inhabitants. In some mysterious way the world is kept in place by the attraction of the sun which exerts a mighty power as the center of earth's system. Thus the earth goes around its orbit and never wanders from its path. As the sun keeps the earth in place, so the Lord, by his attractive power, keeps us in the orbit of his will.

Among the benefits of the sun is *light*. How dull the day is when the sunbeams are not dazzling! There is beauty all around when the sun shines. As the light and heat of the sun are everything to the fields and gardens, so the Lord, as a sun, is the light of the world, banishing its spiritual darkness. When he appears as the sun of righteousness with healing in his wings, the gloom of earth will disappear.

But the sun not only provides us with light; it is also the source of *life*. Invalids have been restored to health by basking in the sun. Plants in the garden, deadlike through the winter, live again as the kindly sun shines on them when summer approaches. Similarly, the Lord as a sun is the source of life, and we live anew when we turn our hearts and faces toward him in penitence and faith. If the Lord God is the sun in the universe of your heart, then may grace be yours to walk in his light and love.

The Murmuring of Innumerable Bees

"They compassed me about like bees." *Psalm 118:12.*

"Sweet is every sound" and "every soul is sweet," said Tennyson, and among these sweet sounds the poet included "the murmuring of innumerable bees." To those who are afraid of bees, their buzzing is not a very sweet sound. In a well-flowered garden bees often surround one, but as a rule they only compass about those who threaten to attack their hives and rob them of the little treasure they have been accumulating for many busy months to sustain their lives during the hard winter. Bees seem to know their enemies as well as their friends and usually do not sting unless there is a cause.

Are there some ways in which we can imitate the busy bee? I think so. We cannot blame bees in the least for compassing about those who set out to rob them of their possessions. Do not tricksters who live by plundering the hard earnings of others deserve to be stung? The skill bees exhibit in building is superb. The hive, or home, is unique in intricacy, ingenuity, and utility. Beauty and order are conspicuous—a less for us to give of our very best, not only in what our hands find to do, but in our service for God. Even clever bees are not perfect, for there are drones among them, just as there are among humans.

Are you among the *busy* bees? In a hive nurse-bees move about softly, caring for the sick and the newborn. In God's family there is need and room for more nurse-bees. Conspicuous among bees' activities is the way they store up food for the future. Cells are filled with honey and then sealed until winter comes and there is urgent need of food. Too often we live only for the present, heedless of preparing for coming days. What folly is ours when we neglect to provide, not only for our future here, but for eternity beyond this vale of tears. Some bees go out to work; some stay at home caring for others, but all share alike. "As his part is that goeth down to the battle, so shall his part be that tarrieth by the stuff: they shall part alike" (1 Sam. 30:24).

Thy Stained Name—from All Stains Free

"Can any good thing come out of Nazareth?" *John 1:46.*

The above question was asked by Nathanael, an inhabitant of a neighboring village who evidently looked upon Nazareth with something of local jealousy and scorn. The form of his question also suggests an ill repute in reference to those who lived there. At the outset let it be made clear that to be called a *Nazarene* was altogether different from being known as a *Nazarite*, a Hebrew under the vow of abstinence. Jesus was a true Nazarite and also a Nazarene—a term equivalent to shame and contempt. He was brought up in Nazareth and was known as "Jesus the Nazarene."

Sneeringly, Nathanael asked, "Can any good thing come out of such a despicable town?" Jesus came out of it, and he was "holy, harmless, undefiled, and separate from sinners." Over his mangled form on the cross they wrote, "Jesus of Nazareth." And as a true Nazarene, he stooped to the lowest depths of ignominy on our behalf. For our salvation he was willing to endure hatred and contempt. Nazareth, however, lost its stain through Christ's contact with the place. He is the cruse of salt flavoring every bitter spring of life. To quote from an unknown writer:

> Though a name of evil holding
>   There was brought the Undefiled.
> Like a dove, a serpent folding,
>   There grew up the Hold Child.
> Nazareth! Cross-like we see
>   Thy stained name, from all stains free.

Contempt, Farewell! And Maiden Pride, Adieu!

"Take heed, that you despise not one of the little ones."
Matthew 18:10.

The Master's warning against the danger of contempt was uttered when the disciples were wrangling for the foremost place in his kingdom. Their pride prevented them from taking a lowly place. The words in the title above, from Shakespeare's *Much Ado About Nothing*, continue: "No glory lives behind the back of such" contempt and pride. The only person fit for the kingdom of heaven is the humblest. The disciples were not childlike, and they were in peril of the contempt accompanying pride. In the New Testament the word *despise* which Jesus used is only once found in a neutral sense and once in a commendable sense. In every other reference it is cast in reproach. The favorable and only exception is that describing Jesus as "despising the shame" (Heb. 12:2). "Take heed that ye *despise* not" (Matt. 18:10).

Scripture is against cherishing contempt toward anything or anybody. Flourishing in an atmosphere of pride, the spirit of contempt is always impoverishing to those who possess it. The word *despise* itself means to "think down upon" or "look down on one." When a person "thinks down upon" others, he or she thinks of them from the exalted position created in his or her own imagination.

Jesus told his disciples not to think down upon the little ones before him but to be clothed with humility. How much more forcible is the warning of Jesus when applied to those who, in the spirit of pride, belittle others! Contempt toward those nobler than they are earns divine condemnation. In fact, said Jesus, they are not godlike since they despise what the Father in heaven values greatly. To the extent that we despise anyone who is humble, we are unlike the Father. Further, we are unlike the angels who guard the little ones if we despise them. Courtiers of heaven, the angels are ever near to those who are childlike in heart and action. May ours be the spirit of the Master himself who was ever meek and lowly in heart.

PART IV

Silence and Remembrance

At last, in our odyssey, we come to the final quarter of our circular journey. In October the artist's fingers itch to capture with brush and paint the loveliest colors nature has spilled over woodlands and hills with an enchanting range of shadows. Some years ago the Chicago *Tribune* ran a series of attractive vignettes on the twelve months of the year, each illustrated by drawings, events, and proverbs. For October the paper had a cartoon entitled "I am the month of splendor and enchantment." Can we say that our lives are adorned with the beauty of the Lord?

Like the dog with a bad name, November finds it hard to escape from its gloomy, unhappy tradition—an unfortunate reputation for being a month of chilly winds, dark days, gloom and fog, and gray skies. Yet, while there is less activity in the woodlands because creatures have begun their winter sleep, November often presents an attractive face and can change from smiling severity to caressing gentleness. In November we celebrate Veterans Day, remembering those who died in a useless war. O God! Why do men make wars?

At last we complete the circle, finding ourselves in December. Extremes meet during this month, for it is the deathbed of another life to come. This month reminds us that the Lord of the years and the potentate of time was born that we might not die or live eternally in the morgue of sin. As we leave this final month in which decay is all around, let us ever treasure the fact that God gave us memory that we might have roses in December.

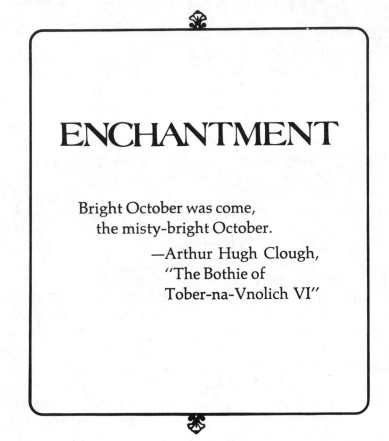

ENCHANTMENT

Bright October was come,
   the misty-bright October.

> —Arthur Hugh Clough,
> "The Bothie of
> Tober-na-Vnolich VI"

The Survival of Unfittest

"Jonathan hath yet a son, who is lame on his feet."
2 Samuel 9:3.

This chapter revolving around David and Mephibosheth is rich in the virtues of loyalty, kindness, and love. The phrase used by the famed biologist Herbert Spencer, "The survival of the fittest," may appear accurate as we observe the struggle for existence. But often God plans that the unfittest shall survive, that when the strongest, bravest, and chiefest pass away, no one remains alive but a Mephibosheth. Saul and Jonathan had been slain in battle, the latter leaving behind a son who was but five years old.

Long years passed, and David, who reigned undisputed over Israel, remembered the covenant he had made with Jonathan. How could he forget that trysting in the fields! So, inquiring about Saul's family, he asked, "Is there yet any that is left in the house of Saul?" and he discovered the crippled son of his dear friend Jonathan. But David took no notice of Mephibosheth's legs and feet. Generously he received this unfit, remaining member of Saul's family and heaped upon him loving-kindness for his father's sake. Years before, when they were close friends, David pledged that he would care for Jonathan's family if he were slain. True to his vow David blessed Mephibosheth, giving him all that had been his father's.

Throughout 2 Samuel 9 we have the refrain, "For Jonathan's sake," and this kindness for another's sake is a parable of the love of God who blesses and enriches us for the sake of his only begotten Son. Sinners may be spiritually lame, poor, and forgotten, but a greater than David, through his grace, restores a lost inheritance and takes the lost and helpless into a rich fellowship with himself. David was not kind to Mephibosheth because of his severe lameness, but for the sake of Jonathan his father. It is thus that God deals with those crippled by sin. Through matchless grace he restores them for the sake of his Son. It is for his sake that God receives and blesses.

Sole Daughter of My House and Heart

"He had one only daughter, about twelve years of age."
Luke 8:42.

When father and mother knelt beside the bed in the Jewish quarter of Capernaum, they hoped against hope that their only child would be spared. An unnoticed feature of the raising of Jairus' daughter is that she was an *only* daughter, possibly like "Ada, sole daughter of my house and heart," about whom Lord Byron wrote in "Childe Harold." How often *one* thing, *one* person, stands at the center of a Gospel scene or story. The shepherd lost *one* sheep; the woman lost *one* coin; the widow of Nain had but *one* son; and in the grief-stricken home of Jairus was *one* daughter. While it is thrilling to know that around the throne of God in heaven *thousands* of children stand, we magnify him for his personal love and grace. "The Son of God Who loved *me*" (Gal. 2:20). An unknown poet wrote:

> *Thou art as much His care, as if beside*
> *Nor man nor angel lived in heaven or earth.*

When his precious solitary child was at the point of death, at the break of day Jairus sought Jesus and in all humility implored him to spare his daughter. The day before the disciples cried "Master" as shipwreck faced them; *fear for themselves* made them call for help. But when Jairus cried "Master," *love for his only child* forced his plea.

What different impulses lead us to kneel before the compassionate Jesus for aid! Reaching the house of death, Jesus emptied it of those who had rudely invaded it, especially the professional mourners who were paid to weep in death chambers. As the Lord of life, he raised the young maid from the dead. Having perfect sincerity, Jesus hates all shams.

An aspect of the miracle is the unfailing thoughtfulness of Jesus seen in his command that the resurrected child should be given food. Jairus and his wife dearly loved their daughter, but in the joy of that hour of restored life they had not noticed that she was hungry. All spiritual awakening is the work of the Spirit, but because the young are the most easily awakened, let us bring them to Jesus before the grave-clothes bind them.

The Sword and the Trowel

"Everyone with one of his hands wrought in his work, and
with the other hand held a weapon." *Nehemiah 4:17.*

Nehemiah, cupbearer to the king of Persia, is conspicuous as one of the
godliest and bravest characters in Scripture. The good hand of the Lord
was upon him in his honorable position in the palace; he had an easy
life and every comfort. But his noble soul was burdened to see Jerusalem
in ruins and he surrendered his lucrative sphere to face hardships and
peril repairing the walls of the city. A greater than Nehemiah was rich
but became poor; he suffered much and died that he might restore sin-
ruined humanity.

Nehemiah 4 records the trials and difficulties confronting Nehemiah
in his patriotic task. Enemies surrounded him, but slowly and surely
the great work was accomplished in the face of much opposition. No true
work that is worth the doing is done easily. But while a most practical
man, conspicuous for his deeds, Nehemiah was preeminently a man of
prayer. Behind the hands holding the sword and the trowel was the
beating heart of prayer, which never hinders the highest service.
Nehemiah's men were both soldiers and builders. Toiling with their
trowels, they held their swords always ready for battle. As they labored,
their ears were alert, and at the sound of the trumpet they would muster.
Actually their work of building the shattered walls was a warfare in
disguise.

What a truth is enshrined in this record for your heart and mine! We
are builders, and the wall is rising. Underneath is a sure foundation,
but as we build, we have to battle, taking to ourselves the whole armor
of God. The trowel of service must be accompanied by the sword of the
Spirit, by which we are able to fight the good fight of faith with all our
might and, in fellowship with Jesus, assist in the building of his church.

293

If You Have Great Talents, Industry Will Improve Them

"Lord, thou deliverest unto me five talents, behold, I have gained beside them five talents more." *Matthew 25:20.*

Sir Joshua Reynolds, the famous artist, said in a lecture to the students of the Royal Academy, "If you have great talents, industry will prove them: but if you have but moderate abilities, industry will supply their deficiency." In our Lord's parable of the talents the man with five talents certainly worked hard and doubled their worth. The man with only one talent was of moderate ability yet failed through lack of industry to multiply what he had. One evident lesson of this parable then is, *Use it or lose it.*

The parables of the ten virgins and the ten talents, if not spoken by Jesus at the same time, were likely intentionally placed by Matthew because of the light one throws on the other. The story of the virgins is a parable of *watching*, while that of the talents is a parable of *working*. As watchers Christians are meant to *work*, and as workers they must *watch*. From an unknown source we learn: "The former parable centres in the *heart-supplies*, while the latter story moved in the sphere of *outward service*, indicating that, in the Christian life, the heart must always come before the hand."

The five virgins failed because they were oversanguine and easy; the one-talent man failed because he was overcareful and afraid. A further lesson to be learned from the talents is that our gifts are proportioned to our power of using them. If we are faithful in the least and over a few things, the Lord will make us rulers over many things. It is not enough to have a gift or gifts. They must be used, for God is disappointed when someone not only misuses a talent, but does nothing with it. Shakespeare wrote in *Measure for Measure*:

Heaven doth with us as we with torches do;
Not light them for themselves; for if our virtues
Did not go forth of us, 'twere all alike
As if we had them not.

Where Jesus Is, 'Tis Heaven There

"Lord, it is good for us to be here." Matthew 17:4.

When Luke gave his report of the transformation, he said that Peter was dazed and dazzled by the outflashing of our Lord's inherent glory and by the appearance of the glorified saints, Moses and Elijah. "Not knowing what he said," Peter voiced, not only his delight at being in such august company, but also his desire to build three tabernacles for the three distinguished ones and stay forever on the mount. Peter erred in retaining the three in association—Moses, the lawgiver; Elijah, the prophet-reformer; Jesus, the promised Messiah. Jesus is not to be looked upon as one among others. When the Master is present, servants must go. So when Peter opened his eyes, he saw "Jesus only" and in so many ways confessed, in the words of Charles Wesley, "Thou, O Christ, art all I want!"

It is, of course, spiritually beneficial to be in the presence of Jesus, living and walking in fellowship with him; and it is good to be numbered with God's people, witnessing with them in a world of sin. But there are other significant applications that can be made concerning this narrative. Peter expressed pleasure when he said, "It is good to be here." When we come to the trials and burdens of life or to a bed of affliction, can we say, "Lord, it is good to be here"? Do we honor him by our loving submission and patient suffering? In our daily task, no matter what our occupation as long as it is legitimate, do we say, "Lord, it is good to be here, for I have opportunities of manifesting forbearance and testifying to thy matchless grace and power"?

If we are truly the Lord's, it is always good to be anywhere, to do anything, as long as he is being glorified by our witness. If our chief aim is to honor him, then no matter where we are, our hearts will say, "Lord, it is good to be here!" Once we reach heaven, from which Moses and Elijah traveled down to the mount, and find ourselves in their company and among the redeemed of all ages and, above all, with our glorified Savior, then with perfect delight we will say, "Lord, it is good to be *here!*"

295

Solitude Is the Mother Country of the Strong

"Jesus went into the Mount of Olives." John 8:1.

This mount holds a unique place in the awe and affection of those who love and follow Jesus, for it was the scene of his periodical solitude, a habitual haunt of his when he detached himself from the crowds to be alone with God. When day was over, everyone went home, but Jesus, with no home of his own, went to the Mount of Olives to be alone and pray. With the daily pressure of preaching, teaching, and miracle-working, at times Jesus "had not leisure so much as to eat" (Mark 6:31), and his season of solitude preserved the poise and power in his life. Even Jesus could not live continually in the limelight.

Poets have ever praised the virtue of solitude. Edward FitzGerald could say, "The thoughtful soul to solitude retires." John Milton wrote in *Comus:*

> *. . . And Wisdom's self*
> *Oft seeks to sweet retired solitude,*
> *Where with her best nurse Contemplation*
> *She plumes her feathers, and lets grow her wings,*
> *That in the various bustle of resort*
> *Were all too ruffled, and sometimes impair'd.*

Milton also reminded us that "solitude sometimes is best society." Shelley confessed, "I love tranquil solitude"; and Wordsworth wrote in "A Poet's Epitaph," "Impulses of deeper birth, have come to him in solitude." He also described "the self-sufficing power of solitude."

We sing that "faith has still its Olivet and love its Galilee." Galilee shared with Olivet the honor of being a habitual resort of Jesus. Has your faith an Olivet and a Galilee? Have you learned that seasons of solitude are the sanity and sanctity of your life and living, that periods of retirement to be alone with God and his word are an imperative necessity? If so, at all cost keep these sacred trysts with him on *your* mount, no matter where it is.

I Loathe Myself When God I See

"Though I be nothing." *2 Corinthians 12:11.*

Self-depreciation is not attractive to those of the world. Instead of singing, "O to be nothing, nothing," they repeat the refrain, "O to be something, something." The philosophy of humanism exalts individuals by telling them that they are all-sufficient in themselves to achieve what they desire. The humanist despises the virtue of self-abnegation and rejects the Pauline doctrine that no good thing dwells in the flesh. Carlyle could write of "the golden-calf of Self-love—the idol of all lovers of self-worship."

Without doubt the greatest figure in New Testament history after Jesus is Paul, who never thought too highly of himself. He wrote, "Though I be nothing" (2 Cor. 12:11); "the least of all saints" (Eph. 3:8); "the chief of sinners" (1 Tim. 1:15); "in me dwelleth no good thing" (Rom. 7:18). The apostle was blissfully content in exalting the Master he dearly loved and sacrificially served. The more he knew and saw of himself, the more humbled in dust before a thrice-holy God he became. The person outside of Christ will and *must* be something, but the lower the Christian falls before God, the happier and holier will be the outcome. The Christian is willing to be nothing that Christ may be everything, for apart from Christ the Christian is less than nothing.

All we are in grace is *by* Christ; all we have is *from* Christ; all we shall be is *through* Christ. We are empty, but he fills us, we are lost and ruined by the Fall, but he saves us; we are naked, but he clothes us; we are helpless, but he strengthens and sustains us. May we be delivered from fancying we deserve more than we receive, either from God or from others. Let us sing with E. E. Hewitt:

Lower and lower; yet higher we rise,
Lifted in Jesus, led on to the skies;
Humbly we follow the way of the Cross,
Then, crowns of glory, and gains for all loss.

In His Good Time

"I called him, but he gave me no answer."
Song of Solomon 5:6.

Shakespeare wrote in *I Henry VI* that "delays have dangerous ends," but this is not so with divine delays, which are ever beneficial since they develop trust and patience in the soul that waits for heaven's response. God's delays in prayer must not be mistaken for denials. Though he tarries, we must wait his good time, for he will surely come to our aid. There are times when needs are pressing and help is urgent but our prayers seem to rebound in our ears as from a brazen sky. God is not deaf or indifferent to our cry, but often when he gives great faith, he tests it by long delays. We may have felt like Jeremiah who said of the God who hears and answers in his good time, "Thou covereth thyself with a cloud, that our prayer should not pass through" (Lam. 3:44).

But all prayers, inspired by the Spirit and offered by sincere hearts, *always* get through and, although not answered immediately, are not unheard. As Charles H. Spurgeon said:

> God keeps a file for our prayers—they are not blown
> away by the wind, they are treasured up in the King's
> archives. This is a registry in the Court of Heaven wherein
> every prayer is recorded. Tried believer, thy Lord hath
> a tear-bottle in which the costly drops of sacred grief are
> put away, and a book in which thy holy groanings are
> numbered. By-and-by, thy suit shall prevail . . . . God's
> long-dated bills will be punctually honoured; we must
> not suffer Satan to shake our confidence in the god of truth
> by pointing to our unanswered prayers.

Fellow believer, are your prayers for the salvation of dear ones unanswered yet? Then do not mistake delay for denial. God is the sovereign Lord who gives according to his own good pleasure. If he is exercising your patience by not opening his gate at once, remember that he can do as he wills with his own. Rest assured, he will answer "in his good time."

Memory, the Bosom-spring of Joy

"This I recall to my mind, therefore have I hope."
Lamentations 3:21.

A Cockney boy when asked, "What is memory?" quickly replied, "The fing yer fogets wiv." Shakespeare's Lady Macbeth says that memory is "the warder of the brain." Memory is not only "the bosom-spring of joy," as Coleridge called it; it is likewise the bosom-spring of eternal anguish, for the rich man in hell found that memory would be part of the flame tormenting him. "Son, remember . . . thou art tormented" (Luke 16:25). Tennyson said that the truth the poet sings is, "That a sorrow's crown of sorrow is remembering happier things."

In his third lamentation Jeremiah recalled that the Lord's mercy and compassion had not failed him through all past affliction and misery, and this stimulated his hope and trust in his compassionate Lord. Memory can become the bondslave of despondency if the mind feeds on the dark foreboding of past sin. But although Jeremiah called to remembrance the cup of mingled gall and wormwood of former days, he transformed the cup into comfort. "Therefore have I hope" (Lam. 3:21). Like a two-edged sword, the prophet's memory first killed his pride and then slew his despair. An unknown author wrote:

> As a general principle, if we would exercise our memories more wisely, we might, in our very darkest distress, strike a match which would instantaneously kindle the lamp of comfort. Memory need not wear a crown of iron, she may encircle her brow with a fillet of gold, all spangled with stars.

The seventeenth-century poet Henry Vaughan wrote:

> *They are all gone into the world of light,*
> *And I alone sit lingering here;*
> *Their very memory is fair and bright,*
> *And my sad thoughts doth clear.*

Great Things Are Done When Men and Mountains Meet

"Get thee up into the high mountain." *Isaiah 40:9.*

The history of Bible mountains confirms these lines of William Blake:

Great things are done when men and mountains meet;
This is not done by jostling in the street.

In the introduction to his book *Peaks and Glaciers* E. H. Blakeney remarked "In all times and among all people the mystery and majesty of the hills have, it may be unconsciously, exercised some benignant influence; there is something in their preternatural calm, their august purity, and their solitude that, while humbling the earth-bound spirit, at the same time lifts it nearer Heaven whence it came." The Vulgate version of Psalm 84:5 reads, "Blessed is the man who, nerved by Thee, hath set his heart on ascents."

Since there is a certain security of elevation about divine purity and goodness, Isaiah called upon Zion to get up into the high mountain. "Thy righteousness is like the great mountains" (Ps. 36:6). Ancient Greeks regarded the hills as the home of the gods. The native name for the crests around Mt. Everest was *Diva Dlunga*—God's seat. We can understand, then, how saints of old lifted up their eyes unto the hills to learn their mystic secret. The higher one climbs some hills, the more one is thrilled with the widening prospect.

Is this not so in spiritual experience? The higher we climb, the clearer view we have of the glory and beauty of him who called the mountains into being. The peaks of many Bible mountains were the stepping stones of deity upon which God and men met. John Ruskin, a fervent lover of hill-climbing, said, "My most intense happinesses have been amongst the mountains." As Paul neared his end, death seemed like gaining the summit of a mountain from which he could view the whole of the faithfulness and love of Jesus, to whom he had committed his soul. "I know whom I have believed" (2 Tim. 1:12). May we prove the blessedness of those who set their hearts on ascents.

300

Our Sanctuary of Peace

"My people shall dwell in quiet resting places."
Isaiah 32:18.

The unregenerate do not experience peace and rest. Their hearts are like the waters of a troubled sea that cannot rest. Jonah found a resting place beneath his gourd, but it withered away, and the runaway prophet was left without shelter. Jesus himself is the quiet resting place of those redeemed by his precious blood, and in him they are safe and sheltered forever. None and nothing can destroy him who is our shelter. The Revised Version translates our text, "My people shall dwell in a peaceable habitation."

Paul called the body of the believer "the earthly house of this tabernacle" (2 Cor. 5:1), which is the soul's brief and fragile house and which Jesus chooses as his peaceable home until the earthly house perishes. The grave, the body's long and gloomy habitation, was to Job "mine house; I have made my bed in the darkness" (Job 17:13). But this is by no means a peaceable habitation. Its silence is that of death.

There is, however, a sure dwelling place for the soul and the body of the child of God, namely, the blessed and perpetual resting place which Jesus called "My Father's house." No plague can come nigh this dwelling. Within it there is room for the great multitude no one can number of the redeemed, for this peaceable habitation has many mansions. The reality of this eternal sanctuary of rest is confirmed by the affirmation of Jesus, "If it were not so, I would have told you" (John 14:2).

Having lived with the Father through the eternal past, Jesus knew all about its peace. John Bunyan described his longing for heaven thus: "Now, just as the gates were opened to let in the men, I looked in after them, and behold, the city shone like the sun. Which, when I had seen, I wished myself among them." Praise God, someday—it may be sooner than we expect—we shall hear a voice for our eternal happiness say, "Come up hither!" Then shall we be at home with the Lord.

301

Have Mercy on Us Worms of Earth

"Have mercy upon me, O God." Psalm 51:1.

Whether William Carey's epitaph had any influence on the prayer of Frederick W. Faber, "God Most High, have mercy on us worms of earth," we have no means of knowing. When brought low by a dangerous illness, the famous missionary to India was asked, "If this sickness should prove to be fatal, Dr. Carey, what passage would you select as the text for your funeral sermon?"

He replied, "Oh, I feel that such a poor sinful creature is unworthy to have anything said about him; but if a funeral sermon must be preached, let it be from the words, 'Have mercy upon me, O God.' " In the same spirit of humility Carey directed in his will that the following inscription and nothing more should be cut on his gravestone:

WILLIAM CAREY, BORN AUGUST 17th, 1761: DIED
A wretched, poor, and helpless worm
On Thy kind arms I fall.

After his death in 1834 Carey's wish was carried out. "Have mercy upon us miserable sinners" is among the prayers of the Anglican church; and mercy, the sinner's initial and fundamental need, is shown by God to the repentant in virtue of him who bore the load of sin in his own body on the tree and by his death canceled our guilt.

In the Apocrypha we find the confession, "We will fall into the hands of the Lord, and not into the hands of men: for as His majesty is, so is His mercy." Robert Browning wrote, "Mercy every way is Infinite," and this divine attribute of mercy seasons justice. Only on the footing of free grace can the holiest and most honored approach God, and those who seek to serve the Lord best are most conscious of sin within themselves. What a precious gospel it is to preach that inexhaustible mercy waits to be gracious to a world of sinners lost and ruined by the Fall. Would that the cry would rise from millions of stricken hearts today, "God be merciful to me, a sinner!"

302

Constancy Lives in Realms Above

"As I was . . . I will be." Joshua 1:5.

The truth of divine constancy runs like a golden thread through Scripture. The Lord is conspicuous as the unchanging and unchangeable companion on life's highway. "I am the Lord, I change not" (Mal. 3:6). Joshua was assured that the divine presence and protection vouchsafed to Moses would likewise be his portion as he assumed command of Israel. The courageous leader proved that God unalterably adhered to all his promises. Reiterating the promise repeated to Joshua, the writer to the Hebrews asserted that "Jesus Christ is the same yesterday, today, and forever" (Heb. 13:8). Persons may change, but Jesus never. Glory to his name!

James, writing of God as "the Father of lights" (1:17), affirmed that "in whom there is no variation or changing shadow" (Charles Williams, tr.). Because of all he is in himself, God cannot vary or change between shadow and substance. All God has ever been, he is and will be forevermore. As Jean Ingelow expressed it:

> The course of God is one. It likes not us
> To think of Him as being acquaint with Change;
> It were beneath him!

Said St. Theresa of Avila, "All things are passing! God never changeth."

Ours is the full confidence that God, having been our help in ages past, will continue to be our hope for years to come. His is an unchanging love. As we retrace the path of the past, we bless him because his goodness has never failed, and thus cheerfully we lay our hands in his for the rest of the way, believing that all he has been he will be until we enter his presence above. What a sheet anchor in the storms of life is God's unchangeableness! Earth's joys may grow dim and its glories pass away, but, as Henry F. Lyte learned, faith sings:

> Change and decay in all around I see;
> O Thou who changest not, abide with me.

Beauty, Truth, and Love in Thee Are One

"Let the beauty of the Lord be on us." *Psalm 90:17*.

Scripture has much to say about beauty as associated with God, persons, and things. But what exactly is this quality? The dictionary explains beauty as being "a combination of qualities that delights the sight or mind." We connect beauty mainly with the features and form of the body.

Absalom was renowned for his beauty, to which his luxurious hair contributed but which, alas, brought about his death. If only he had been as good as he was beautiful! Doubtless this rebellious son inherited his beauty from his father, for David is described as being of "a beautiful countenance, and goodly to look to" (1 Sam. 16:12). But, as we say, "Beauty is skin deep," and disease or accident can quickly distort a lovely face.

When the Bible speaks about "beholding the beauty of the Lord," it does not imply facial beauty. Since no one has seen God at any time, one cannot describe God's features. Commentaries explain the phrase "the beauty of the Lord" as "the delight of the Lord" or meditation on the graciousness of God. Beauty, Truth and Love in Thee are one, and we are called to worship him in "the beauty of holiness."

Keats said, "Beauty is truth, truth beauty." Certainly God loves beauty, for he created a beautiful world. John Milton spoke of beauty as "Nature's coin" and as "Nature's brag." Dr. A. J. Gossip, unique Scottish preacher of a past decade, loved to tell the story of the great explorer, Mungo Park. After journeying days and miles in the desolate wilds of China, Park quite suddenly saw at his feet a little blue flower and said gently, "God has been here!" Although God made all things bright and beautiful, his beauty he would have us adorn is an inner spiritual beauty. This is his "diadem of beauty" for his people. In Gossip's hymn to intellectual beauty are lines we can lift to a higher source:

*Spirit of Beauty, Thou canst consecrate
With thine own hues all Thou dost shine upon,
Of human thought or form.*

His Word Is His Bond

"I trust in thy word." *Psalm 119:42.*

We have different ways of describing those who say one thing and do another or those whose word is not to be relied on: "He's not a man of his word"; "He's a double-dealer, promising one thing, but doing another"; "He never says what he means"; "His deeds contradict his promises." A person can be trusted only when words and actions harmonize. "Suit the action to the word, the word to the action," said Shakespeare in Hamlet, and this is what God always does. He spoke and it was done. Emerson told us that "words and deeds are quite indifferent modes of divine energy. Words are also actions, and actions are a kind of words."

David could trust what God had said because he knew that what God had promised, he was able and would fulfill. Over and over again the psalmist had proved that God would not lie, that not one good word of his would fail, that he was not only in his words most wonderful, but most sure in all his ways.

A promise is God's bond, and he will keep it. Trusting in his word, we set our minds at rest and wait calmly and in confidence for the fulfillment of his promise. Believing that God is as good as his word, we fear no foe, dread no trial, because we know that he will be faithful in undertaking for us as he said he would. Knowing that there must always be a performance of those things the Lord tells us in his Word, we must believe a promise suited to our need, plead it, rely on it, and expect its fulfillment.

If we cannot take God's Word and depend upon it, what can we trust? Our comfort and encouragement is that divine truths have been tried by numberless saints down the ages and have been found faithful. Trusting in God's unalterable Word brought them, as it brings us, peace of mind, joy to the soul, and all that is necessary in time of need.

What Light through Yonder Window Breaks

"Bind this line of scarlet thread in the window."
Joshua 2:18.

A window was the way of escape for the two spies befriended by Rahab. After hiding them at the peril of her life, "she let them down by a cord through the window." The scarlet thread from the same window was to be a true token that, when Joshua invaded Jericho, Rahab and all her relatives would be delivered from death.

What an apt illustration this presents of an alarmed and repentant sinner, saved by grace through promise, relying on the scarlet sign because of the declared Word! Calvary is the scarlet thread in God's window assuring us of safety when his righteous judgments are abroad. John Milton wrote, "At my window bid Good-Morrow," but there can only be a "Good-Morrow" for you if the scarlet thread hangs from the window of your heart. If God does not see his Son's blood upon you and yours, he cannot pass over you.

Doubtless, the same scarlet cord that preserved the spies preserved Rahab and her family. One proviso that the spies made was that no soldier would attack Rahab's house when Jericho was under siege and no relative of hers would be taken captive and killed if he or she were under the token of the scarlet thread. We can imagine with what zest Rahab went round gathering her parents and all their household to bring them with haste to the house of safety. Her own kith and kin were saved from death purely for Rahab's sake. When Joshua finally entered Jericho, light broke through Rahab's window for all who were behind it, with its scarlet token dangling.

Thrice happy are we if all the members of our family are in the house of safety, free from condemnation because they are in Christ Jesus. Can it be that you still have a dear, unsaved loved one? Then by divine grace may you be enabled to bring them behind the shelter of Calvary's scarlet thread before it is too late.

Less Than We Deserve

"I will correct you in measure." Jeremiah 30:11.

It causes us to walk humbly before God as we constantly remember that because of his mercy we are not rewarded according to our iniquities. If we were, we would not be able to stand before him. Sin merits correction, and love sends it, but we are corrected in measure, not according to the desert of sin. Earlier in his prophecy Jeremiah prayed, "O Lord, correct me . . . not in thine anger, lest thou bring me to nothing [diminish me]" (Jer. 10:24). Toward the end of Jeremiah's prophecy the Lord said to him, "I will make a full end of all nations . . . but I will not make a full end of thee, but correct thee in measure; yet will I not leave thee wholly unpunished" (Jer. 46:28).

The discipline of God as the righteous Judge is at once retributive and reformative. David prayed, "O Lord, rebuke me not in thine anger, neither in thy hot displeasure. Have mercy upon me, O Lord!" (Ps. 6:1, 2). So great is God's mercy toward us that he does not deal with us after our sins. With his Father's heart he pities us and corrects us in measure. "Thou our God hast requited us less than our iniquities deserve" (Ezra 9:13). "It is of the Lord's mercies, that we are not consumed, because his compassions fail not" (Lam. 3:22).

As our Father he chastens us, not in full, but in measure; not in wrath, but in love; not to destroy us, but to save us. As his children we are in constant need of his correction, and it would not be right for him never to reprove us. Because God loves us, he rebukes and chastens us. An unidentified author wrote:

> *Father, if Thou must reprove*
> *For all that I have done,*
> *Not in anger, but in love,*
> *Chastise Thy wayward son:*
> *Correct with kind severity,*
> *And bring me home to Thee.*

Like—But Oh How Different!

"Who made thee to differ from another?" 1 Corinthians 4:7.

In an ethnical sense the world's multitudes are alike in that all are descendants of our first parents, Adam and Eve. We are, however, totally different in respect to nationality, color of skin, customs, habits, and religions. Out of over three billion inhabitants of this globe, no two persons can be found exactly alike. One will differ from the other, as one star differs from another in glory. True, in the case of twins of like sex, there may be very strong resemblances; yet a close study will reveal contrasts. John Wesley said that when God fashioned him he broke the mold. Well, there has not been another like this mighty revivalist who became father of the great Methodist Church!

When Paul asked the Corinthians, "Who made thee to differ from another?" he was dealing with gifts and positions in the early church and with those who were somewhat puffed up over their possessions. In respect to the source of the various gifts exercised there was no difference. None could be attained by any personal excellence; all were the free gift of God.

A wide difference is stressed, however, when it comes to one's relationship to God. In this age of grace there is no difference between Jews and Gentiles, for all are sinners and need the same Savior. Upon Israel of old, God laid the necessity of separating the clean from the unclean, putting a difference between them, and likewise between his redeemed people and surrounding nations. The call in this Christian era is to come out from the godless and to be separated unto the Lord. What a vast difference there is between those quickened by the Spirit and made alive unto God and those dead in trespasses and sins! The regret is that the line is not as distinctly drawn as it should be. Little difference is observable between some who confess to be Christ's and those making no profession.

308

Dear to God, Dearer We Cannot Be

"He that toucheth you, toucheth the apple of his eye."
Zechariah 2:8.

Zechariah, the prophet of hope, loved to dwell upon the infinite tenderness of God in dealing with his people who had been visited with sore judgments, reduced to wretched straits, and left despised. Returning to their own country after a period of captivity in an alien land, the people were like brands plucked from the burning; they were badly scorched. Tears of deep contrition were theirs, and in his love and pity God assured them of future protection and safety. He would guard them as "the apple of his eye."

There is no part of the human frame so safely protected as the apple, or pupil, of the eye. F. B. Meyer, the popular English pastor and speaker who died in 1929, reminded us, "The strong frontal bones, the brow or eyelash to intercept the dust, the lid to protect from scorching glare, the sensitive tear-glands incessantly pouring their crystal tides over its surface—what a wealth of delicate machinery for its safety and health!" We use the phrase "the apple of his eye" to symbolize a most cherished object.

Redeemed by the blood of his Son, the church is God's most cherished object of affection, and he is ever near to defend and cleanse her. Those who persecute the faithful persecute their Master, as Saul of Tarsus, persecuting the church, heard Jesus say, "Saul, Saul, why persecutest thou me?" (Acts 9:4). Seeking to ill-treat the saints, Saul was ill-treating their Savior even though Jesus was in heaven, for his saints and he are one.

Is it not consoling to know that we are as near and dear to Jehovah as the apple of his eye, that safe shelter is ours under the shadow of his wings, as Zechariah further declared? If we are in need of discipline, he will not suffer others to give it to us but tenderly apply it himself. Since we have his kind care, loving sympathy, and constant protection, we should be joyful. How wonderful are the ways of him who has been our help in the past and is our hope for years to come! God's existence is passed in helping weakness.

309

Such Things As Were Most Precious to Me

"He is precious . . . precious blood." *1 Peter 1:19, 2:7.*

In Shakespeare's *Macbeth* Macduff replies to Malcolm:

> *But I must also feel it as a man.*
> *I cannot but remember such things were*
> *That were most precious to me.*

Laurence Sterne, seventeenth-century essayist, wrote of "Dear sensibility! source inexhausted of all that's precious in our joys, or costly in our sorrows." The adjective *precious* figures often in Peter's vocabulary. He never failed to remember such things as were precious to his heart. The apostle reveled in God's "*precious* promises" (2 Pet. 1:4); in the trial of his faith which was much more *precious* to him than gold, in "the *precious* blood of Christ" (1 Pet. 1:19), in Christ the one "chosen of God, and *precious*" (1 Pet. 2:4), in the possession of a "*precious* faith" (1 Pet. 1:7), and in Christ as being "*precious* to you which believe." To them Christ is "the aroma from life to life" (2 Cor. 2:16). The Revised Version of "He is precious" (1 Pet. 1:7) reads in the Amplified Bible, "For you therefore that believe in the *preciousness.*" He is precious in himself and is the source of all that is precious to the believer. We sing with an unidentified hymn writer:

> *Our Saviour is more precious far*
> *Than life, and all its comforts are;*
> *More precious than our daily food;*
> *More precious than our vital blood.*

As we think of every name he wears, every virtue he bears, every relation he fills, every office he sustains, none can be compared with him. Do you value him above all others, love him as you do no other, prefer him above all things, and consider him altogether lovely and beyond all human wealth and worth? The more you come to know of him, the more you will prize him.

Boundless, Endless, and Sublime

"Is the Spirit of the Lord straightened?" Micah 2:7.

In "Childe Harold" Byron eloquently described creation as God's "glorious mirror" in which was seen his form, "boundless, endless, and sublime, the image of Eternity." As the Spirit played a vital part in the creation of our marvelous universe, he can never be straightened in his activities since he too is "boundless, endless, and sublime." His hand is never shortened that it cannot redeem or deliver, nor his ear heavy that it cannot hear the cry of sorrow for sin.

When we think of the vast, unnumbered, unreclaimed multitudes in the world, it would seem as if the power of the Spirit is limited and feeble. If he is omnipotent, then surely the knowledge of God's salvation should have transfigured this sinful world before now. But we are blameworthy, not the Spirit of grace. The church has been straightened, unconcerned, and negligent in her mission to reach earth's millions who cry, "Come and help us, or we die." There are no restraints with God's Spirit when it comes to the evangelization of a lost world. Must we not confess that we have been living far below our privileges as those regenerated and indwelt by the omnipotent Spirit? If his mighty hand is withheld in blessing, the fault is ours, not his.

Have we grieved the Spirit, quenched his operations, sown to the flesh instead of to him, and thereby caused him to restrict his activities? Jesus, the Son of God with power, could not do mighty works because of unbelief; and Israel long ago, by her lack of dedication, "limited the Holy One of Israel" (Ps. 78:41). Without the mighty Spirit we can do nothing, but with him controlling every phase of life there is no limit to what he is able to accomplish through us. This old world has yet to see what he can do through those who give him the unrestricted control of their lives.

Let Me Hide Myself in Thee

"I flee unto thee to hide." Psalm 143:9.

Individuals seek refuge from their mistakes, trials, disappointments, and conflicts in different ways. Many drink to hide from their sins and sorrows. Others flee into suicide as the way out of their anguish. Of old, when forced from home through deceit, Jacob fled to Laban; the murderer hastened to a city of refuge provided for the man slayer; Asa sought physicians for relief; Saul, whose refuge was once in God, hurried to the witch; Ephraim in his peril found his way to King Jareb for shelter and help. But the child of God has no other refuge than God himself who is his "refuge and strength" and his "hiding-place." The psalmist, harassed by foes, cried to God, "I flee unto thee to hide me" (143:9).

How Satan outwits himself when he drives us to our God who presents himself as our "shelter in the time of storm"! We are ever in danger from sin, self, and Satan; and fear, painful although groundless, may be ours because we are unable to defend ourselves or to overcome our opposers. Yet what wisdom is ours if we see the storm approaching and make for the covert to hide for safety and comfort. May we be found at all times fleeing to Jehovah who is ever "a very present help in trouble."

Fleeing from the world, the flesh, and the Devil, may we flee to Jesus, for other refuge have we none. His ear is ever open to hear our cry; his heart always yearns to shelter us; his hand is ever ready to deliver and protect . Let us flee to him by prayer in faith and hope for his deliverance. We shall then sing with an unknown hymn writer:

> *Happy soul, that free from harms,*
> *Rests within his Shepherd's arms!*
> *Who his quiet shall molest?*
> *Who shall violate his rest?*

Grow Old Along with Me

"Such an one as Paul the aged." *Philemon 9.*

As I write this meditation, the ninetieth milestone of my life's pilgrimage is not far away. Therefore, I feel qualified to meditate upon old age. Paul was not old in years when he wrote of himself as being "aged," for he finished his course around sixty years of age. But his life of unexampled labor and suffering in prisons and chains, as well as physical disability, made him prematurely old and withered. Thus this reference to being aged has a peculiar beauty and pathos about it and is a stirring appeal to those of us not far from the end of the road.

In his letter to Titus, Paul urged the "older men to be temperate, dignified, sensible, sound in faith, in love, in perseverance" (2:2), and the apostle certainly practiced what he preached. Physical vigor and youth may vanish, but there is a power outside the domain of nature for those who wait upon the Lord for renewal of strength. Caleb, at age eighty-five, drew his spiritual strength from God who was also the source of his courage. Was this not his boast when he said, "As yet I am as strong this day as I was in the day that Moses sent me" [forty years previously] as my strength was then, even so is my strength now" (Josh 14:11)?

If an infirmity has crept over our bodies, we must guard against its creeping over our souls. If our feet cannot take us out into public service as they used to do, there is much work we can do on our knees in spiritual intercession for the church and the world. That most eloquent Scottish divine, James Guthrie, long now with the Lord, once wrote:

> They say I am growing old because my hair is silvered,
> and there are crow's-feet on my forehead, and my step
> is not as firm and elastic as before. But they are mistaken.
> That is not me. The knees are weak, but the knees are
> not me. The brow is wrinkled, but the brow is not me.
> This is the house I live in. But I am young—younger than
> ever I was before.

Are you an aged pilgrim? Then recall Robert Browning's words: "Grow old along with me! The best is yet to be."

313

The Sweet Omniscience of Love

"Your Father knoweth what things ye have need of, before
ye ask him." *Matthew 6:8.*

If this assertion of Jesus is true—and it is—then why waste breath
asking God for what he already knows we need? The simple answer is
because he said, "Ask, and ye shall receive" (John 16:24). What a
precious and consolatory truth there is in this statement found in the
Sermon on the Mount!

Your Father. Such a privileged relationship is ours through the
finished work of the cross and the regenerating power of the Holy Spirit.
Jesus taught his own to look up into the face of God and address him
as their Father in heaven. God is not the Father of all. His fatherhood
is based upon the Saviorhood of his Son.

Knoweth. Jesus here emphasized the foreknowledge and omniscience
of his Father—attributes associated with him throughout Scripture.
There is no personal detail—past, present, and future—of your life
and mine beyond his ken. Nothing escapes the eye of him whose grace
covers our life from commencement to the end.

What things ye need. It will be noted that this means the Father's
knowledge of what we need and not our own estimation. All circumstances are minutely and absolutely known to him. Whether the needs
are physical, material, or spiritual, he has a register of them all; because
of his omnipotence he can meet any need according to his riches in
glory. How comforting it is to believe that before the heart can recite
its need the loving Father is on his way to meet it!

Before ye ask him. Before we enter his presence with our plea for help,
God is cognizant of the burden of our spirit. He has already bottled
our tears and recorded beforehand what his omniscient mind knows are
our needs. His knowledge is perfect, and our needs are real. When the
twain meet, what relief is ours. Let us rest in all he is in himself.

Secret and Insidious Perils

"Moth and rust doth consume." *Matthew 6:19.*

Jesus was master of the art of simple, easy-to-understand illustrations in his enforcement of truth. He could see "sermons in stones, and books in brooks," as Shakespeare wrote in *As You Like It*. Here, for example, in dealing with the ways treasure can be lost, he suggested that the *moth* and the *rust* represent the more secret, subtle, and insidious perils which eat away slowly and silently at our treasures. What truths do the conjunction of these consumers suggest?

The moth. Looking silky, beautiful, and innocent as it flits about in the twilight of the day, the moth seems a little, harmless, innocent creature; yet what destruction it can cause. It can hide and burrow among costly garments and riddle them with holes until they are only fit to be burned. The moth can stand for what we call little sins, but there is no such thing as a little sin, for sin, no matter how minute we think it is, is sin. Seemingly harmless and innocent thoughts, imaginations, and desires are heedlessly admitted into the inner life and gradually corrupt and consume one's moral and spiritual strength.

The rust. Without doubt, rust is the symbol of neglect. Tools and utensils never rust if kept clean and in constant use. Science has provided us with lotions to prevent rust. The use of talents can be lost through neglect, as Bishop Westcott acknowledged when he said that his absorption in theological studies consumed his gift of song. Negligence is just as destructive as rust and must be guarded against. To neglect God's great salvation is to be in peril of being eternally lost.

Jesus prefaced his warnings against the moth and the rust with the exclamation "Beware!" May he enable us to be ever on our guard against the deadly peril of both. Moth and rust may seem harmless, and therein lies their subtle and most deadly danger. Let us beware of giving shelter to anything, no matter how innocent looking, that would consume us.

The Bounds of Freedom Wider Yet

"The Word of God is not bound." 2 Timothy 2:9.

Paul found deep satisfaction in calling himself, not a prisoner of any Roman emperor, but "the prisoner of Jesus Christ" (Eph. 3:1) who had permitted his prison chains for the gospel's sake. In the passage before us Paul used his bondage as a striking contrast to the unfettered word he loved and lived to preach. "I suffer hardship unto bonds, as a malefactor; but the word of God is not bound" (2 Tim. 2:9, RV). Roman authority might cast Paul into the dungeon and chain his hands and feet, but it could not prevent the gospel he preached from traveling on its free, untrammeled way. The apostle's foes tried to circumscribe his influence and to retard the spread of the Christian truths he declared, but—and you can feel something of the glow in his heart—he exultantly declared, "The Word of God is not bound!"

Godless persons may imprison those who preach the Word, but they cannot clamp chains upon it or stifle and silence its voice. Because it is God's infallible Word, it must run, have free course, and be abundantly glorified as the Word that liveth and abideth forever.

During the reign of Charles II the state tried to silence John Bunyan by throwing him into Bedford Gaol. But within his cell he wrote *Grace Abounding* and dreamed of *Pilgrim's Progress* which, next to the Bible, enjoys the largest circulation of any Christian book today. From that Gaol the Word for which Bunyan suffered ran on its unfettered way through the world. Communism may silence preachers in cruel ways and try to expel the Word of God from those under the sway of such an atheistic philosophy. But it will yet reveal itself as the unfettered Word, freeing those bound with the chains of their own godless systems of government. Praise God, for his Word that cannot be bound!

316

God's Nightingales

"In the night his song shall be with me." *Psalm 42:8.*
"God . . . who giveth songs in the night." *Job 35:10.*

The nightingale seems to be one of the favorite birds among poets; many have dwelt upon its characteristic feature of singing in the night. In *Romeo and Juliet* Shakespeare said of this twang-throated singer, "Nightly she sings on yond pomegranate tree." The bard also dwelt on what the nightingale could do if only "she should sing by day." John Higly, of the fifteenth century, wrote, "O 'tis the ravished nightingale . . . Her woes at midnight rise . . . The moon not waking till she sings." Andrew Marvell described the songstress as "sitting so late . . . Studying all the summer night, Her matchless songs doth meditate." John Fletcher, who died in 1625, gave us these lines in his "Faithful Shepherdess":

> *The nightingale among the thick-leaved Spring,*
> *That sits alone in sorrow, and doth sing*
> *Whole nights away in mourning.*

John Milton's frequent references to the nightingale indicate how he loved this bird. He too described its habit of singing in the night in *Paradise Lost:*

> *. . . All but the wakeful nightingale;*
> *She all night her amorous descant sung;*
> *Silence was pleased . . . .*

God too has his nightingales who are able to sing their songs in the night of trial, sorrow, or separation. Paul and Silas, fettered with chains and sitting on the cold floor of their prison cell at the mignight hour, could sing praises unto God whose ear could hear no sublimer music since he gave his human nightingales their songs.

Even when we come to walk through the dark valley of death, the cheerful song of faith is, "Thou art with me." A proverb has it that "a nightingale cannot sing in a cage," but this is not so with those to whom God gives songs in the night. Madame Guyon in prison confinement could pen her wonderful poem:

> *A little bird I am, shut in from fields of air,*
> *And in my cage I sit and sing, to Him who placed me there.*

Have you come to a night of grief and loss? Then let your heart sing unto the Lord.

317

Perseverance Keeps Honor Bright

"The race is not to the swift, nor the battle to the strong."
Ecclesiastes 9:11.

Among the wise sayings of Solomon none is more eloquent in praise of perseverance than the one before us. Far too many of us start well, but we never get there. We lack what is known as "stickability." Matthew Henry's comment on the passage is significant: "One would think that the lightest of foot should, in running, win the prize; and yet *the race is not* always *to the swift*, some accident happens to retard them, or they are too secure, . . . and let those that are slower get the start of them. One would think that, in fighting, the most numerous and powerful army should be always victorious, and, in single combat, that the bold and mighty champion would win; . . . but *the battle is not* always *to the strong*." Young David in his slaughter of Goliath and the rout of the Philistines proved that the weak can carry the day against formidable power. Frances Ridley Havergal has the line, "The swift is not the safe, and the sweet is not the strong." Prayer and perseverance count in the long run.

The ancient fable by Aesop about the hare and the tortoise illustrates the doggerell we used to sing, "Go on, go on, go on!" The proud hare laughed at the short feet and crawl of the tortoise. But the latter in confidence said, "Though you be swift as the wind I will beat you in a race." The hare accepted the challenge, and they decided that a fox should choose the course and name the goal. Well, the day came for the race, and the hare and tortoise left the starting line together. With its native speed the hare was soon far ahead of the tortoise that lumbered on with a slow but steady pace. Feeling that the race was in the bag, the hare fell fast asleep. Awaking, on he ran, thinking the tortoise was still behind, but on reaching the goal, he found there the tortoise whose perseverance won him the race.

We read that Jesus set his feet steadfastly toward Jerusalem and never halted until he reached there to die upon a tree. Paul could say, "By the grace of God, I am what I am (1 Cor. 15:10). May the same God inspire our perseverance in the race set before us.

318

Bring Me My Chariot of Fire

"There appeared a chariot of fire, and horses of fire."
2 Kings 2:11.

As the result of sin's entrance into the beautiful world God created, countless millions, from Adam and Eve down the ages to the present hour, have passed into eternity through the tunnel of death, with the exception of two godly men, Enoch and Elijah. All persons, whether Christian or unsaved, will continue to leave the world by way of the grave until Jesus returns for his church when all the redeemed, living at that glorious moment, will be caught up to meet the Lord in the air and thus, like Enoch and Elijah, will not taste death.

What are some of the truths to be gleaned from Elijah's sudden, glorious, and dramatic translation to glory? First, he had an inner conviction that he was about to meet the God he had so faithfully served. When persons live in close communion with God, as Elijah did, they become very sensitive to divine purposes. They can catch the whisperings of heaven.

When Elijah's last day on earth came, he spent it quietly doing his work. The companionship of Elijah and Elisha was precious during those last days. Elijah knew that Elisha had a heart like his own and thus wanted him near when his unusual disappearance occurred. When the hour arrived, it seemed to Elisha that twenty thousand chariots surrounded Elijah, along with the angels doing God's bidding as a flame of fire. As the prophet of fire, Elijah had defied Ahab, "The God that answereth by fire, let him be God (1 Kings 18:24). Elijah left earth, not in quiet peacefulness like Enoch before him, but in the whirlwind and the flame of his career into the rest of God.

Elisha not only received Elijah's mantle—the badge of his prophetic calling—but a double portion of his master's loyal spirit. The only eye that saw Elijah in the chariot of fire and caught up to heaven in a whirlwind was Elisha's. The first to see the risen Jesus was Mary. This is the sight love receives. Such love is not blind but has the keenest of all sight.

319

Sore Let and Hindering in Running the Race

"The spirit suffered them not." Acts 16:7.

The Holy Spirit not only *constrains*, but *restrains*, as Paul proved when he was intent on preaching the gospel, first in Asia and then, when the door was closed, in Bithynia. But as sincere as he was to spread the truth, in both cases, the Spirit of Jesus did not permit Paul to go on his mission. Because of his intimate knowledge of the Spirit's nature and ministry, the apostle doubtless bowed in submission, believing that he knew best.

There are some *hinderings* we can fully understand. For instance, God intervened to prevent Balaam from carrying out his intention to curse Israel. He restrained Herod from fulfilling his cruel purpose to kill the infant Jesus. It seems right for God to bring the devices of the wicked to nought, for such action is in harmony with God's character.

On the other hand, it is hard to understand that some of the disappointments and frustrated good purposes are the work of the Spirit. Paul knew that Asia was a magnificent field for evangelism; yet he was "forbidden of the Holy Spirit to speak the word in Asia" (Acts 16:6). Divine interference thwarted the apostle's plan, but Paul's faith did not break down as, possibly, ours would have done. It is hard for those who are zealous to spread the gospel to understand that the closing of some doors can be the act of a loving God. Because of his omniscience and foresight, he knows best. What we must believe is that God is as truly in the prohibitions, hindrances, and disappointments of life as he is in its fulfillments, joys, and blessings. God is ever thinking upon us for our good, even when he closes a door.

Who Shall Ever Find Joy's Language?

"We joy in God." Romans 5:11.

The whole verse of Robert Bridges in his poem "Growth of Love" is true of divine joy:

> *Ah heavenly joy! But who hath ever heard,*
> *Who hath seen joy, or who shall ever find*
> *Joy's language? There is neither speech nor word;*
> *Nought but itself to teach it to mankind.*

We do not joy in our feelings because they fluctuate and change; we do not joy in our friends, for death robs us of them; we do not joy in our possessions, for they are liable to take wings and fly away. *We joy in God.* Although the exercise of this joy may be more apparent at some times than others, the object of our joy is eternally the same. Thus we joy and rejoice in God as our heavenly Father who cares for us as his children, as our friend who sticks closer than a brother, befriending us at all times, and as the God of all comfort upholding and sustaining us during the trials and sorrows of life.

Such a deep-seated joy, unspeakable and full of glory, is an emotion we cannot produce. It comes to us from God, for "the fruit of the Spirit is . . . joy" (Gal. 5:22). This divine joy is the privilege of every child of God on the basis of the faithful work of his beloved Son at Calvary. All charges against him have been blotted out. He is freely and fully forgiven and justified from all things and stands before God in Christ, accepted, beloved, and blessed. Now, at peace with God and made a son of God, the believer's exceeding joy is God. Can you say that *your* joy is *in* and *from* God? To quote an unknown source:

> *The earthly joys lay palpable, A taint in each, distinct as well;*
> *The heavenly flitted, faint and rare, Above them, but as truly were*
> *Faintless, so is their nature best.*

Well might we pray: Lord, evermore, give us these untainted heavenly joys!

SILENCE
and
REMEMBRANCE

November's sky is chill and drear,
November's leaf is red and sear.

—Sir Walter Scott,
"Marmion"

The Grand Perhaps

"Perhaps he therefore departed for a season."
Philemon 15, 16.

We may not experience that every *perhaps* is "grand," as Robert Browning suggested, but Paul wanted Philemon to know that perhaps Onesimus was parted from him for a while as a servant, that he might have him forever as a brother beloved. Thus for Philemon this would be a "grand perhaps." Now that Onesimus was a Christian, Paul could give some of God's reasons why the one-time slave had forsaken Colosse. But he felt there might be other reasons beyond his knowledge. An unknown poet of the eighteenth century wrote of

> *Dreams that bring us little comfort, heavenly promises that lapse*
> *Into some remote* It may be, *into some forlorn* Perhaps.

But from God's side the mists that seem to hang about many of his intentions and doings are never forlorn. God has his own secret stairs to fulfill his journeys. While uncertainty may be ours, constraining us to say, "Perhaps this is his design" or "It may be this is his purpose," God acts unerringly even though we cannot predict his exact aim. It should be enough that we are in his hands and that with him there are no *perhapses.* He is able to tune the lights and shadows, the joys and griefs, into glorious harmony. We only limit his wisdom and his power if we try to forecast infallibly his methods.

An old Scottish saint cried, "I do not know by what door he will approach. I thought he would come by the way of the hills, and, lo, he came by the way of the valleys!" Dr. Alexander Maclaren's comment on the above verse is worthy of note:

> We are not to be too sure of what God means by such
> and such a thing, as some are wont to be, as if we had been
> sworn of God's privy-council. . . . A humble *perhaps*
> often grows into a *verily, verily*—and a hasty, over-
> confident *verily, verily* often dwindles to a hesitating
> *perhaps.* Let us not be in too great a hurry to make sure
> that we have the key of the cabinet where God keeps His
> purposes, but content ourselves with *perhaps* when we
> are interpreting the often questionable ways of His
> providence, each of which has many meanings and
> many ends.

Trust God: See All, nor Be Afraid

"I will not be afraid of ten thousands of people, that have
set themselves against me round about." *Psalm 3:6.*

The psalmist presented us with many passages urging us to the unreservedness of trust, ever honoring God who loves his people to depend
upon him in simple, childlike confidence. David was not scared by ten
thousands of people although nothing could look worse to human sight
than such an array of enemies. Despite appearances, David had a calm
born of faith. Others might have said, "All these things are against me,
and ruin stares me in the face," but not so the psalmist who, through his
trust in God, had a loophole of escape and could boast, "I will not be
afraid."

Similar circumstances confronted Martin Luther as he journeyed
toward Worms. His dear friend heard that the enemies of the Reformation were going to treat him as a heretic and sent Luther the message,
"Do not enter Worms!" But he sent back the challenge to his confidant,
Spalatin, "Go tell your master, that even should there be as many devils
in Worms as tiles on housetops, still I would enter it." And as we know,
he did. Luther said, "I was then undaunted, I feared nothing."

How do we act when, in our Christian witness, we find ourselves
surrounded by hostile forces, seen and unseen, as well as adverse
circumstances? If we walk by sight, fear will grip our hearts and defeat
will be ours. If, however, we walk by faith, believing that greater is
he who is in us than the enemy against us, then with all confidence we
can say with David, "I will not be afraid."

To trust only when appearances are favorable is to sail only with
the wind and tide, to believe only when we can see. May ours be that
unreservedness of faith enabling us to trust God come what will. In
triumph Job could confess, "Though he slay me, yet will I trust him!"
(13:15). Let our prayer be, "Lord, give me that unreserved faith enabling me to trust thee unreservedly, despite all appearances. Amen!"

Ingratitude, Thou Marble-hearted Fiend

"Be ye thankful." Colossians 3:15.

That Shakespeare abhorred thanklessness is seen in his frequent condemnation of it. In addition to his description from *King Lear* given in the above title, we have the following song from *As You Like It:*

> *Blow, blow, thou winter wind,*
> *Thou art not so unkind*
> *As man's ingratitude.*

Wordsworth wrote of the lack of gratitude, "It hath oftener left me mourning." Paul said that one evidence of godlessness is, "Neither were thankful" (Rom. 1:21). A trait of godliness is "the giving of thanks."

As those who are the Lord's, we have so much to be grateful for since we are surrounded by mercies—physical, material, temporal, spiritual. As we think of our salvation, are we not thankful that God chose us in his beloved Son before the foundation of the world and that he sent him to be the propitiation for our sins and to make us meet for heaven? How we should strive to live as glad, grateful, and loving children and thereby rejoice the heart of our heavenly Father who emptied heaven of the best for our redemption!

Having his grace in our hearts, his infallible Word in our hands, his mercies in our homes and in our daily lives, we should be found giving thanks continually to his name. May we ever guard against harboring the marble-hearted fiend of ingratitude in our hearts. If thanklessness has been ours, let us confess it before the Lord, mourn over it, and ask him to fill our souls with daily praise for his unmerited grace and goodness. May he enable us to live as thoughtful dependents upon his bounty and as grateful, loving children, praising him from whom all blessings flow. Joseph Addison, the seventeenth-century poet, wrote:

> *Through all eternity to Thee,*
> *A joyful song I'll raise;*
> *For O, eternity's too short*
> *To utter all Thy praise.*

Thy Sweet Converse and Love So Deeply Joined

"I will speak of the glorious honour of thy majesty."
Psalm 145:5.

John Milton was right in joining converse and love, for out of the heart proceeds conversation, whether sweet or sour. Therefore, it is imperative to keep our hearts with all diligence, for out of it are the issues, not only of life, but of lips. Much is said in Scripture about *conversation.* We are to order our conversation aright, to live and labor as becomes the Gospel, to be holy in all manner of conversation, and to be examples of those using chaste conversation.

In some references the word *conversation* implies manner of life rather than, explicitly, the words of our lips. The psalmist had no doubt as to the content of his converse. "I will speak," he said, "of the glorious honour of thy majesty." In general, the habitual converse of the world is low, with buying and selling, gossiping, and trifling matters forming the staple subjects of talk. Those of the earth are earthly, and as their hopes, interests, and enjoyments, so their conversation. Where the treasure is, there will the heart be also; and where the heart is, there generally will be the tongue also. Out of the abundance of the heart, the mouth speaks.

It is not to be supposed for one moment that because we are Christians we must shut out from our conversation all reference to the ordinary affairs of daily life and business, for we have to earn our bread by labor and talk to people of the world. What we have to watch is becoming worldly in our tone or, as Scripture states it, "order our conversation aright" (Ps. 50:23). The psalmist would have us remember that we are not only to speak *to* God but speak *about* him, particularly of "the glorious honour of thy majesty." The word used for *speak* does not mean an occasional reference to all God is in himself, but "speaking at large," not merely "alluding to, incidentally" but "entering into particulars," as though one took delight in expatiating on all that is involved in the majesty and mercy of the Lord. May we never be ashamed to "talk of his doings."

He Has Not Escaped Who Drags His Chain

"Our soul is escaped as a bird out of the snare."
Psalm 124:7.

The escape the Lord makes possible from the snares of the satanic trapper is complete in that the delivered one is also freed from the chains. But those who profess to have escaped condemnation are still in the trap if they drag their chains as the above proverb suggests. The dominant thought of the psalm before us is the perfect help Jehovah provides for his people when they are surrounded by circumstances that would destroy them.

Often through our own disobedience to the revealed Word of God we involve ourselves in entanglements. Unable to extricate ourselves from a perilous position, we are brought to realize that only by divine action can we escape. Whatever temptation may face us, a way of escape is provided. Peter said that only through the knowledge and experience of Jesus as Savior can we "escape the pollution of the world" (2 Pet. 1:4, RV). We are warned to be aware of the wiles of the Devil as he seeks to enslave us. We have no idea how crafty he is and how cleverly he hides his snares. As F. B. Beyer expressed it:

> Quite unexpectedly he begins to weave the meshes of some
> net around the soul, and seems about to hold it his
> captive. And then, all suddenly, the strong and deft hand
> of our Heavenly Friend interposes, as we sometimes
> interpose on behalf of a struggling insect in a spider's
> web. The snare falls into a tangle heap, and the soul
> is free.

I hope that you have the assurance that you have fully escaped from satanic snares and are now as free as a bird in the air. "Make me a captive, Lord, and then I shall be free," wrote George Matheson. To those who prefer captivity in sin and remain blind to their bondage, the solemn question comes, "How shall we escape, if we neglect so great a salvation?" (Heb. 2:3). If they die in their sin, there can be no escape from eternal condemnation.

Faith Shines Equal, Arming Me from Fear

"Believe the Lord your God." *2 Chronicles 20:20.*

Emily Brontë's "Last Lines" prove that she herself was "surely anchor'd on the stedfast rock of immortality." How moving is the first verse in her poem:

> *No coward soul is mine,*
> *No trembles in the World's storm-troubled sphere;*
> *I see Heaven's glories shine,*
> *And faith shines equal, arming me from fear.*

In the believer, faith and fear cannot exist together. Believing that the Lord is almighty, the Christian is armed against fear. David could confess, "God is my refuge and strength, and a very present help in trouble, Therefore will I not fear" (Ps. 46:1, 2). When such "faith shines equal," then we can laugh at impossibilities and cry, "It shall be done." The proper object of our active faith is not God as the God of nature, but God in Christ through whom he is our covenant God, all sufficient, ever propitious, gracious, taking pleasure in us, and ever ready to undertake for us.

Believing in such a God produces peace of heart, zeal, humility, strength to accomplish his will, and deliverance out of every difficulty. So "have faith in God." We first of all receive faith *from* God since it is a gift he bestows upon sinners who accept his salvation. Faith then is an attribute he increases in those who are saved by his grace.

But the aspect of faith our basic text exhorts us to manifest is faith *in* God, an exercise he requires and approves. If Christ returned today, would he find such a faith in our hearts—faith in himself as the sovereign one, faith in his Word as being true and faithful, faith in his presence, knowing that he will never leave us, faith in his power since nothing is too hard for him, faith in his faithfulness which is as steadfast as the mountains and abides forever? "This is the victory that overcometh the world, even our faith" (1 John 5:4) in one who is supreme. Keep believing!

Gladly Would He Learn and Gladly Teach

"Thou art a teacher come from God." *John 3:2.*

Chaucer's axiom is certainly descriptive of the Lord Jesus who delighted to do the Father's will and who learned many things by obedience to that will. Having come to make the glad tidings of the gospel possible, Jesus manifested great joy of heart as he fulfilled his ministry as a teacher from God. Teaching is ennobled by the fact that all three persons of the Trinity are presented in the character of teachers. Of the Father it is said, "I am thy God that teacheth thee" (Isa. 48:17). "Who teacheth like Him?" (Job 36:22); "He teacheth thee to profit" (Isa. 48:17). Of the Son it is recorded, "He began to do and teach" (Acts 1:1); "He taught men" (Matt. 7:29). Of the Holy Spirit Jesus promised, "He shall teach you all things" (John 14:26); "The Holy Spirit will teach you what to say" (Luke 12:12). Then, after the Ascension of Jesus, the apostles became conspicuous as teachers, found "daily teaching in the temple" (Acts 5:25). Paul gloried in his mission as "a teacher of the Gentiles."

Among the gifts to the church are teachers, with women being exhorted to be "teachers of good things." Nicodemus said that Jesus was a teacher *sent from God,* indicating that Jesus came with all divine authority and divine inspiration. The miracles he performed authenticated that he came to rule by the power of truth, not by the sword. All teachers of the Word, whether in the home or the church, must look upon their mission as being *from* God and essential therefore to be undertaken *for* God.

What glorious victories the patient teaching of Jesus through some three years achieved in the lives of his disciples, as their noble ministry in the Acts proves! At times flesh and blood find the slow, painstaking, persistent teaching hard and disappointing, but in eternity the Great Teacher himself will graciously reward those who were teachers after his example and for him. So whether we have the privilege of teaching in pulpit, Sunday school, or home, may we be found teaching transgressors the ways of the Lord.

Ye Are Living Poems

"We are his workmanship." *Ephesians 2:10.*

In his verses to children Longfellow said:

> *Ye are better than all the ballads,*
> *That ever were sung or said;*
> *For ye are living poems,*
> *And all the rest are dead.*

Living poems! Evidently *poem* was the symbol of saints. In writing to the Ephesians Paul said that they were God's *workmanship*, the Greek word for which is *poema*, transliterated as our word *poem*. If we lack the gift to compose poems, we love to read inspiring, poetical productions. The meter varies in poems in the way that the course of one life differs from another.

The word Paul used for *workmanship* is only used once elsewhere, also by the apostle. It is found in his premise that the universe is a revelation of the power and deity of the Creator, "The things that are made" (Ps. 45:1)—*poema.* The two poetic masterpieces of God are the universe, brought into being by his fiat, "He spake and it was done" (Gen. 1:24), and the born-again believer, "created in Christ Jesus unto good works." In both references *poema* suggests something produced with effort, object, and design.

It is wonderful that all who are in Christ form the highest, finest, and most beautiful expression of his thought and purpose. They are masterpieces upon whom he bestowed his best and therefore surpass his first creation which only cost God his breath. As God's new creation we represent the precious blood of his beloved. As the couplet expresses it:

> *'Twas great to call a world from naught*
> *'Twas greater to redeem.*

We ourselves and our works are of God's poetic creation. Poems as well as poets, we say, are born, not made. A sinner becomes God's poem by the new birth, and thereafter his good works, not of the flesh, but of God, eloquently express the rhythm and music of a divine creation. Are others blessed as they read the verse of your life as God's poem?

No Pains—No Gains

"I know . . . thy labor, and thy patience."
Revelation 2:2.

In his commendation of the church at Ephesus Jesus used two very forceful words for our English word *patience*. He said, "Thou haste borne, and hast *patience*" and "for my name's sake hast *laboured*, and hast not fainted" (Rev. 2:3). *Labor* in the original language implies "suffering" or "weariness," hence, exhausting toil. The word is associated with the term often used to describe the arduous apostolic labors: "Labour in the Lord" (Rom. 16:12); "Labour more abundantly" (1 Cor. 15:10). The thought implied is that there was no easy, leisurely task, but hard labor involving maximum physical strength and energy.

While the word *patience* comes from a root meaning "staying" or "to wait," it does not suggest mere endurance of the inevitable, for Christ could have relieved himself of his sufferings (Heb. 12:2, 3; Matt. 26:53). *Patience* implies the heroic, brave persistence which, as Christians, we are not only to *bear* but to *contend*.

In his sermon "On Patience" Henry Barrow, sixteenth-century English church reformer, defined it as "that virtue which qualifieth us to bear all conditions and all events, by God's disposal incident to us, with such apprehensions and persuasions of mind, such dispositions and affections of heart, such external deportment and practices of life as God requireth and good reason directeth." The words *bear* and *borne* are related to the words Paul used to urge believers to bear each other's burdens. Zeuxis, the fifth-century B.C. Greek artist, was asked why he spent so much labor and patience on a picture. He replied, "I paint for eternity!"

Can we say that we are laborious and patient in light of eternity where rewards are to be given to all who have labored in the Lord and patiently awaited their Master's return? Every person's work is to be tried by fire to test its quality, the standard being "No pains—no gains." Presently we are in constant conflict with evil, but we must never become weary *in* or *of* the contest. Utter devotedness to Christ must be ours, no matter how hard the task or the endurance required.

331

Habit Rules the Unreflecting Herd

"Accustomed to do evil." Jeremiah 13:23.

Jeremiah's indictment of the habitual sinners of his time is a commentary on Wordsworth's axiom about habit ruling the unreflecting herd. One habit followed another until the evil people became fixed or accustomed to their corrupt ways and could no more change their course of life than a leopard could remove his spots. Hannah More of the early nineteenth century gave us this couplet:

> *Small habits, well pursued betimes*
> *May reach the dignity of crimes.*

The following verse is attributed to Charles Reade, a nineteenth-century English writer:

> *Sow an act, and you reap a habit,*
> *Sow a habit, and you reap a character.*
> *Sow a character, and you reap a destiny.*

There are some things we never had to learn and became accustomed to because they were natural. We were made with the ability to breathe, move, cry, eat, and drink. But we were not born with other abilities which have become habits by doing them over and over again.

In many respects we are made up of *habits*. Doing a thing once does not make a habit. "One swallow does not make a summer," but it is on the way to it. May the good Lord deliver us from any bad habit, for only he can break the fetter that binds us. We read that Jesus "went about doing good" (Acts 10:38). He was "accustomed to do good" in contrast to those Jeremiah wrote about as being "accustomed to do evil."

Are we sincere in cultivating good habits that will result in a Christ-like character and a glorious destiny? The ennobling habits of prayer, reading the Bible, and seeking the fellowship of God's people force the world to become strangely dim in the light of his glory and grace. Ours must be a constant watchfulness and a resolute and self-denying effort if we desire to become accustomed to pleasing God.

Tears and Smiles Like Us He Knew

"Jesus wept." John 11:35.

While the Gospels do not mention the smiles of Jesus, they have something to say of his tears. Yet, as C. F. Alexander in his hymn "Once in Royal David's City" goes on to say, "He feeleth for our sadness, He shareth in our gladness." Although there are only three references to his dropping of warm tears, his must have been "a long drip of human tears." When he was only twelve years of age, Jesus declared his God-given mission in the world, only to find that his brothers and sisters did not believe in him. Living in a home in which he was not understood must have cost Jesus many tears. From early manhood, he was a Man of Sorrows.

The shortest and sweetest text in the Bible is "Jesus wept." These two words have been blessed by God to the hearts of countless thousands, for next to the comfort of knowing that he shed his blood for us is reading that he shed tears for his enemies as well as for his friends. When Jesus rode in lowly guise into Jerusalem with Hosannas, "he beheld the city and wept" (Luke 19:41). Those tears of grief and compassion were for a lost city rejecting his love and grace. A few days later, in dark Gethsemane, he shed not only his tears but great drops of blood as "he offered up prayers and supplications with strong crying and tears" (Heb. 5:7). Such a depth of agony we will never understand.

The other occasion of his tears was in Bethany when death claimed his friend whom he loved. Being told that Lazarus was dead, "Jesus wept!" On Olivet he wept for foes resolved and doomed to perish. In the garden his liquid agony revealed what he was enduring for us. At the grave of Lazarus he wept in sympathy with bereaved loved ones. And in all cases his tears were the result of heart anguish for others. No one has ever suffered as much as Jesus did in his own heart. He still offers prayers and supplications since he ever lives to make intercession for us, but without strong crying and tears. For him all tears have been wiped away; yet he is the same sympathizing Jesus and would have us follow his example by weeping for those who weep. Can it be that we have become too dry-eyed?

Fine Nets and Stratagems to Catch Us In

"Surely in vain the net is spread in the sight of any bird."
Proverbs 1:17.

A double meaning is suggested by Solomon's assertion. Some say that no bird is so foolish as to hop into a net which is surely spread for it. While the bird has a little head and little brain, it does not have so little wit as to do that. Others think that Solomon meant to say that even if a bird sees you spread the net it has not wisdom enough to know what it means and will hop into it.

While there may be some doubt as to what Solomon thought the birds might do, there is no uncertainty at all as to the lesson to be gathered from his saying. If we are foolish enough to go into the net of sin, spread by the Devil for our destruction, to gather a few crumbs of worldly pleasure, then we are easily gulled. The word *gull* is said to be derived from birds who come down from the Arctic regions to fish in flocks in our harbors and coasts. They are easily caught. This may be an insult to the gulls who are not so readily gulled as some humans who find their hearts tangled in amorous nets.

Are we not warned of the wiles, or stratagems, of the Devil and told that of ourselves we have no wisdom to detect his shrewdness as the archdeceiver? We are told that he is a "roaring lion" (1 Pet. 5:8). God gave lions their roar so that everybody could keep out of their way. Satan may spread his net in our sight, but he cannot compel us to go unto it. If our ears and eyes are open, he spreads his net in vain. His cleverly laid nets are surrounded with piles of his victims; yet there is deliverance for them as, like fluttering birds, they entangle themselves worse in the meshes. Satan spread nets for Jesus to walk into, but Jesus' anointed eyes could see them. He came to "proclaim deliverance to the captives, and to set at liberty them that are bruised" (Luke 4:18). If we have escaped as a bird out of the snare of the fowler, we should never cease to praise him who rescued us or cease to tell those who are still trapped of the glorious rescue Jesus can accomplish for them.

334

Hark, the Glad Sound!

"Blessed is the people that know the joyful sound."
Psalm 89:15.

The American Standard Bible gives us this version of our text: "How blessed are the people who know the blast of the trumpet, and shout of joy." This verse is akin to a similar passage: "With trumpets and the sound of the horn / Shout joyfully before the King, the Lord" (Ps. 98:6). The world abounds in sounds. Many are delightful; others are discordant.

Note first the joyful nature of the sound mentioned by the psalmist. How we love the sound of good, inspiring music and of the warbling birds! But there is a sound sweeter than all other sounds reaching the inner ear of the soul. It is the voice singing to us out of Scripture of the love of God in Christ Jesus. As the hymn by Priscilla J. Owens puts it, "We have heard the joyful sound—Jesus saves!" Such a sound is joyful because it tells us how we can be emancipated from sin's guilt and power and made new creatures in Christ.

Second, "Blessed is the people that know." Those who know this joyful sound of sins forgiven are indeed *blessed*. The word *know* implies more than a mere mental comprehension. It includes a deep personal experience. Some people may not hear a joyful sound easily detected by others, either because they are deaf or cup their ears. The godless have ears but hear not simply because they close their ears.

If a treasure were left us in a will, the same would be joyful to hear about, but if we did not claim it or failed to acquaint ourselves with such a fact, then we would lose a blessing. If possessions are willed to us, we must know all about them and believe the provision of the will and stake all that is ours. The same applies to all the precious, spiritual legacies willed to us by the one who died for us. Blessedness and joy become ours as we know of and claim all that is ours through grace.

In Confidence Shall Be Your Strength

"Cast not away therefore your confidence." *Hebrews 10:35.*

Bible references to *confidence* and its cognates are numerous and, taken together, throw much light on the nature and necessity of such a quality. Bishop Charles John Ellicott gave us the reading, "Cast not away therefore your boldness, seeing it hath a great recompence," and then commented, "To *cast away boldness* is the opposite of 'holding fast the boldness of the hope,' Heb. 3:6; the one belongs to the endurance of the faithful servant, the other to the cowardice of the man who draws back, Heb. 3:12, 16, 18. This verse and the next are closely connected: Hold fast your boldness, seeing that to it belongs great reward; hold it fast, for *he that endureth to the end shall be saved.*" Following the usage of the Authorized Version word *confidence,* we have the writer of Hebrews saying, "[We have confidence] to enter into the holy place by the blood of Jesus" (10:19, RV).

In these days of modernistic approach to fundamental truths of Scripture, doubt is cast upon the efficaciousness of the blood of Jesus to remove sin. Its never-failing power to cleanse from all sin is one aspect of confidence we must not throw away. Virgil had a saying, "Nowhere is confidence safe." It is certainly not safe in many theological training centers today. Unfortunately, too many young men learn to doubt the beliefs they once held and enter the ministry believing their doubts. Arthur Hugh Clough gave us this verse:

> *In controversial foul impureness*
> *The Peace that is thy light to thee*
> *Quench not! In faith and inner sureness*
> *Possess thy soul and let it be.*

Our confidence in the articles of the faith, once delivered unto the saints, will often be assailed and sharply tried, but we must seek grace to hold fast to our confidence until the end, knowing that a great reward awaits us for our unshaken trust in all God has revealed in his Word. Without being contentious, we must earnestly contend for the faith, casting none of it away.

Approach My Soul the Mercy Seat

"Rebekah went to enquire of the Lord." *Genesis 25:22.*

After twenty years of marriage Isaac and Rebekah were still childless, but prayer to God prevailed, and the great trial of faith ended. Realizing that there was more than one child struggling in her womb, Rebekah inquired of the Lord. She learned that she would give birth to two children who in turn would become the progenitors of two nations or "two manner of people," namely, the house of Jacob and the house of Esau (Obad. 18).

Rebekah left us an excellent example to imitate. God, of course, commands us to inquire of him. Did he not say, "I will be enquired of" (Ezek. 36:37)? Joshua and his men greatly erred when they failed to ask counsel of the Lord in respect to the deceit of the Gibeonites. When trouble overtook Job and his mind was perplexed over what God had permitted, he approached the mercy seat and prayed, "Show me wherefore thou contendest with me" (Job. 10:2).

Are you disturbed and confused over the trials and disappointments that have come your way? Go and inquire of the Lord. Ask him for the design of your tears, and he will instruct you and unfold the reason *why* the dark threads are as needful as those of gold and silver. A proverb has it, "Too much inquiring is bad." We fail from too little inquiry of the Lord. Although heaven's Inquiry office never closes, we are not persuaded, as we ought to be, that whatever our circumstances or trials may be the ear of the Lord is ever open to hear our request. His hand is ready to undertake for us.

If painful and distressing experiences overtake us, may we not be found despondent or full of complaint over God's providential dealings, but going to a throne of grace, inquiring of the Lord the reason for our chastisement. David is often described as inquiring of the Lord in the varied crises of his life and receiving all necessary guidance and direction. May this be our constant act and attitude.

I Sing the Progress of a Deathless Soul

"The path of the just . . . shineth more and more unto the perfect day." *Proverbs 4:18.*

For the pilgrim with his deathless soul there must be unhindered progress as he journeys from the City of Destruction to the Celestial City. Since he has been justified by grace, his path must be as the shining light that "shineth more and more unto the perfect day." He cannot remain static in his pilgrimage. If he is not going forward, then he is retreating.

Scripture gives us various descriptions of our spiritual progression: It is "of life unto life"; "faith to faith"; "grace to grace"; "from glory to glory"; "face to face"; "from strength to strength"; "from day to day"; and "more and more." Robert Browning could write of "Progress, man's distinctive mark alone." It should be the distinctive mark of the new person in Christ Jesus. Browning also reminded us that:

> *. . . Progress is*
> *The law of life, man is not man as yet.*

We are not what we should be or shall be, but, like Paul, we follow on, for progress is the law of our life in Christ, and his love perfects what it begins. Much is said regarding our growth as the children of God. Our faith should be found growing exceedingly in the grace and knowledge of the Savior and into a holy temple in the Lord. Can we confess that spiritual growth is ours, that our path "shineth more and more unto the perfect day"? The sentiment Isaac Watts expressed should illustrate our progress in eternal matters:

> *Just such is a Christian; his course he begins*
> *Like the sun in the mist when he mourns for his sins,*
> *And melts into tears; then he breaks out and shines,*
> *But when he comes nearer to finish his race,*
> *Like a fine setting sun, he looks richer in grace,*
> *And gives a sure hope, at the end of his days*
> *Of rising in brighter array!*

338

My Great Taskmaster's Eye

"When thou was under the fig tree, I saw thee." *John 1:48.*

It was when John Milton reached the age of twenty-three that he penned the lines:

All is, if I have grace to use it so,
As ever in my great Task-Master's eye.

Joseph Addison gave us this precious verse:

The Lord my Pasture shall prepare,
And feed me with a Shepherd's Care;
His Presence shall my wants supply,
And guard me with a watchful Eye.

Scripture has much to say about the Master's omniscient, ever-open eye. Nathanael, praying under the fig tree, did not know that the watchful eyes of Jesus saw him on his knees and was surprised when Jesus told him, "I saw thee."

We can never hide from the divine eyes as they scan the whole earth. They saw Adam and Eve when they sought to conceal themselves among the trees of Eden; they saw Abraham as he was about to plunge the knife into his son's heart and stopped him; they saw Hagar in the wilderness when she kissed her boy, Ishmael, and left him to die in the agony of thirst, but *her eyes* were opened to see a well of water; they saw Elijah in the lonely cave, and he was startled by the question, "What dost thou here, Elijah?"

Each of us can say of the Lord, "Thine eye seeth *me!*" Omnipresent, he is present everywhere; omniscient, he sees the needs of his redeemed ones no matter where they are. If his eye is on the odd sparrow and marks its fall, then surely, as those he died to save, we are of more value to him than many sparrows. What pains him as his eyes are upon us is that which is contrary to his character and will. Nathanael was praying at his hallowed spot under the fig tree when Jesus beheld him, and his loving eyes beam with delight as he sees you and me in the spot we have hallowed as a little sanctuary. "Thou God seest me!"

You Told a Lie, an Odious Damned Lie

"They kept back part of the price." *Acts 5:2.*

In Shakespeare's *Othello* Emilia uses these condemning lines:

> *You told a lie, an odious damned lie!*
> *Upon my soul, a lie! a wicked lie!*

Byron asked, "What is a lie?" and provided the answer, " 'Tis but the truth in masquerade." The lie Ananias and Sapphira told was most odious and wicked because it was truth in masquerade, for they had professed to have sold all the possessions for the Lord's cause and had given Peter *all* they had received in payment.

The tragic story of these two disciples is that they kept back, for themselves, part of the price received. For lying against the Holy Spirit in this way they were both smitten with sudden death. The doomed deceivers wanted to imitate the complete surrender of Barnabas who sold *all* he had and gave *all* he secured in payment to the Lord. Proudly and plausibly, Ananias and Sapphira presented to Peter a certain part of what their land brought as if it had been the whole amount. But God revealed to Peter their hypocrisy, and a few minutes later they were corpses, lying stiff and cold at the spot where they dropped dead.

The same incomplete obedience and partial dedication was Saul's sin when he declared that he had slain *everything* belonging to Amalek and said to Samuel, "I have performed the commandment of the Lord" (1 Sam. 15:13). But Samuel discerned his lie and said, "What meaneth then this bleating of the sheep in mine ears?" (1 Sam. 15:14). Are we not humbled as we reflect upon such triflings with God? We have professed to have our all on his altar; yet ours was but a partial surrender, only part of the price. May we be saved from acting a lie, and may we ever cherish the tender strings, checking us in the path of falsehood in any vow we may make. May he who is the truth constantly cleanse us from all secret faults.

The Roots of Sin Are There

"Lest any root of bitterness springing up, trouble you."
Hebrews 12:15.

There can be little doubt that the writer to the Hebrews had in mind the solemn warning Moses set before Israel about the sin and terrible punishment of idolatry. He ended with the words, "Lest there should be among you a root that beareth gall and words." These last words are given in the margin as "poisonous herb," implying that the root from which sin springs is not only bitter, but poisonous (Deut. 29:18).

One idol worshiper in a community of believers can bring into it a root of bitter poison. Achan did not suffer alone as a root of avarice; all Israel likewise suffered. Peter also referred to Moses' warning when he exposed Simon Magus, who, above all other men, proved a root of bitter poison in the early church.

A root is hidden in the ground, and we become aware of it only when fruit or flowers appear. When a person with the root of poisonous influence in the heart enters an assembly of believers, its appearance brings disruption and bitterness into the church. An evil root may now lurk hidden in some heart, but when fruit appears, it will bear a terrible harvest of misery to many.

We should be found searching our own souls to discover if there is any root of bitterness growing in the soil. Then, with all prayer and thoroughness, we should root it out before it can spring up to cause trouble to ourselves and to others. A root is always growing as long as it is left living in the ground. By nature it cannot remain inactive but is always spreading out beneath the surface before it reveals itself in branch and leaf. Likewise the longer sin remains in the heart, the stronger it grows and the harder it becomes to kill.

The nature of the fruit corresponds to the nature of the root; if the root is bitter, it produces bitter fruit. But the root can be dealt with drastically and made to bear fruits of righteousness. On the way to Damascus the bitter root in Saul of Tarsus was transformed by a flash of Christ's redeeming love. With the root of a renewed nature implanted, Saul became the greatest figure in the New Testament next to Jesus who himself was a root out of the dry ground.

341

The Last Enemy Destroyed by Emmanuel

"O grave, I will be thy destruction." *Hosea 13:14.*

Among ancient Greek stories is this one about the city of Athens doomed to supply each year a tribute of youths and maidens to the monster of Crete. However, the hero Theseus embarked with the crew and accompanied the victims that he might beard the dreadful ogre in his den and, slaying him, forever free his native city from the burden of death under which it had groaned.

Did not the prophet Hosea predict the victory of Jesus, our heavenly Theseus, when he affirmed that he would deliver from the power of the grave? "O death, I will be thy plague! O grave, I will be thy destruction" (13:14). Is this not the same paean of victory Paul joined in when he exclaimed, "O death, where is thy sting? O grave, where is thy victory?" (I Cor. 15:55).

When Jesus clothed himself with the garment of our humanity it was with the glorious purpose of becoming *Death's* death, and, at Calvary, by dying, death he slew. Now the saint can sing, "The fear of death has gone forever." In the Revelation of Jesus Christ afforded the Apostle John, Jesus is depicted as having the keys of death hanging at his girdle, indicating that all power is his to shut so that none can open, and to open so that none can shut. How blessed it is to know that the hour is not far distant when death, as the last enemy, is forever vanquished by him, who was dead, but is now alive forevermore! Till then, when we come to walk through the valley of the shadow of death, we have no fear, for the Deathless One himself is with us to lead us to his heavenly abode in which there is no death. Evan Hopkins wrote:

> *Work on, then, Lord, till on my soul*
> *Eternal Light shall break,*
> *And, in Thy likeness perfected,*
> *I "satisfied" shall wake.*

342

A Wise and Masterly Inactivity

"Their strength is to sit still." *Isaiah 30:7.*

This title is taken from a speech by Sir James Mackintosh, Scottish philosopher and historian who died in 1832, in which he said, "The House of Commons, faithful in their system, remained in a wise and masterly inactivity." Isaiah would have us experience the strength gained from a certain form of inactivity, namely, sitting still—a great trial for those who are mad in their pursuit for action or who must always be "up and doing." Theirs would be great achievement if only they could learn to be "down and dying to self-energy."

Isaiah recorded how the Jews wanted to have a sense of security in the midst of their foes and sought to get it by forming an alliance with their ancient masters and oppressors on the bank of the Nile. Displeased at this effort, God told his people that the strength of Pharaoh would be their shame, and their trust in the shadow of Egypt, their confusion. Such a security as they sought would not profit them. Their strength could only be found by sitting still under God's protection and providence.

To *sit still* does not imply an idle bodily composure but a humble dependence upon God, in contrast to wandering about seeking help from various sources. Those who put their confidence in any creature rather than in the Creator will sooner or later find it a reproach to them. Martha was "careful and cumbered" (Luke 10:40) about many things, but her sister Mary found her strength sitting at the feet of Jesus. Moses assured Israel of divine deliverance when escape from the Egyptians seemed hopeless. "Fear ye not, stand still, and see the salvation of the Lord, which he will shew you today" (Exod. 14:13). All the people could do was to "stand still," facing, as they were, graves in the sea. Standing still did not mean physical inactivity, for God commanded the people to "go forward," but he implied trust in the divine promise, "The Lord shall fight *for* you, and ye shall hold your peace" (Exod. 14:13). Spiritual strength is ours as we wait *before* the Lord and wait *for* him to work.

343

Be Famous Then by Wisdom

"Four things which . . . exceeding wise." *Proverbs 30:24.*

The wise and their wisdom form favorite themes for poets. For instance, John Milton had much to say about them. Here is a greatly admired verse of his:

> *The childhood shows the man,*
> *As morning shows the day. Be famous then*
> *By wisdom, as thy empire must extend,*
> *So let extend thy mind o'er all the world.*

Solomon, remarkably endowed by God with wisdom, included the saying of another wise man, Agur, in his Proverbs. Ants, conies, locusts, and spiders were cited by Agur as being "little upon the earth, but they are exceeding wise."

Ants have the instinct to prepare for winter, and thus they gather their food in summer for future needs. Unfortunately, many humans are not so wise as the small ants. Time, money, and strength are wasted, and when the winter of trial or of old age comes, help has to be sought from others. Have you been wise enough to prepare for eternity?

Cronies may be a "feeble folk, yet make they their houses in the rocks." These wise creatures, similar in their habits to wild rabbits, make their homes in stony places where their enemies cannot reach them. Instinct and experience prompt other creatures as well to seek the safety of strong places. Has wisdom been ours to find in God our refuge and hiding place? In the East locusts are large and travel in companies. If they were few in number, they would have little power; so they are wise enough to stay and work together. In their unity there is strength.

We usually shun spiders, but the fourteenth-century liberator and king of Scotland, Robert Bruce, in his cave learned the lesson of perseverance by watching a spider try again and again to weave its web. When things are difficult think of the wise spider.

If we would be as wise as serpents, our highest wisdom can only be found in "the only wise Saviour" (Jude 25), who has been made to us "the Wisdom of God" (1 Cor. 1:24).

Such Are the Gates of Paradise

"Go through, go through the gates." *Isaiah 62:10.*

From the first reference to gates in Scripture—Lot sitting in the gate of Sodom (Gen. 19:1)—to the last reference of the twelve gates of pearl which John described in the Book of Revelation, gates of all sorts are mentioned hundreds of times. In our meditation let us think of some gates we ourselves must go through. First, there are gates which God arranges for us to go through whether we will or not, namely, the gates of life and death. At birth we enter the gate of life, and the one who tenderly brought us through this one will graciously lead us through the gate of death to himself if we have entered the new life in Christ.

Next there are gates we must shun, namely, the world, the flesh, and the Devil. To go willingly through these three gates ultimately means going through the gates of hell. John Bunyan in his dream saw that there was a way to hell, even from the gates of heaven.

Third, there are gates we should strive to enter. Jesus used the illustration of two gates open to all sinners, the narrow gate leading to eternal life and the wide gate through which the unrepentant go to eternal condemnation. Faith is one of the principal gates into peace with God, as is prayer. Tennyson wrote of "battering the gates of Heaven with storms of prayer."

Then mention must be made of two gates that shut us in for eternity, that close forever behind us. In his portrayal of the rich man and Lazarus in eternity Jesus emphasized how the gate was barred for each in their respective spheres. "There is a great gulf fixed: so that they which would pass from hence to you cannot; neither can they pass to us, that would come from thence" (Luke 16:26). The pearly gates of paradise exclude "dogs, and sorcerers, and idolators" (Rev. 22:15) forever from eternal bliss and encircle forever all those who obey the call, "Go through, go through the gates" (Isa. 62:10) into the joy of the Lord. How blessed we are if we have entered the open gates of his righteousness!

He Did Entreat Me Past All Saying Nay

"But they constrained him, saying, Abide with us."
Luke 24:29.

This precious portion of Scripture records one of the distinct appearances of Jesus after his resurrection and is one of the most moving passages in the four Gospels. Two disciples had been at Calvary and witnessed the bitter end. Full of sorrow, they journeyed home to Emmaus, some seven miles from Jerusalem where Jesus died. They were companions in grief and were doubtless rehearsing all they could remember of Jesus' life, teaching, suffering, and death.

While thus communing, the two sad men were joined by a stranger, but they did not recognize him as the one they were mourning, for "he appeared in another form." Asking them about the subject of their conversation, Jesus, although he knew what it was all the time, heard from their lips the story of his last hours and of how crushed their hopes were by his death. Then came our Lord's matchless exposition concerning himself, and the two men were at their village before they knew it. Jesus "made as though he would have gone further." This pretense on his part does not imply anything false. He *was* going on and would have gone on but for the entreaty to tarry with them. "They constrained him, saying, Abide with us." They pressed him not to go on his journey. The Lord loves to be entreated by his people.

Ruth said, "Intreat me not to leave thee." Gideon said to the illustrious angel, "Depart not hence, I pray thee." This repeated plea, "I pray thee," proves that the Lord, in love, often tries our faith as he appears to go on. When the invitation came "Abide with us," Jesus responded, and a glorious revelation came to those willing to give him shelter. Those two disciples could not bring themselves to part with one who had done so much for them.

While "Abide with Me" has become the most popular of our evening hymns, we do not have to entreat Jesus to remain, for we have his own promise, "I will never leave thee, nor forsake thee." Read backwards, it means the same, "Thee forsake, nor thee leave, never will I."

Human Nature's Daily Food

"Give ye them to eat." *Matthew 14:16.*

In the Anglican church there is a Sunday observed in the middle of Lent, forty days before Easter, which is known as Refreshment Sunday. It is so called because in the Gospel reading for the day there is something about people resting in the fields, eating divinely provided food they found refreshing and nourishing. It is the miracle of Christ feeding the five thousand.

Miracles are shadows telling us of something spiritual behind them, and the miracle Jesus performed at the close of a busy day was a parable of all he is as the bread of life. There was *the recognition of need*, for the Master said, "They have nothing to eat" (Mark 8:2). He knew the multitude who had followed him would starve if food were not forthcoming. He is still concerned about the natural daily food of his own and taught us to pray, "Give us this day our daily bread."

Then there was *the recognition of order* in performing the miracle, for Jesus commanded the people to "sit down in groups in order" (Luke 9:14). If the thousands present had been allowed to be all jumbled up together, serving them would have been a hard task. That day Jesus revealed that order is heaven's first law. Are we not enjoined to walk orderly?

Further, there is *the recognition of the use of what we have.* The villages were too far away to buy food, and the disciples produced the five loaves and two fishes found among them. With these a miracle was performed that satisfied the hunger of a vast crowd. Little is much if God is in it, and that day God the Son multiplied what a boy gave him. If we have one talent and fully devote it to him, he will increase it to ten talents. Why not let him make much of the little we have?

There was also *the recognition of waste*, for the fragments of food were gathered into twelve baskets for use later on. Jesus was careful about those "leftovers." Should we not shun any willful waste? The axiom has it, "Waste not, want not!"

Last, there is *the recognition of himself* as the one who is able to feed our souls as we feed our stomachs. Does he not feed us with himself and with his promises? Well might we pray, "Lord feed me, or I'll die."

347

Shining Ones, Whose Faces Shone As the Light

"Shine as lights in the world, holding forth the word of life." *Philippians 2:15, 16.*

Doubtless all of us are familiar with the description John Bunyan gave in *Pilgrim's Progress* of Christian and Hopeful drawing near to the deep river of death where they met two shining ones whose raiment shone like gold and whose faces shone as the light. Being thus illuminated, they were able to lead the two pilgrims into the city as they emerged from the river. Bunyan was not portraying angels in his figure of "shining ones," but all saints who should shine as lights in the world. The sphere in which they are to shine is a whole world lost in the darkness of sin.

As Jesus was about to leave his disciples, he prayed, not that they should be taken out of the world, but left in it to witness, whether in darkest heathenism or in the dark places of the city where we live. Absence of light not only means darkness but *danger*, as we experience when a blackout occurs because of electrical failure. The question is, Are we—you and I—helping to banish the spiritual darkness in the little piece of the world we represent?

Then it is also necessary to think, not merely of the place where the light is to shine, but of *what* the light is in itself. The word Paul used for *lights* means "luminaries" and it is the same word found at creation, "Let there be lights in the firmament of heaven" (Gen. 1:14). We are to shine as the stars that come twinkling one by one from out the azure sky, scattering beams of grace to all around us. The sacred light we shine with is not self-created but comes from him who declared himself to be "The light of the world" (John 8:12). Our light then is reflected and "shining more and more unto the perfect day." Paul makes it clear that the manner of our shining is associated with the Word of life. We are to *hold forth* as a lamp to our feet and a light to our path.

God made the sun, moon, and stars to shine for the benefit of his world, and as his new creation, we are to display the illuminating Word so that it can be seen by those who are perishing in the darkness of sin and who are in danger of eternal darkness. Have you been a star in someone's sky?

Do It and Make Excuses

"They all with one consent began to make excuse."
Luke 14:18.

The ancient proverb, used as the title for this meditation, is so true of those cited in the Bible as having made excuses, for they indulged in an act of disobedience and then, when exposed, excused themselves. The first one in the world to make an excuse was the first man, Adam. Forbidden by God to touch the tree of knowledge, Adam and Eve tasted of its fruit. Then, smitten with conviction, they foolishly tried to hide from God. Called from his hiding place, Adam crept out and heard the question, "Hast thou eaten of the tree?" (Gen. 3:11). His excuse was ready: Eve gave me the fruit; it is not my fault. Then God looked at Eve. She too had thought up her excuse and said, "The serpent, the wicked serpent beguiled me and I did eat" (Gen. 3:13). From then on we have a succession of "their thoughts the mean while accusing or else excusing one another" (Rom. 2:15), as Paul put it.

No matter how good an excuse, it is impossible to persuade oneself, and very rarely anyone else, that the excuse is truth. An anonymous poet has left us these lines:

> *Oftentimes the excusing of a fault*
> *Doth make the fault worse by the excuse;*
> *As patches set upon a little breach*
> *Discredit more a hiding of the fault*
> *Than did the fault before it was so patched.*

The Duke of Wellington is credited with having said that a person good at making excuses is seldom good for anything else. This is certainly true of those Jesus described as being invited to a great supper but who with "one consent," or all alike, came up with excuses which were disguised lies. As those who profess to be the Lord's, *excuses* is a word that should not be in our vocabulary. If we have erred, it is folly to excuse ourselves. It is better to confess our fault and claim anew the blood of Jesus who is able to cleanse us from all sin.

Be Swift in All Obedience

"According to all that God commanded Noah, so did he."
Genesis 6:22.

Noah will ever remain, not only as a model worker, but as a sterling example of obedience to God, for in accordance to the divine command, this man who walked with God crossed every *t* and dotted every *i*. Although he was not a shipbuilder, living in a seaport town Noah was commissioned to build a large ship the like of which had never been heard of before. How easy it would have been for Noah to make excuses and to reply truthfully to God, "I know nothing about building ships, nor do my sons, and there are no ship carpenters around I can engage to help me." But Noah did not raise the slightest objection and went to work at once. Implicitly, he obeyed God and fashioned the ship, or ark, to divine specifications.

To the godless around, the story of a coming flood and the ship in building to be the means of escape for Noah and his family seemed an idle tale. They must have thought godly Noah a bit of a nut, but on he went in a fearless way to obey God. We read four times that "as God commanded Noah, so did he." Willing to obey God, he found that nothing was too hard for him, and as with Paul, Noah proved that he could do all things through him who strengthened him for his gigantic task.

Have we learned that God's commands are his enablings, that what he asks of us he always imparts strength to obey? "Faithful is He Who called you, *Who also will do it*" (1 Thess. 5:24). One day Charles Wesley said to his famous brother, "If I had a pair of wings I would fly away." John Wesley replied, "If God told thee to fly, he would give thee a pair of wings."

May we never be found saying *I can't* to anything God tells us to do. At the marriage in Cana, Mary, the mother of our Lord, said to the servants of the house, "Whatsoever he saith unto you *do it*" (John 2:5). And they did, helping thereby in the miracle of turning water into wine. With Shakespeare in *Henry VIII* may we learn to say:

> *The will of heaven be done, and the King's pleasure*
> *By me obeyed.*

350

Little Things Are Infinitely the Most Important

"By little and little." *Exodus 23:30.*

Both Scripture and human experience agree with Arthur Conan Doyle who wrote, "It has long been an axiom of mine that the little things are infinitely the most important." By little and little the Canaanites were driven out of their land by the Israelites; and your heart and life and mine are what Canaan was when the Israelites succeeded—full of wild beasts, or lusts, evil thoughts, and desires. But little by little as God's sanctifying grace works in us, more of the territory of our lives becomes his. We must guard against those little sins and faults that spoil Christian character—the little foxes that spoil the grapes. We must not look with suspicion and even contempt upon that which is outwardly insignificant. It is folly to despise the day of some things.

The whole record of great scientific discoveries and inventions suffices to show that the apparently trivial may be of vast importance. The falling of an apple led to the discovery of the law of gravitation; the steam issuing from a kettle was the starting point of the steam engine. Greatness of little things can also be seen in nature as Julia Fletcher Carney wrote:

> *Little drops of water, little grains of sand*
> *Make the mighty ocean, and the pleasant land.*

Tennyson wrote of how he came "to be grateful at last for a little thing." Are we? Bethlehem-Ephratah was little among the thousands of Judah; yet out of it came the mighty ruler. That little things count in human life was suggested by Hannah More in these lines:

> *The sober comfort, all the peace which springs*
> *From the large aggregate of little things;*
> *On these small cares of daughter, wife, and friend,*
> *The almost sacred joys of home depend.*

Wordsworth would have us remember:

> *That best portions of a man's life*
> *His little, nameless, unremembered acts,*
> *Of kindness and of love.*

A Portion of the Eternal

"The Lord is my portion." *Psalm 119:57.*

One of the most wonderful aspects of our Lord's being is that each of us can look up and claim him as our own. The humblest believer can turn his eyes upon him and say, "Thou art *my* portion, O Lord." The king of Babylon graciously provided for Jehoiachin "every day a portion . . . all the days of his life" (Jer. 52:34). Is Jesus your daily portion, the one you appropriate for the needs of each day? Too many try to exist on a very meager portion of him who is ever ready to bless us with his fullness. Describing the position of the enduring dead when they awake, Shelley affirmed that they will become "a portion of the Eternal." But are not these redeemed by the blood, whether on earth or in heaven, a portion of the eternal? "The Lord's portion is his people," declared Moses (Deut. 32:9). As we by faith endeavor to possess all we have in him, in like manner he is never satisfied until he possesses all we are and have. Are we giving him a full portion to feed upon? It is consoling to sing the words written by Anna L. Waring:

> *"Thou art my Portion," saith my soul,*
> *Ten thousand voices say,*
> *And the music of their glad Amen*
> *Will never die away.*

But can he turn to you and me and say with sublime music in his voice, "Thou art *my* portion"?

DEATH
YET LIFE

In a drear-nighted December,
Too happy, happy tree,
Thy branches ne'er remember
Their green felicity.

—John Keats, *Stanzas*

My Mind Aspire to Higher Things

"Friend, go up higher." *Luke 14:10.*

Tennyson agreed with Sir Philip Sidney's aspiration for "higher things," for in his *In Memoriam* we have these impressive lines:

> *I held it truth, with him who sings*
> *To one clear harp in divers tones,*
> *That men may rise on stepping-stones*
> *Of their dead selves to higher things.*

Spiritual elevation should be our constant aim as expressed in the well-known hymn by Sarah F. Adams, "Nearer, my God, to Thee, Nearer to Thee."

We fail to bear in mind, however, that humiliation is the ladder to elevation, that to go up higher we must be willing to go down lower. Jesus took upon himself the form of a servant and humbled himself to the brutal death of a cross, but thereafter he was highly exalted and given a name above every name. If we are to go up higher, we must die to self-praise and self-dependence and become more distressed over our spiritual penury.

Ours must be a separation from the world in so far as its godless pleasures and practices are concerned. We cannot climb higher if the things of earth are not growing dim in the light of his glory and grace. Contamination prevents elevation. Matthew Henry's comment is apt: "The way to *rise high*, is, to *begin low*. Thou shalt have honour and respect before those that sit with thee. . . . Honour appears the brighter for shining *out of obscurity*."

A parable from an ancient source says that three men were bidden to a feast. One sat highest, "for," said he, "I am a prince." The other, next, "for," said he, "I am a wise man." The other, lowest, "for," said he, "I am a humble man." The king, seated at the head of the table, placed the humble man highest and put the prince lowest. As God ever delights in exalting those of low degree, may he always find us low at his feet, recognizing that without him we are nothing, have nothing, and can do nothing. Only thus can we rise higher.

Treasure of Light in Earthen Vessels

"Empty pitchers, and lamps within the pitchers."
Judges 7:16.

What a stirring chapter this is in the Book of Judges! In Israel's sad days God raised up Gideon, and thousands flocked to follow his brave leadership. Out of the thirty thousand soldiers he chose three hundred, and dividing them into three companies, he gave each man a ram's horn and an earthen pitcher or vessel with a light hidden in it. At midnight Gideon grouped his valiant three hundred around the tents of Midian and Amalek and silently and unseen moved them closer and closer to the sleeping foes. Then, when Gideon blew a great blast on his own horn, every man did the same, and all cried, "The sword of the Lord and of Gideon" (Judges 7:18). All broke their pitchers, and the lights flashed forth. The robber army was startled from sleep by the sound of the horns and shouting, and seeing the flashing lights moving through the darkness, they were overtaken by panic and fled, only to be pursued by Gideon's band and killed. This is the great victory the gallant judge achieved for Israel.

One wonders whether Paul had this incident in mind and applied it when he wrote: "God, who commanded the light to shine out of darkness, hath shined in our hearts, to give the light of the knowledge of the glory of God in the face of Jesus Christ. But we have this treasure [treasure of light] in earthen vessels, that the excellency of the power may be of God, and not of us" (2 Cor. 4:6, 7). The pitcher, the outflashing of the lights at night, and the excellent power that gained the victory hold a precious lesson for our hearts. Poor, weak, and fragile though we may be, as vessels we carry a divine light and life which cannot be destroyed and which can shine worth and win glorious victories for God who is able to fill the weakest with strength for his work. In ourselves we are vessels of neither gold nor silver, but of clay, like earthen vessels. Yet, when the excellent light and power of God are revealed through us, what marvelous things are accomplished.

Prayer is the Breath of the Soul

"Pray without ceasing." *I Thess. 5:17.*

Christians cannot live, naturally, without constantly breathing. So, too, they cannot live, spiritually, without prayer, which is their vital breath and native air. And they should be encouraged as they remember that God's ears are ever open to listen to their unceasing petitions. What Paul was doubtless teaching the Thessalonians was the necessity of cultivating the habit of prayer, that as their needs were constantly returning, so their intercessions should be constantly ascending to him who is always ready to listen and answer according to his own wisdom and word.

Does not our prayer-hearing and prayer-answering Father in heaven beseech us to look to him for all our needs and assure us that if what we ask for is according to his will, then it is as pleasant for him to answer our prayers as it is to listen to them? Does he not invite, exhort, and command us to pray always and in everything? But we are so slow to learn that every object that meets the life, every circumstance that occurs, every act in which we engage can afford matter for prayer, if properly viewed. If prayer is allowed to dwindle into a mere duty or into cold, stereotyped forms, occasionally offered, or if it becomes more of a burden than a blessing, then we are heading for spiritual death. Because prayer is the breath of the soul may it become easy for us to pray and as naturally and as constantly as it is to breathe God's fresh air all around us. If we would be spiritually healthy, we must never relax our breathing exercises, particularly in the morning ere we face the heat and burden of the day.

The Irish hymn writer, James Montgomery, sang:

> *Prayer is the Christian's vital breath,*
> *The Christian's native air,*
> *His watchword at the gates of death;*
> *He enters heaven with prayer.*

356

You May Be Mistaken

"The Lord is God of the hills, but he is not the God of
the valleys." *1 Kings 20:28.*

Oliver Cromwell, in a letter to the General Assembly of the Church of
Scotland in 1650, wrote, "I beseech you, in the bowels of Christ, think
it possible you may be mistaken." The best of persons make mistakes.
In his speech at the Mansion House, London, 1899, Edward John
Phelps said, "The man who makes no mistakes does not usually make
anything." The only person the world has ever known who never made
a mistake was the Lord Jesus.

King Ben-hadad, ruler of the Syrians, made a colossal mistake as he
discovered to his cost when he declared that the God of the hills was
not the God of the Valleys. The king went against a small handful of
God's people, and they defeated him, causing him to flee. Ignorantly,
Ben-hadad put his reverse in battle down to the fact that it had been
fought on the hills. Returning with a larger army and keeping away from
the hills, he kept to the valleys, doubtless with the idea that he would
be keeping out of the way of Israel's God. But again he was routed and
made to escape for his life. Thus two defeats forced Ben-hadad to believe
that God is not only the God of the hills, but of the valleys also.

The king's mistake of thinking God is in one place and not in another
is a common one today. There are those who think God is in the church
but not in their business, and they often act as if God were not omnipresent and omniscient. There is no place where God is not, whether
it be hills or valleys. David asked, "Whither shall I flee from thy
presence?" (Ps. 139:7), and answered his own question by saying that
if he took the wings of the morning to fly to uttermost parts he would
find God waiting for him there. In the desert with only a stone as a
pillow, fleeing Jacob had a dream that God was in *all* places. When he
awoke, he confessed, "Surely the Lord is in *this* place; and I knew it
not" (Gen. 28:16). My friend, whether you be on the mountaintop
sparkling with light or in the valley of shadows, remember that God
is round about you.

All Chance-Direction Which Thou Canst Not See

"And a certain man drew a bow at a venture."
1 Kings 22:34.

What we call *chance* means the way things fall out, leaving things to risk, probability. But Alexander Pope reminded us that a chance can be a direction we cannot see. John Milton would have us think of:

> *That power*
> *Which erring men call* Chance.

What the captains, with their special commission to kill the king of Israel, failed to do, a Syrian common soldier accomplished. Taking aim at one of the enemy, the soldier drew a bow by chance, and away the arrow sped, piercing not another ordinary soldier but the king of Israel himself.

Often our words and deeds are like that Syrian soldier, shooting chance arrows, well-aimed at something but striking a target we had not expected—God giving them a direction we could not see. Doubtless, if the soldier who drew a bow at venture had been told that he would shoot the king and win the battle, he would have laughed and said, "Not I!"

Is this principle not often seen in the things we do? Some of the greatest consequences come out of the smallest chance actions. Invading Scotland, the Danes prepared for a night attack on the sleeping garrison, and all of them crept forward barefooted, but one of the Danes stepped on a large thistle which made him cry out. That cry aroused the sleeping Scottish soldiers, and springing to arms, they drove the Danes back. What we must learn from that Syrian soldier is that there are really no unimportant deeds or words. An unkind word may escape our lips without any purpose on our part really to hurt anybody, but it goes like a poisoned arrow into another heart. The arrow hits a mark we did not expect. Of this we can be certain: if all the arrows we shoot are kind, helping, Christlike words and actions, direction from heaven will guide them to beneficial ends.

Dig for Victory

"Make this valley full of ditches." *2 Kings 3:16, 17.*

During World War II enemy action destroyed many ships bringing food to Britain from various parts of the world. People were forced to use food ration books, and a popular national slogan was "Dig for Victory." Gardens, fields, and almost every green patch were made to produce the necessary vegetables for consumption. It was something like this in Elisha's time when a large army, shut up in a dry and thirsty valley, was commanded by God to dig ditches to hold water. The people had to dig in faith, for there was no trace or sign of rain or water anywhere to fill the trenches once dug. But the prophet said dig, assuring them that God would fill the valley ditches, which he did for "the country was filled with water."

Have we discovered that our main business in life is to dig ditches in dry valleys? It is useless to sing "Showers of blessings we need" if trenches in life have not been cut to receive the heavenly supply. In the Lord's parable, the unjust steward who had wasted his goods and faced famine said, "I cannot dig" (Luke 16:3). But he got down to his spade and dug himself out of difficulties.

Are we digging trenches in our own hearts and in the lives of the children at home and in Sunday school that can be filled with the water of life, strengthening ourselves and preparing others to breathe the air and share the blessedness of heaven? Surely no task is comparable to that of preparing channels through which the Spirit of God may flow into our own hearts and through them to others. There may be no cloud in the sky, no sound of wind, no evidence of water anywhere, but as we *dig* in faith, making every preparation for revival, the *deluge* will come. God has promised to fill our trenches with that water which if any man drink he will never thirst again. What a solemn responsibility it is to prepare the way of the Lord.

An Ancient Timekeeper

"The dial of Ahaz." 2 Kings 20:11.

The clever Chaldeans are credited with being the first to invent the sundial to help them by day; at night they reckoned time by observing the movements of the stars. Now we have all kinds of timekeepers which are a vast improvement on the sundial which had to be fixed properly, with its finger pointing toward the north, if correct time were needed. Many of these old sundials can still be seen in churchyards, in old church towers, and in ancient marketplaces. Usually, these dials carry mottoes from which we can gather spiritual lessons. Many of these mottoes indicate the limited use of dials: "I do not take account of the hours unless they are bright"; "I reckon only the sunny hours"; "What's the good of a sundial in the shade?" Since dials require plenty of sun, they are of no use on dull days, and, of course, they are useless at night. Certainly, it is good to look on the bright side of life, but human experience is made up of both sunny hours and dark and gloomy ones.

Another quotation on many a dial is *tempus fugit*, meaning "time flies." The shadow moving along the dial reminded everybody that time did pass away, and that it was incumbent upon them to be on time and to make the most of time, or, as the Bible puts it, "Redeeming the time" (Eph. 5:16).

For King Hezekiah the finger on the dial of Ahaz went back ten degrees as a sign that he would not die but would live another fifteen years. As a guide in life, the dial is disappointing because of its variableness. It may teach us to live admirably in the sunshine but does nothing to prepare us when trouble comes. It may tell accurately the time of day when the sun shines, but its company is no good when night falls. As creatures of time we need a guide without limitation who is able to direct us in the darkest hour as well as in the brightest. We have such a guide in him who has promised to guide us with his eye. Another dial has a Bible text as its motto which we must make our own. "Yet a little while is the light with you. Walk while ye have the light" (John 12:35).

360

A Little Boy Who Was King

"Josiah was eight years old when he began to reign."
2 Kings 22:1.

Josiah was only a child of eight when he became the king to rule over the Jews. This youngest king in Israel's history has a parallel in English history in Edward VI who was sometimes called the "Josiah of England" since he became king at nine years of age. Like Josiah, Edward had a reverence for God and his Word. As a boy he saw somebody get a large Bible to stand on, not being tall enough to reach something on a shelf, and the young king said, "You must not stand upon the Bible, it is God's Book." What a joy it would be if only we could see more boys—and men—loving and honoring the Bible and treating it with the reverence it deserves.

Both Josiah and Edward VI, who became kings in early life, turned out to be the best of kings. Josiah had a wicked father, Amon, but a very good mother, Jedidolah, who doubtless had a good share in her noble child's doing that which was right in the sight of the Lord. For those who are surrounded by the young, whether at home or in Sunday school, it is imperative to remember that young children can be brought to reign in life by Jesus Christ.

Josiah was eight years old when he began to reign, and in the eighth year of his reign he *began* to seek after God, that is, when he was fifteen years of age. From childhood Josiah had loved everything about God. Loving God's house, then in a bad state, he set about repairing it. When the Book of the Law was found and read, Josiah tore his clothes and joined in the repentance of his people. God was pleased with the youthful king because "his heart was tender," and when at fifteen years of age Josiah began thirsting after God in a more intense way, what a rich reward was his in his godly reign. If you are a parent or if you have the care of the young, may grace and patience be yours to teach the young at your side to do that which is right in the sight of the Lord.

The Polished Corners of the Temple

"Glistering stones." *1 Chronicles 29:2.*

Among the most valuable things David prepared for the Temple he was not permitted to build were all manner of precious stones. What the exact nature of these costly gems were is not easy to determine. The American Standard Bible gives us "stones of antimonys" for "glistering stones." The Revised Standard Version at Isaiah 54:11 has "stones in antimony" for "thy stones with fair colours." Antimony is a bright, silvery-white, metallic substance used in many ways. Applied to the stones David stored up to adorn the Temple, antimony can suggest their sparkling beauty and splendor.

Smooth and brilliant stones can be made more beautiful by being polished with their own dust. Roughly cut and coarse at first, a diamond for instance, is rubbed and rubbed again with diamond dust and thus made to sparkle. We say that "experience teaches fools." But this proverb is only partially true, for experience also teaches those who are wise. As "living stones" we take on a better polish as we rub against our old sins and mistakes and learn to leave them behind. When we learn from our failures, they become like the dust of our old selves to make our lives "glistering" for him, the brilliant chief cornerstone.

Peter's tears of repentance over his denial washed his heart and gave him a more polished witness for the Master. Peter reminded us that all who come in repentance and faith to Jesus as to "a living stone, rejected by men, but choice and precious in the sight of God" (1 Pet. 2:4) are themselves made "as living stones, built up as a spiritual house" and shine before the Lord in his temple forever and ever. While here below, our heavenly lapidary, the Holy Spirit, is unceasingly active removing all that is coarse and rough in the Lord's jewels, as the redeemed are called. As cornerstones we are being polished after the similitude of a palace or being cut as diamonds to adorn his palace with its gates of pearl.

A Lot of Little Things

"She fastened it with a pin." Judges 16:13–14.

The Bible is the most fascinating Book in the world to those who love and study it under the inspiration of its divine author. For instance, have you noticed that it even speaks about *pins*—little things we often lose more of than use? The three or four references to such appears to indicate a means of fastening. Ezra said, "Give us a pin," words we often repeat if we want to fasten some cloth material together. It must be understood that the pin Delilah used to entangle Samson's hair and the pins of the Tabernacle were not the same kind of article as the common steel pins we can buy so cheaply today. Doubtless, they were made of wood and fashioned more like pegs.

But let us see what lessons a slim, shiny, sharp-pointed pin can teach us. We have a saying, "You could have heard a pin drop," which means it is silent and noiseless in action. Is this not how the Holy Spirit works in heart and mind? Another old expression is, "Bright as a new pin." If a child is clever, he is referred to as being bright. As a child Jesus grew in wisdom, and he will ever remain a shining example to the young.

Further, pins are of little use if they are blunt. To fulfill their function they must be sharp. When Paul wrote, "Diligent in business serving the Lord" (Rom. 12:11) he implied that we must not be dull or blunted in any way. Pins may be a lot of little things, but the smallest pin has both a point and a head—the former being necessary to pierce the torn garment to be repaired, and the latter to prevent its going too far. We speak of one who is a success in life as having "a good head." A pin's head seems to say, "I stop here." Do we not need grace to guide us when to start and when to stop? All who work with pins know only too well that a crooked pin cannot fulfill its purpose. Jesus died and rose again that crooked lives might be made straight and then fit for his use.

What's in a Name?

"Hadassah, that is Esther." *Esther 2:7.*

Although no divine name is found in the Book of Esther, there is no other book in the Bible in which divine providence is more conspicuous. God is shown as overruling in the affairs of his own people in a foreign land. Secretly he works until his purpose is achieved. "Standeth God within the shadows, keeping watch above His own," wrote James R. Lowell.

Esther the orphan girl was brought up by Mordecai, her cousin, who treated her as his own daughter, and she is the central figure of the book bearing her name. What intrigues we see in the double name given the young Jewess by the sacred historian—Hadassah and Esther. Names and their meaning are an absorbing theme.

Hadassah was the original name of this fair and beautiful exile, an interesting name meaning a myrtle. Mordecai took this precious plant into his home long before the Persian king took her into his palace, and nurtured her until she became a lovely plant of renown. Her physical beauty was matched by an inner loveliness of soul. Too often a beautiful face is spoiled by an unholy heart.

But Hadassah's name was changed to *Esther* which means a star. And a star shines forever. Even when she became a great queen, Esther's fear of God and humility shone like a star. The story of Persia's happy queen can be summed up in a sentence, namely, that through God's overruling providence the myrtle became a star. Esther grew up like a *myrtle* and came to glow like a *star.* Her character illustrated the significance of her two names. A myrtle is ever green and cheers the winter as well as the summer. Its leaves also have a sweet fragrance. God would have his myrtles ever fruitful and fragrant. A star sparkles because God clothed it with light. There it shines, "Up above the world so high, like a diamond in the sky." If the true myrtle characteristics are ours, then we shall shine as the stars forever. As myrtles, we too shall become stars.

The Liberal Deviseth Liberal Things

"He giveth more grace." *James 4:6,* RV.

James the Practical, as he has been called, was also a preacher of the generosity of God who, being liberal-hearted, devises liberal things for humankind. "He giveth to *all* men liberally" (1:5). James remembered the word of the Lord Jesus that "whoever hath, to him shall be given, and he shall have more abundance" (Matt. 13:12), and so he wrote, "He giveth more grace," or grace upon grace.

God never limits the supply, nor is he ever weary of giving, though we are of asking and receiving his ever-expanding grace. The width of God's sympathy is seen in that he gives to all. *Whosoever will* may beg at his footstool, for he is most catholic minded. As for his bounty, James described it as liberal. God always gives with an open hand, never meagerly, partially, or grudgingly. He loves a cheerful giver since his is an unmeasured and unmerited grace. If he gives joy, it is always unspeakable.

The magnanimity of God's liberal heart comes out in James' phrase, "God . . . upbraideth not" (1:5). He blesses all who seek his abundance in the gentlest way. "He mingles no acids with His honeycomb. . . . He is too eager for my temporal and spiritual wealth to mar the welcome gift with the harsh word," said an unidentified writer.

Further, James leaves us in no doubt as to the certainty of God's response to what we ask him if we lack, not only wisdom, but other virtues, making us more effective witnesses. It shall be *given him*! From experience James himself knew how liberally God answered prayer. It was said that the apostle's knees were hard as a camel's because of his continual kneeling before God. How encouraging it is to know that we cannot carry to our generous God a petition which dismays or boggles him and that the more we desire, the more he will grant! In 1873 P. P. Bliss wrote a hymn that focused on James 4:6:

> *Have you on the Lord believed?*
> *Still there's more to follow;*
> *Of His grace have you received?*
> *Still there's more to follow.*

Strives in His Little World of Man

"Why dost thou strive against God?" *Job 33:13.*

The American Standard Bible gives this verse a softer tone: "Why do you complain against Him, That He does not give an account of all His doings?" As he does according to his will which is perfect, why should God give an account to the little world of humankind of what he does? The call is, "Be silent, O all flesh, before the Lord!" (Zech. 2:13). Because he is the omnipotent God, he is not responsible to puny humans who often complains about divine providence. But he is not accountable to any and will not be questioned by the curious or called to an account by the proud and curious.

With our finite minds we cannot fully understand the divine purpose behind many of the perplexing experiences of life, but when we see him face to face, then all will be made clear, and we shall bless the hand that guided and the heart that planned. Because of the perfection of his character, he demands that we trust him where we cannot trace him and be acquiescent on the ground of the promises of his Word. To strive against him or to resist him is actually rebellion and treason, for his designs, although mysterious to us, are always gracious and good, and his ways are all righteous. In his ode to Napoleon Bonaparte, Byron had this verse:

> 'Tis done—but yesterday a King!
> And armed with Kings to strive—
> And now thou art a nameless thing;
> So abject—yet alive!

Those who continually strive against the King of kings, against his Word, his commands, and some of the dispensations of his providence, become as nameless things and abject. His wisdom is infinite; his love is unchangeable; and his power is unlimited. Therefore, let us not strive against but submit to his perfect will and trust him completely.

For His Bounty—There Was No Winter In't

"God said, Ask what I shall give thee." *1 Kings 3:5.*

Actually, God presented Solomon with a blank check to draw what he liked from heaven's never-failing treasury. But the young king took no undue advantage of God's bounty which knows no winter of scarcity. All Solomon desired was "an understanding heart to judge thy people, that I may discern between good and bad" (1 Kings 3:9), and God bountifully supplied Solomon with unusual wisdom so that "there was none like thee before thee, neither after thee shall any arise like unto thee" (1 Kings 3:12). We link God's request, "Ask what I shall give thee," to Christ's word to his own, "Ask, and ye shall receive" (John 16:24), to emphasize that heaven does not respond indiscriminately and give us anything we ask for—"Ye ask and receive not, because ye ask amiss" (Jas. 4:3). Had Solomon asked for long life, riches, or the life of his enemies, he would have asked amiss and not received. Scripture must be balanced by Scripture. John said, "We know that we have the petitions that we desired of him" (1 John 5:15), but he was careful to affirm that God only responds to requests, "If we ask any thing *according to his will*, he heareth us" (1 John 5:14). Therefore, in all the things we ask for, there must be the observance of this proviso—*according to his will.*

God always gives freely and plentifully when there is harmony between his will and our petition. Having boundless resources, he is never straitened in himself and constantly asks us to avail ourselves of all we have in him in whom there dwelleth "all the treasures of wisdom and knowledge" (Col. 2:3). Like Solomon, we can pray for wisdom since our understandings need to be enlightened and our wills brought into perfect harmony with the will of God and our affections fixed on him and on holy and heavenly things. From an unknown source we read:

> *My life, my crown, my heaven, Thou art!*
> *Oh, may I find in Thee my heart.*

Out of Debt, Out of Danger

"Owe nothing to anyone, except the loving one another."
Romans 13:8, Handley Moule.

What a better place this old world of ours would be to live in if only all of us shared the expressed hatred of Charles H. Spurgeon, nineteenth-century preacher, for *dirt*, *debt*, and the *Devil*. In a most congenial way Paul closed his precepts of civil order with the universal command to love. As those forgiven for our spiritual debts we must avoid absolutely the social disloyalty of debt and, with watchful care, pay every creditor in full. How striking is Emerson's phrase, "Pay every debt, as if God wrote the bill!" All who have been redeemed by the blood of Jesus should be prompt and punctual in payments and should not be guilty of rash speculations resulting in heavy debt, which is a breach of the divine precept. They should live within their means and not bring disgrace upon their Christian witness by contracting debts they are unable to pay. Too often, in order to keep up with the Joneses, large debts are incurred that become a burden.

As believers we should be more concerned about adorning the doctrine of God our Savior than about spending money we do not have to keep up appearances. The one debt we are to be deep in is that of love. Said Handley Moule, eighteenth-century English bishop of Durham, "Love is to be a perpetual and inexhaustible debt, not as if repudiated or neglected, but as always due and always paying." And an unknown writer said:

Let those who bear the Christian name their holy vows fulfil;
The saints—the followers of the Lamb—are men of honour still.

Like a Living Coal His Heart Was

"Thou shalt heap coals of fire upon his head."
Proverbs 25:21, 22.

How impressive is Longfellow's description of Hiawatha whose:

Heart was hot within him,
Like a living coal his heart was.

Only those whose hearts are warm like living coal can practice the injunction of Solomon and earn divine reward. In ancient times the process of melting and purifying metal was crude. Rough nuggets of gold were hard to soften, and the refiner would not only have fire beneath a crucible but would pile fire all around it and over it until it was buried in fire with heat reaching the metal from beneath, around, and above. Heaping coals of fire on the head of the crucible greatly helped to melt and refine the silver.

The application is not hard to discover. The scribes and Pharisees had broken the divine law regarding love of the brethren and of enemies. Their hearts were not hot with love within them. When Jesus came, he gave the old commandment new life by his wonderful example of loving us, even when we were his enemies. Long patience was his, but he knew that the gold of hard hearts melts slowly. Burying them in the warmth of his love, he heaped coals of fire upon them until his foes were made friends.

The divine way to treat those in need of succor and kindness is to mollify them as the refiner melts his metal in the crucible, not only by putting it over the fire, but by heaping coals of fire upon it. We can transform enemies into friends only by acting toward them in a loving, friendly manner. Nothing can nourish those in need like "the milk of human kindness." The psalmist's heart was strangely warmed by the marvelous kindness God showered upon him in a strange city. When we love our enemies, bless those that curse us, do good to those who hate us, and pray for those who despitefully treat us and persecute us, we heap coals of Calvary's fire upon their hearts and heads.

Adversary versus Advocate

"Joshua . . . standing before the angel of the Lord, and
Satan standing at his right hand to resist him."
Zechariah 3:1.

In his most illuminating commentary on Zechariah F. B. Meyer said
that the one thought which pervades the prophecy of Zechariah is
"Hope, for he is pre-eminently the Prophet, as Peter is the Apostle, of
Hope." This feature is clearly evident in the chapter before us, taken
up, as it is, with the divine rebuke of Satan. In the opening verses there
is conflict between the adversary and the advocate, with the latter
proving victorious over the former. Some writers suggest that "the
angel of the Lord" is a person of high dignity in the angelic realm; he
may have been Jesus in one of his preincarnation appearances. But
that could hardly be so here in light of Zechariah 1:12, 13, where the
personality of this special angel of the Lord is distinct from the Lord
himself.

Satan, whose name means *adversary,* has been the adversary of
humankind from man's creation. Satan was justly rebuked by the Lord,
for "who shall lay anything to the charge of God's chosen?" The saints
of God are still accused by Satan who ever stands by to resist them as
they seek to live and witness for the Lord. But their source of relief and
victory is the knowledge that Jesus, their mediator and advocate, is
standing by, enabling them to resist all the fiery darts of the satanic
adversary. When assailed by Satan, let this be our constant encouragement that Jesus is standing by our right hand to preserve us against
those who would condemn us. Paul, when heavily assailed by hellish
influences, had no one standing by him, but he could say, "Notwithstanding, the Lord stood with me, and strengthened me" (2 Tim. 4:17).
Anne Steele of the eighteenth century wrote:

> *Look up, my soul, with cheerful eye,*
> *See where the great Redeemer stands*
> *The glorious Advocate on high.*

Clear Shining after Rain

"Not joyous but grievous; nevertheless afterward."
Hebrew 12:11.

The writer of this wonderful Epistle was dealing with God's chastening his redeemed children and also with the results of every pain God permits them to feel. He would have us know that the ripest benefits are sorrow-borne. William Cowper, whose "Olney Hymns" gave us the title of this meditation, also wrote in "Epistle to a Protestant Lady" that:

The path of sorrow, and that path alone
Leads to the Land where sorrow is unknown.

Divine searching and scourging are not joyous but grievous; nevertheless afterward we come to bless the hand that guided and the heart that planned even though part of the plan was pain.

How full of significance is *afterward!* How despairing it would be if there were no *afterward* to explain the meaning of our tears! Scripture is replete with records of saints like Joseph, Hannah, and Job who, severely tried and tested, came to experience a blessed afterward. God's discipline of his redeemed children is never misguided but always wisely administered for their profit. Those who allow themselves to be corrected by it come to prove its beneficial and blessed results. Harsh plowing yields joyful, bountiful harvests.

From an unknown source we learn that the believer "grows rich by his losses, rises by his falls, lives by dying, and becomes full of being emptied." His grievous afflictions result in the peaceable fruit of righteousness in this life and the full vintage of joy in the *afterward* of heaven. There are times when the heart is perplexed over what God may permit in life, but patience must be allowed to do her perfect work. The *cross* may be our lot today, but tomorrow, the *crown*. A hymn writer declared:

We may not fully understand
How underneath God's chastening hand
Pain is fulfilling love's command
But afterward!

371

His Droppings of Warm Tears

"I tell you even weeping, that they are the enemies of the cross of Christ." *Philippians 3:18.*

Those warm Christlike tears of Paul dropped, not only over those who were utterly godless and positively hostile to the idea of a man dying for their sins, but over those who professed Christ and sought shelter beneath his cross. Paul's tears, his liquid agony, over those in the Philippian church indicate at once the tenderness of the mourner and the awfulness and certainty of the coming ruin of those who were enemies of the cross because they did not see in it the evil of sin. They had the horrible belief that although under grace they could give the reins to sin instead of being strangers to its attractions. They would not submit to the authority or confirm themselves to the example of Christ who died upon the cross. To them Christian *liberty*, which Paul preached, meant *license*. Continuing in sin, that grace may abound, those Antinomian Philippians made themselves the enemies of the cross. Having thus "turned the grace of God into lasciviousness" (Jude 4) they earned for themselves the severe judgment of destruction.

If the cross is all our glory, then we must never by conduct or conversation bring disgrace upon it. We must strive in every possible way to advance its victory, spread its glory, and bring sinners to trust him who was crucified upon it for their salvation. Because that wondrous cross is the foundation of our hope, the key opening the gates of paradise, the object of angelic wonder, and the cause of Satan's everlasting destruction, it should give us pain to be considered its enemy in any way.

May grace be ours never to be ashamed *of* the old rugged cross or a shame *to* it. May he who died in our room and stead enable us to glory in his cross, spread its glories, declare its triumphs, and hold it up in the face of a sinful world as its only hope for life, here and hereafter.

Every Fool Will Be Meddling

"He that . . . meddleth . . . is like one that taketh a dog by
the ears." *Proverbs 26:17.*

This proverb must be seen in light of the times when Solomon penned
it. The Jews, failing to understand that a dog could be trained for useful
service, sadly neglected it until it became an unclean animal and a by-
word for reproach. To call anyone *a dog* was the greatest insult. Sometimes a few dogs would snarl and quarrel over a morsel of food in the
street, and a man would try to seize the most angry dog in the group
by the ears and drag it away. But the longer he held the ears, the more
exhausted he became, and letting go, he was bitten by the dog.

Solomon makes the point that anyone meddling with strife that has
no personal application is likely to be bitten. If the passerby had let the
dog alone, its fit of temper would have subsided, and the animal would
have left the street in peace.

What a lesson for meddlers! As Solomon goes on to say, only fools
meddle with strife not belonging to them and only add fuel to the fire.
Further, it is foolish to meddle so as to cause a quarrel, as some misguided folks are fond of doing. If a friend becomes ill-tempered, one
should not vex him or her still further. "A soft answer turneth away
wrath; but grievous words stir up strife" (Prov. 15:1). It is always
unsafe to meddle in other people's affairs if we can do no good. The
golden rule for our conduct at ail times and under all circumstances was
laid down by Jesus: "Whatsoever ye would that men should do to you,
do ye even so to them" (Matt. 7:12). It was he who made peace by the
blood of his cross and who can enable us to be at peace among ourselves.

Thou Hast Conquered, O Galilean

"A stronger than he shall come upon him." *Luke 11:22.*

In our Lord's discourse about casting out demons there is no doubt that his illustration symbolized his victory over Satan. A strong armed man was guarding his palace and his goods, and a stronger man came and conquered him, taking from him the armor he trusted.

As the stronger, Jesus came upon the boasted strong man and overcame him. Thus, through the life, death, and resurrection of Jesus, Satan is a conquered foe. We sing about marching *on* to victory. Actually, since Calvary, we march *from* victory. Triumph over all satanic foes, as well as the security of our redemption, was in his final cry of conquest, "It is finished" (John 19:30).

Now, by faith, we make his victory our own. Satan still vaunts his strength as the enemy of all righteousness and as the unwearied foe of the saints. We know only too well that he excites to sin, accusing us of sin before God and striving to overcome our faith in God and his Word. But as the result of Calvary's victory over Satan, we can steadfastly and successfully resist him through all that Christ, his grand opponent, is to us.

Satan may be a deadly serpent, but Jesus is the brazen serpent which heals. Satan is still a roaring lion whose roars warn us of his attacks, but Jesus is the prevailing lion of the tribe of Judah. Satan, as a wolf, seeks to harry the little flock, but Jesus is the Good Shepherd and protects his sheep. Satan is ever our foe, but Jesus is our abiding friend. Satan is a liar and the father of lies, but Jesus is the Truth. Satan is branded as the accuser, but Jesus is extolled as the advocate. Satan is portrayed as the prince of darkness, but Jesus is the light of the world and of life. Satan has the evil reputation of being a murderer since the beginning of humankind, but Jesus is the resurrection. Satan boasts his power and position as the god of this world, but Jesus is God over all and is stronger than the world's hellish deity. We sing with A. C. Dixon:

Jesus is stronger than Satan and sin, Satan to Jesus must bow;
Therefore I triumph without and within; Jesus saves me now.

The Household of Continuance

"Evening, and morning, and at noon, will I pray."
Psalm 55:17.

The church of the living God is composed of those who represent the "household of continuance" in the spiritual grace of prayer. Paul, agreeing with the psalmist, said that we must "continue in prayer, and watch in the same with thanksgiving" (Col. 4:2) and "pray without ceasing" (1 Thess. 5:17). Praying at morning, noon, and night implies that prayer must be considered a *habit* or that we should speak to God at all times and in all places whether there are immediate occasions for its exercise or not.

St. Augustine expressed the hope that when Christ appeared for his translation he would find him either praying or preaching. Such continuance in prayer is independent of *place* or *time*. Some are slavishly dependent upon a place, which can become a hindrance to true prayer. An aged minister asked a plain, prayerful servant girl how she would interpret Paul's exhortation about praying continuously. "Can you pray all the time with so many things to do?"

The girl's reply was, "Yes, Sir, the more I have to do, the more I pray. When I awake in the morning, I pray, 'Lord, open the eyes of my understanding.' While I am dressing, I pray that I may be clothed with the robe of righteousness. When I have washed, I ask for the cleansing of the blood. As I begin my work, I pray for strength equal for my day. As I sweep the floors, I pray God to sweep all dirt from my heart with His besom. Then, as I prepare the meals, I ask God to feed with His manna and the sincere milk of the Word. When busy caring for the little children in the house, I ask my heavenly Father to carry me as His child. And so, on through the day, Sir, everything I do furnishes me with a thought for prayer."

The minister was overwhelmed and said, "Well, Mary, you have certainly learned how to pray without ceasing."

Have we? We sing of prayer as the "Christian's vital breath," but is it? If we cease to breathe, physically, we die. Unconsciously we breathe without ceasing and so live. Place and posture in prayer are observed at given times, but to *continue* in prayer means praying at all times and in all places and having one's life itself a *prayer*.

Thought Is the Child of Action

"I will run the way of thy commandment, when thou shalt enlarge my heart." *Psalm 119:32.*

Benjamin Disraeli gave us the dictum, "Experience is the child of Thought, and Thought is the child of Action." *Running* implies vigorous action, but, said David, we must run on the track of the divine Book. To run and not be weary is dependent upon the enlargement of heart. The strong action of the heart in all holy things comes as the result of the Spirit's operation upon it. Only those who wait upon the Lord can run without weariness.

Our great physician knows that all spiritual disease is heart disease which must be remedied before there can come effective action in service. Athletes know that running is a strong, healthy movement of the whole body, requiring energy and necessitating a sound heart. We cannot run in the way of God's commandments except in the strength and vigor he calls "enlargement of heart," which means a love for and cheerfulness in doing the will of God.

Walking and sitting Christians are more common than *running* Christians, who make haste and delay not. Paul described the Christian life as a race which we must all have to run, and run well, if we would win the prize. When there is enlargement of the heart by God, there is an outgoing beyond all the limits self-ease would impose. Heartiness as action for God depends upon the heart cleansed, and kept clean, by him.

Our hearts must be daily enlarged to take in the ever-growing thoughts of God. When he fills the heart to the limit, he enlarges its capacity to receive more, and so the faster we run. We recognize that *walk* is often used to denote the habitual obedience of our life in Christ, but the term *run* signifies the energy of such a life. Scripture also has a good deal to say about rest, and some hold that this and not action is the rule and privilege of a Christian's life. But it is neither. The Christian's privilege is rest for the soul; the Christian's rule must be action for the energies. Rest is justification in Christ's blood; action is the power and unction of the Holy Spirit.

None of Self, and All of Thee

"Not I, but Christ." Galatians 2:20.

Paul ever practiced what he preached. Galatians 2:20 is the imperative rule he laid down for himself and for every child of God. This rule smites yet heals, beggars and exalts. It strips the believer of all self-interest and self-glory and then changes emptiness into fullness and defeat into victory. May each of us, with Paul, experience what it is to give Christ the preeminent position in all things.

Theodore Monod in his heart-searching hymn traced the gradual step from *I* to *Christ:* "All of self, and none of Thee"; "Some of self, and some of Thee"; "Less of self, and more of Thee"; "None of self, and all of Thee." And this should be our ruling passion.

The impressive Keswick hymn, bearing the initials A.A.F., exemplifies our text:

Not I, but Christ, be honoured, loved, exalted,
Not I, but Christ, be seen be known and heard;
Not I, but Christ, in ev'ry look and action,
Not I, but Christ, in every thought and word.

Not I, but Christ, to gentle soothe in sorrow,
Not I, but Christ, to wipe the falling tear;
Not I, but Christ, to lift the weary burden,
Not I, but Christ, to hush away all fear.

Christ, only Christ, no idle word e'er falling,
Christ, only Christ, no needless bustling sound;
Christ, only Christ, no self-important bearing,
Christ, only Christ, no trace of I be found.

Not I, but Christ, my every need supplying,
Not I, but Christ, my strength and health to be;
Christ, only Christ, for spirit, soul, and body,
Christ, only Christ, live then Thy life in me.

Christ, only Christ, ere long will fill my vision,
Glory excelling soon, full soon I'll see;
Christ, only Christ, my every wish fulfilling,
Christ, only Christ, my all in all to be.

The question of paramount importance is, Does Jesus reign supreme in your life and mine? Count Zinzendorf never tired of saying, "I have only one passion, it is *He!*" Are we consumed by such a passion?

377

Veni, Veni, Emmanuel!

"They shall call his name Emmanuel, which being
interpreted is, *God with us.*" *Isaiah 7:14; Matthew 8:23.*

Among the prophetic, symbolic names given to Jesus, none is more
expressive of his condescension in being made in the likeness of man
than that of *Emmanuel.* The sign Isaiah gave the people was of goodwill
to Israel and particularly to the House of David which, though its fulfillment would be some five hundred years later, brought much assurance
to the nation that God would not cast it off. A Messiah would come on
a glorious mission, wrapped up in a glorious name—*Emmanuel,* "God
with us!" James Mason Neale's translation of a ninth-century Latin
chant reminds us of Israel's hope:

> *O come, O come, Emmanuel*
> *And ransom captive Israel.*

Matthew opened his Gospel by announcing the supernatural birth of
this heavenly being, "breaking His way to earth through a virgin's
womb in fulfillment of the prophecy that He should be called *Emmanuel,*
or 'God with us.' " Both the names *Jesus* and *Emmanuel* belong to him
who came as the manifestation of God to humankind, as the God-man.
Since *Jesus* means "Jehovah–Savior," both names are freighted with
an implication of the deity of its bearer. Had he not been *Emmanuel,* he
could not have been Jesus the Savior. How comforting is this precious
name Emmanuel! God is our nature; he is with us in our sorrows and
trials, in our lives and service, in our homes, and at the end of the road
translating us to Emmanuel's land above. We sing with John Newton:

> *Sweeter sounds than music knows,*
> *Charm me in Immanuel's name;*
> *All her hopes before my spirit owes,*
> *To His birth, His cross, His shame.*

378

Lessons from a Spider's Web

"The hypocrite's hope shall perish . . . whose trust shall
be a spider's web." *Job 8:13, 14.*

While we are all fascinated as we watch spiders weave their beautiful
webs, we nevertheless think them horrid insects and seek to destroy
them. Yet, in spite of our aversion to spiders, we must not forget that
they only fulfill the instinct which an all-wise Creator implanted within
them and they are of much value to us in diminishing the swarms of
insects by which we are molested. Bereft of these wily hunters, we
should be plagued like the Egyptians of old with flies.

While popular prejudice has always been against the spider, earning
the unknown poet's description that it is "cunning and fierce, mixture
abhorr'd" because of the way it decoys the little fly into its parlor, we
can imitate its prowess in seeking to destroy that which is evil. We all
know about the lesson King Robert the Bruce learned while hiding in a
cave from his foes. He watched as a spider tried again and again to
weave its web.

The spider's skill as a weaver is remarkable, for its web, though frail,
is a marvelous production, distinguished by beauty of design, fineness
of construction, and sensitivity to touch. Alexander Pope's couplet
expresses it:

> The spider's touch, *how exquisitely fine,*
> *Feels at each thread and lives along the line.*

The whole fabric is spun out of its own body and is a part of the spider's
life. Thus it should be with our service for the Master which comes out
of a life utterly given to him. But with all its beauty, wonder, and
design, the spider's web is so easily destroyed. Job made this application when he reminded us that the hypocrite's hope, so cleverly conceived, will perish as a fragile web. His hope is the creation of his own
fancy and therefore doomed.

Threefold Cord of Gospel Truth

"Keep in memory . . . Christ died for our sins . . . thanks be unto God for the victory." *1 Corinthians 15:2, 3, 57.*

The well-known American novelist, Peter DeVries, in an article "The Age of Innocence," described how he helped a young Chicago girl to whom he became attached in his youth. Catechism classes were held in the basement of the Dutch Reformed church, and Peter helped the youthful Greta brush up on her lesson so that she could appear to be sound in doctrine. He posed the question that would be asked of her by the examiner, "What three things are necessary for thee that thou mayest live and die happily?"

"*First*, how great are my sins and miseries," she gave the answer.

"*Second*, how may I be . . . let's see . . . Delivered. Delivered from my sins."

"*Third*, How may I express my gratitude to God for this deliverance?"

Recognition, emancipation, and adoration are the aspects of our faith we must not forget. We must keep in memory the necessity of the recognition of our sinful condition before a thrice-holy God and repentance or contrition because of such. The order is "repent" and then "believe the Gospel." Discovering how great are our sins, we must turn in penitence and faith to him who died for our sins and experience the perfect deliverance he made possible from the penalty and thralldom of those sins. Paul would have us remember that this deliverance is of a threefold nature: *past, present, perspective* (2 Cor. 1:10). Would that the multitudes around us fettered by iniquity could experience the glorious deliverance, the blood of the cross secured! What else can this blood-bought emancipation result in but adoration. We express our gratitude to God when, with Paul, we exultingly cry, "Thanks be unto God for the victory" (1 Cor. 15:57). Such gratitude not only escapes our lips but is manifested in a life of obedience and devotion to him who died for our sins. But not until we join the ransomed throng above, who washed their robes and made them white in the blood of the lamb, shall we praise, worship, and adore him as he merits.

Brothers All in Honor

"This honour have all the saints." *Psalm 149:9.*

All who are saved by divine grace are brothers and sisters in grace and thus share equally in the honor of being a people near unto the Lord and living with the high praises of God in their mouth, and a two-edged sword in their hand. Honor becomes an empty bubble if we do not realize how signally we have been honored of God. When asked to cover the stars on his uniform, Lord Nelson replied, "In honour I gained them, and in honour I will die with them." All we have through grace was gained for us by the honor of our substitute, which has become one eternal honor. This honor, it will be noted, is the possession only of the *saints*.

Who and what is a saint? In the Roman Catholic Church a member must have achieved eminence in some particular way and have been dead for many years before being canonized as a saint. But all God's saints are living and have been redeemed by the blood of his Son, with some being more saintly than others.

Among all the titles given the believers in Scripture, *saint* is the most expressive one of the lives they must live as followers of their holy Lord. "Be ye holy, for I am holy" (1 Pet. 1:16). Called to be saints, what is our honor? It is being born again of incorruptible seed, even of the Word of God by the Spirit, being acknowledged as the sons of God, being closely allied to him who died for our sins, being heirs of God and joint-heirs with Jesus, being forever freed from the slavery of sin to serve our heavenly deliverer in liberty, having him as our representative and advocate on high, knowing that when he appears in glory it will be for our glorification, being appointed to sit with Jesus in the judgment of angels and in his universal reign. Are we confident and conscious of these great privileges and living under their sanctifying influence? Then sing with an unknown hymn writer:

> *Pause, my soul, adore and wonder,*
> *Grace hath put me in the number*
> *of the Saviour's family!*

381

O Living Waters, Rise within Me Evermore

"Spring up, O well; sing ye unto it." Numbers 21:17.

Although this is the only reference in Scripture to the well of Beor, it became famous because it was the subject and object of a divine promise. God had told Moses to gather the thirst-stricken people to the place and there he would give them water. The remembrance of that provision, and the blessings brought by that spring for the Jews and their cattle, remained green in the memories of the people who fashioned it into strange traditions. As the people slaked their thirst, filled their vessels, and watered their cattle, they burst forth into that song of joy of which we have only a fragment, "Spring up, O well; sing ye unto it."

In a time of revival, when there is a marvelous upspringing of the Holy Spirit's power in the salvation of the lost and the quickening of saints, what holy joy there is. There is an acute spiritual thirst today, and multitudes are dying in sin because of the lack of the water of life. May ours be the sincere, heartfelt prayer, "Spring up, O well."

May the Spirit so possess all preachers of the Word that out of them living waters will flow to those smitten with thirst. As we think of the well of Beor, we are reminded of another hot day, hundreds of years later, when another leader, thirsty and weary, sat by Jacob's well at Sychar and promised a more refreshing water that would spring up into life eternal. We must remember, however, that what God has promised to give we must earnestly inquire after and prepare for. That well of Beor was the object of effort, for we read that "the nobles digged it with their staves" (Num. 21:18). As Charles H. Spurgeon put it:

> The Lord would have us active in obtaining grace. Our staves are ill adapted for digging in the sand, but we must use them to the utmost of our ability. Prayer must not be neglected; the assembling of ourselves together must not be forsaken; ordinances must not be slighted. The Lord will give His grace most plenteously, but not in the way of idleness. Let us, then, bestir ourselves to seek Him in whom are all our fresh springs.

May there spring up that marvelous grace of God in fountains over the whole earth, causing the dry places to blossom as the rose and to be beauteous as the garden of the Lord.

The Lamp That Ever Shines

"The commandment is a lamp, and the law is light."
Proverbs 6:23.

Solomon must have had in mind his father's use of the lighted lamp as a simile of Scripture, for David had written, "Thy word is a lamp unto my feet and a light unto my path" (Ps. 119:105). God has hung up in the heavens the lamp of the sun, moon, and stars to pour a flood of light upon the darkness of earth, but a *light* still brighter than the sun and which, like the sun, never goes out, never sets, never requires trimming or relighting like a lamp of our making, is the light of truth in God's holy Word.

Such is the nature of this perpetual, infallible lamp that it gives more than we can use, shines brighter when trial and sorrow make life darkest, and can shed its light through the valley of the shadow of death to the very gate of heaven.

A lamp is of no use if there be no light within it. Thus, if there is any distinction between these two figures of speech, *lamp* and *light*, we can think of the *lamp* as the written Word itself—the Bible, printed and bound up and ready to be read and studied. The *light* is the Holy Spirit within it who inspired holy men of old to fashion the lamp and who ever waits to shed light upon its precepts and promises and enlighten our minds to understand and receive them. "The letter killeth—the Spirit giveth life—and light" (source unknown).

It is comforting to know that we can take this divine lamp and hold it, making it our very own to throw light upon our way as we journey through life. From another unknown source we learn that the Bible is indeed the light of our dark sky:

> *A lantern to our footsteps*
> *Shines on from age to age.*

When the Spirit shines through the lamp, he brings the truth to sight, causing the commandments and counsels to shed a searching light upon our hearts and lives. How right William Cowper was when he wrote that

> *A glory gilds the sacred page,*
> *Majestic, like the sun:*
> *It gives its light to every age;*
> *It gives, but borrows none.*

383

To Endless Years the Same

"Thou art the same . . . thy years shall have no end."
Psalm 102:27.

The psalmist speaks of God's unchanging, unending years throughout the generations. The earth and the heavens he fashioned have grown old like a garment and have disappeared, but "thou art the same." Since God is the ever-present deity, the division of time into past, present, and future has no relevance to his existence. "From everlasting to everlasting" he is God to whom a thousand years are but a day. We may spend our years as a tale that is told, but as the one without beginning and ending, God has no such tale to tell. Time is broken up for us into years, months, weeks, and days, but to God, from eternity to eternity is one unbroken whole.

Until time shall be no more, our earthly lives will be made up of sections of time. Occasionally, we should pause and take stock to discover whether we have been a profit or a loss to the king himself. Have we come short in holiness, spiritual advancement, faithfulness, and diligence? If so, let us repent and correct the balance and have the king blot out the handwriting against us.

Further, we cannot but be grateful that although "time, like an ever-rolling stream" may have borne dear ones away, God has been gracious in filling the vacant place in heart and home with more of his own abiding presence. What else can we do but raise our Ebenezer and trust in the promise that all God has been he will continue to be in all the future holds for us. "The Lord hath been mindful of us: he will bless us . . . . We will bless the Lord" (Ps. 115:12, 18).